AMERICAN SEX MACHINES

THE HIDDEN HISTORY OF SEX AT THE U.S. PATENT OFFICE

Hoag Levins

Adams Media Corporation
Holbrook, Massachusetts

Published by Adams Media Corporation.
260 Center Street, Holbrook, MA 02343

ISBN: 1-55850-534-2
Printed in the United States of America.

J I H G F E D C B A

Levins, Hoag.
American sex machines : the hidden history of sex at the U. S. Patent Office / Hoag Levins.
    p.   cm.
Includes bibliographical references and index.
ISBN 1-55850-534-2 (pbk.)
    1. Sex customs—United States—History.   2. Sex customs—United States—Miscellanea.   3. Sex—Miscellanea.   4. Patents—United States History.   5. United States.   Patent Office—History.
    I. Title.
HQ18.U5L488   1996
613.9'5—dc20   95-52750
                                                CIP

This book is available at quantity discounts for bulk purchases.
For information, call 1-800-872-5627.

Visit our home page at *http://www.adamsmedia.com*

Contents

Acknowledgments

A number of individuals and institutions assisted me as I assembled raw data for this project. I am grateful to designer and graphic artist John Goschke for re-executing many of the patent drawings from faded microfilm originals. Patrick Levins also provided graphic art services. I appreciate the efforts of Ray Durrance and the staff of Associated Information Consultants, Inc., of Ann Arbor, Michigan, in locating and retrieving many of the obscure historical documents required. Jonathan Scherer, a former U.S. Patent Office attorney and current member of the Washington, D.C., patent law firm of Jacobson, Price, Holman and Stern was retained to provide patent searching services during the early stages of this project. Additional research assistance was provided by Christopher Papalas of the department of Anthropology of the University of Michigan; Terry Lehr, Assistant Curator for Research of the Baker-Cederberg Museum & Archives in Rochester, New York; Mrs. Willard C. Bunney of the Rochester Historical Society; Carol Sandler of the Strong Museum of Rochester; and Jeffrey Barr, Director of the North Baker Library of the California Historical Society, San Francisco, California. Sandy Levins and Al Peak provided invaluable manuscript review and other crucial support services. However, all conclusions and interpretations are solely my own, as are any mistakes.

Introduction

This book grew out of my chance discovery that the U.S. Patent Office—one of the most conservative and meticulous data-gathering organizations that has ever existed—has been accumulating and preserving a unique collection of patents that documents over 150 years of American sexual innovations. Gathered together, as they are here for the first time, these patents offer us an unprecedented new way of looking at the evolution of American sexual attitudes and practices.

A talent for mechanical innovation has always been one of the central and distinctive features of the American character—a fact officially recognized as early as 1787, when the Constitutional Convention both invented our system of government and created the Patent Office as one of its central institutions. Created on the eve of the Industrial Revolution, the patent system was designed to encourage inventors to share their mechanical, chemical, and agricultural discoveries as a way of accelerating the growth of an American manufacturing economy.

Left to their own devices, inventors are naturally inclined to keep inventions that have commercial value secret. The patent system offered them a deal. In return for their agreement to create a permanent and public file explaining their discovery, they would be granted exclusive control over its manufacture, sale, and commercial exploitation for a period of seventeen years.

By law, each patent must be a "teaching document," instructing the reader in all the important dimensions of an invention's design.

Patent applicants are also required to describe the problems or deficiencies that their invention is designed to correct. As a result, Patent Office files offer an invaluable record of the difficulties and frustrations Americans of all eras have encountered as part of their daily lives. A hundred years later, a patent can be analyzed for the evidence it provides concerning the social, psychological, moral, and technical attitudes and aptitudes of its day.

The information these patents contain is all the more valuable because of the disciplined and dispassionate manner is which the data is collected and evaluated. Traditionally, patent examiners—the gatekeepers who review and pass judgment over nearly every word of every patent—have been highly trained engineering and legal professionals with an abiding sense of dedication to the system they administer. Nuance, overstatement, ambiguity, and frivolous observations are all proscribed from patent applications—creating historical documents that are rich in detailed observation and careful explanation.

Overall, my research located more than eight hundred patents related to human sexuality—stretching back in time to 1846 and ranging from vaginal implements carved out of whalebone to condoms enhanced with embedded musical computer chips. These patents are not filed in any particular place in the Patent Office, but are scattered throughout their records of more prosaic agricultural and mechanical inventions.

Some of the Patent Office documents contain information that is available nowhere else. For example, the Patent Office is the only national agency that has systematically recorded information about the development of sexual devices during the Victorian era—an era when such products were strictly enforced by federal laws, backed by frequent police raids.

Since the patent system focuses exclusively on documenting innovative concepts, rather than tracking their effectiveness, safety, or commercial viability, there's no way of telling just how many of these eight hundred devices were actually produced for sale. In this regard, it is important for readers to appreciate that many of the concepts and implements described in this book are potentially hazardous. The older sex patents are often based on outdated—and often bizarre—theories about human physiology. At the same time, many of the modern sex patents have not yet been evaluated by the authorities—such as the U.S. Food and Drug Administration—whose approval would be necessary before they could be sold to the public.

Grouped in roughly chronological order and by general mechanical type, these sex patents offer a hidden history of American sexual attitudes—from our Puritan roots, to the sexual and technological revolutions of recent decades, to today's tug-of-war over family values and safe sex. A number of the devices—particularly those from the post-World War II years—have become commonplace items of commerce and personal hygiene. Others are stunningly *uncommon*—erotic, cruel, weird, or just a little sad. Yet all were produced by inventors who believed that they had identified an important need in their society, or a new market opportunity lucrative enough to justify the considerable expense and effort that a patent application requires. Taken together, they offer a striking new perspective on the often strange intersections of American ingenuity and human sexual behavior.

—Hoag Levins

1

The Original Sex Patent

When the American revolution ended with the surrender of the British at Yorktown in 1781, the new nation that emerged was hardly more than two hundred miles wide. According to historians John D'Emilio and Estelle Friedman, it was a hardscrabble society where "strong family ties, the predominance of self-contained farms, (and) the small size of the towns all led to the maintenance of strong traditions in church and state. In most places the official religion was the old Puritan creed, brought from England and differing little from the original Calvinism with its predestination and its strict adherence to the Bible as the revealed word of God." A core concern of this transplanted old-world morality was the tight control of all human sexual conduct. In their history of sexual traditions, John D'Emilio and Estelle B. Freedman wrote that "in Puritan theology, the entire community had responsibility for upholding morality . . . Moreover, individuals could not easily engage in illicit sex without being noticed in the close-knit towns . . . In the Chesapeake, as in New England, church and court prosecuted sinners, levying fines on or whipping those who fornicated, committed adultery, sodomy, or rape . . . In Maryland . . . unmarried couples who had sex could receive up to twenty lashes and could be fined as much as five hundred pounds of tobacco."

However, after the defeat of the British in 1781 other, less visible, revolutions began in the social and technological order of the former colonies. By the time of George Washington's death in 1799, the fundamental nature of American life and business had already been reshaped by a new national passion for things mechanical. The creation and potentially profitable use of mechanical contrivances had emerged as a force almost rivaling religion in its attraction of the imagination and daily aspirations of many individual citizens.

By the time Thomas Jefferson died in 1826, the river banks of the eastern seaboard had sprouted clusters of mills and factories surrounded by mazes of warehouses, dwellings, shops, and places of entertainment. The noise, color, and commercial vibrancy of such places was a siren song, and their anonymity promised a welcome refuge from the restrictive lifestyle of farms and rural crossroads towns. James Reed wrote that "the search for economic opportunity was leading the young away from their communities of origin. Geographical mobility weakened kinship ties and forced the newly married to be more dependent on their own consciences or internalized standards of conduct in ordering their lives. Economic change was also altering the roles of men and women within the family." The speed and scope of these changes were, in turn, greatly impacted by another new invention that simultaneously created and fed on public controversy and social conflict: the improved printing press.

Printing Press Improvements

By the 1830s, the same inventive energies that were changing the manufacture of everything from firearms to farm equipment were also altering the process of pressing inked characters onto paper. A series of new advancements involving ink making, paper handling, typesetting, and mechanized presses allowed factory-like printing operations to produce hundreds or even thousands of newspapers or books in the same time it had previously taken one-sheet, hand-cranked presses to produce a few dozen. This revolution in the capacity and economies of the printing business resulted in an explosion of publishing companies whose overall product was the first mass communications network.

Advertisements in newspapers traveling in saddlebags, fur pouches, and barge barrels provided mail-order merchants with markets of previously unthinkable size and diversity. The circulation of books and newspapers throughout an increasingly literate population also created a new kind of intimate, life-shaping connection between the individual and the daily experiences of the larger society. Even readers who lived in physical isolation could be exposed to a steady stream of new and often provocative ideas from the cities, where changing social and sexual values were the subject of often raucous public debate.

For instance, in New York City in 1831, former school superintendent and newspaper editor Robert Dale Owen published *Moral Physiology: A Brief and Plain Treatise on the Population Question*. It was the first book on contraceptive methods by an American author. A scholarly work recommending withdrawal as the primary means of preventing pregnancy, it was reprinted seven times during the first twelve months after its release—an extraordinary level of demand for a book in that period. Historian James Reed wrote that the controversy sparked by Owen's book "marked the beginning of a national debate over the morality and safety of contraceptive practice. In an age that proclaimed the ability of every person to save his soul and get rich, America began consuming self-help books . . . (which) provided a forum for discussion not only of family limitation but of the proper relationship between the family and society, as well as the role of man and woman within the family."

In 1832 Dr. Charles Knowlton, a respected Massachusetts physician, published *Fruits of Philosophy, or the Private Companion of Young Married People*, the first book to describe the use of mechanical hand-pump devices—syringes—to inject cleansing fluids into the vagina. Dr. Knowlton encouraged contraception by vigorous irrigation of the vagina to wash out or chemically destroy deposited semen. He explained how to use astringent vegetable brews such as green tea and boiled hemlock bark to kill the "animalcules" he believed to be the active agent in semen. Vilified by the clergy, Dr. Knowlton was formally charged with obscenity by a minister in Taunton, Massachusetts. He was tried in court, found guilty, and fined. In Lowell, Massachusetts, a community leader filed additional obscenity charges that resulted in another trial, in which Dr. Knowlton was found guilty and sentenced to three months of hard labor in jail. By 1840, despite such widespread condemnations and controversies, Dr. Knowlton's book had sold an incredible 10,000 authorized copies and had been extensively bootlegged by local printers.

Sex Product Advertising

Such commercial success did not go unnoticed. Growing numbers of entrepreneurs sought to exploit the obvious public desire for information, products and services related to the avoidance or termination of pregnancy. In *Woman's Body, Woman's Right: A Social History of Birth Control in America,* Linda Gordon explained: "Advertisements for abortifacients were plentiful. Newspapers printed many ads like these: 'Portuguese Female Pills, not to be used during pregnancy for they will cause miscarriage.' As the denomination 'French' almost always indicated some contraceptive device, so 'Portuguese' always referred to an abortifacient. Another standard euphemism for abortion was 'relief' or 'removing obstacles.' 'A Great and Sure Remedy for Married Ladies—The Portuguese Female Pills always give immediate relief . . . Price $5 . . .' Many such ads were actually offering emmenagogues, medicines to stimulate menstruation when it was late or irregular. Thus they were called 'Female Regulators' and advertised without mentioning even the euphemisms for abortion."

"So bold and competitive was the market for abortion," wrote Ellen Chesler, "that journalists began to question, not so much its morality, as its independence from any regulation whatsoever in terms of price, quality or availability to the unwed." Former barbers, brothel managers, patent medicine wagoneers, and any number of other self-proclaimed "doctors" set up shop in the booming new trade now estimated to have terminated one of every five pregnancies by the late 1840s. Unfortunately, the various caustic chemical solutions, boiled vegetable poisons, sharp blades, pointed wires, and other odd tools inserted to conduct these procedures also produced toxic reactions, infections, and hemorrhages that ended the lives of increasing numbers of women and created a public scandal. Mainstream medical practitioners, clergymen, social reformers, and politicians decried abortion in an ever more organized manner. Some were concerned with the moral aspects of the issue; others with the practical—and often fatal—outcome of internal surgical procedures performed by untrained individuals competing directly with established physicians.

Homemade Condoms

The rising political hue against abortion as well as the justified fear of its frequently harmful consequences intensified market pressures that already favored contraceptive devices. The problem was, there weren't many available. Condoms of processed sheep gut were available, but problematic. Fitted with a top tie string to cinch them securely about the penis, they had to be carefully washed out, dried, and stored after each use because of their rarity and expense. While some literature explained how housewives could purchase raw animal intestines from local butcher shops and make their own condoms, it's not difficult to imagine how most women responded to such an aesthetically bereft idea.

Meanwhile, inventors and manufacturers competed to provide better mechanical means to achieve the same ends. Newspapers had begun running ads for mail-order purchases of syringes and powders required for the douching methods popularized in 1830s books. The first versions of a commercial "vaginal sponge" barrier were being offered for sale. German doctors reported new vaginal barrier-type inventions: one used wax molds of the upper vagina to cast cervical caps to block passage of semen into the uterus; another was a vaginal diaphragm device made from an early form of the vulcanized rubber just invented and still being perfected by Charles Goodyear.

It was in this milieu in 1845, two floors above the Rochester, New York, riverfront, that dentist John Beers abruptly diverted his inventive attentions from molars and gums to vaginas, completing the invention that would be granted America's first sex patent.

Dr. John Beers

When Dr. Beers arrived in Rochester in 1839, it was the country's first frontier "boom" town. Built around the falls where the Genesee River flowed into Lake Ontario, Rochester was a cobblestone and wood-frame metropolis of grain speculators, shipping magnates, and financiers.

Nicknamed "Flour City," Rochester had the largest grain mills in the world, boasting some of the most complex machinery of their time. They were one of the reasons the city had a large community of tradesmen as well as a communal fascination with gadgetry and invention. This was the very dawn of the Industrial Revolution and America was a civilization suddenly seized, as in a mythical vision, with the idea that a man of modest means who created some new and useful contrivance might propel himself to that position of status now more revered than European royalty—the American millionaire.

One of the first seven dentists to set up shop in Rochester, Dr. Beers was also an avid mechanical tinker and inventor. He had to be. Dentists had to fashion most of their own implements and appliances and thus be skilled as metallurgists, machinists, carpenters, and sculptors. This focus on the engineering and fabrication problems presented by carved

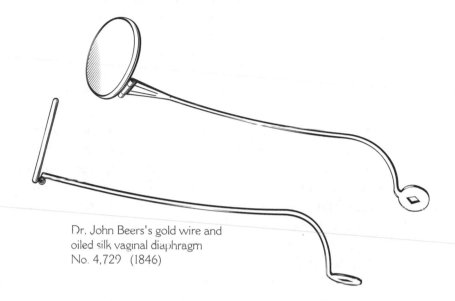

Dr. John Beers's gold wire and
oiled silk vaginal diaphragm
No. 4,729 (1846)

teeth, hinged plates, corrosion-resistant spring systems, gold wire
anchors, drilling implements, and extraction tools made dentistry one
of the most mechanically intensive trades of the time.

In 1845, at a workbench lit by flickering whale oil lamps, Dr. Beers
crossed the concept of the sturdy, gold-coated wire constructions and
miniature hinges of his dental work with the idea that a temporary
barrier inserted into the vagina could prevent semen from entering
the uterus. He worked to define and perfect a mechanical device that
could prevent conception; that would not unduly interrupt a pleasurable sexual coupling; that offered females an implement with which
they could take control of their own sexuality; and that was a
manufactured product which could be profitably marketed for its
advantages over abortion, gut condoms, crude cervical caps, and
poisonous liquid douches.

In early 1846, Dr. Beers completed his design and had two
colleagues—a local bookbinder and an attorney—sign their names as

witnesses to the drawings and descriptions he sent off to the U.S. Patent Office's new headquarters at F and Eighth Streets in Washington, D.C. Dr. Beers informed Patent Commissioner Edmund Burke that he was applying for a patent on a new invention he called a "Wife's Protector" that was designed to prevent conception. The invention was a diaphragm made of oiled silk stretched across a hoop made of gold and "platina" wire.

"To use this instrument," Dr. Beers wrote to the patent examiners, "the hoop is to be pressed down upon the handle by the thumb of the right hand, turning it edgewise, and then introduced into the vagina, when, immediately after having passed the sphincter, and the bones of the pelvis, it extends itself to its natural position, nearly at right angles with the rod or stem, and as it is farther introduced, the handle is to be turned downward 1/4 of a circle. In this position the membrane on the hoop is made to completely cover the os uteri, thus entirely preventing the semen from entering the uterus, without which (it is assumed) conception can not take place."

One can only imagine the discussions that went on between the Patent Commissioner and his two examiners about this unusual patent submission. Ultimately, they concluded that the Beers diaphragm was a new mechanical concept that was potentially useful and, thus, met the requirements for a patent grant. On August 28, 1846, they issued the dentist U.S. patent number 4,729—an event that seems likely to have generated significant interest and discussion among Dr. Beers's Rochester peers, given the rarity and perceived prestige of patent awards in this era.

The Aftermath of Beers's Invention

There is no documentation about how the city's close-knit society of moral reformist business professionals responded to Dr. Beers's triumph of becoming the first inventor to receive a patent for a device designed to facilitate more carefree sexual relations. But it is known that about twenty months after the U.S. Patent Office granted his patent, Dr. Beers closed his dental practice, packed his household belongings, and vacated his flat. He then joined the throng of eighty thousand easterners thronging to the California territory at the news of gold strikes at Sutter's mill. They would turn the wilderness of the Sacramento valley into a rich and unrestrained series of boom towns. Beers established a dental practice in San Francisco, and would go on to receive other U.S. patents for the landmark concept of dental crowns, as well as for improvements in the process of gold sluicing.

Historically, Beers's 1846 gold ring diaphragm patent was unique not only because it was the first that directly addressed human intercourse, but also because it embodied such a straightforward affirmation of sexual pleasure.

Beers's work helped alert droves of other inventors to the commercial possibilities of proprietary sex inventions. Between the 1840s and 1901—a period roughly covering the Victorian era—more than two hundred patents relating to human sexuality were granted by the Patent Office.

But the attitude inherent in most of these subsequent devices was markedly different from that of the upbeat Dr. Beers. The new wave of inventors sought to adapt the materials and concepts of an accelerating Industrial Revolution to a much darker vision—the forcible control and suppression of human sexual instinct.

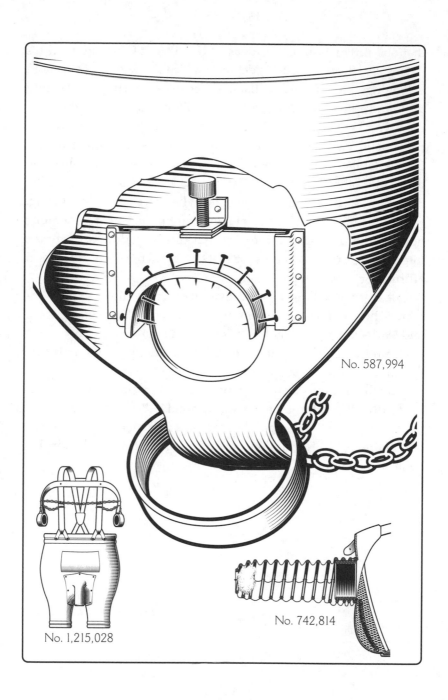

No. 587,994

No. 1,215,028

No. 742,814

2

America's Assault on the Solitary Vice

Although we tend to think of them as "physicians," the medical practitioners of the 1700s were actually closer to what we know as shamans than medical doctors. Heirs to a culture that still believed in possession by evil spirits, they also believed that the "pull" of the moon was responsible for menstruation as well as madness in humans. They dissected cadavers to learn how the soul physically connected to the nervous system, and debated whether yellow fever epidemics were caused by swamp gas or by God taking vengeance against communities that tolerated such sinful activities as dance halls.

The intellectual tenor of these times is succinctly captured in the writings of Simon-Andre Tissot, a French physician and author whose works were widely circulated on both sides of the Atlantic. In 1758 Dr. Tissot wrote *Onanism*, a book that explained why masturbation was harmful to the human nervous system and brain. The book's title was derived from a story in the Bible's Book of Genesis, in which Judah commanded his son, Onan, to impregnate his sister-in-law shortly after her husband was killed. Apparently not anxious to have sex with his brother's wife, Onan withdrew before orgasm, ejaculating on the ground. He was subsequently struck dead by God. The original moral of this story was the importance of obedience: Onan died after he disobeyed his father. However, European religious authorities held that Onan's use of a woman's vagina to excite himself to orgasm, coupled with his conscious attempt to avoid impregnating his partner, constituted an act of masturbation—the sin for which he was slain by God.

In *Onanism*, Dr. Tissot explained his belief that masturbation increased blood pressure inside the skull in a way that irreparably damaged the nervous system and caused insanity. The book's twelve lively chapters provided case histories of persons who were said to have died of consumption, gone mad, become impotent, or been rendered feeble, crippled, blind, or deaf by masturbation.

"Coming from an unimpeachable medical authority, Tissot's book had a profound effect on medical thought," explained historian E. H. Hare. "By the end of the eighteenth century the masturbatory hypothesis was widely accepted throughout Europe and America."

One of those who embraced the idea of a masturbation-insanity link was Benjamin Rush, Chief Surgeon of the Continental Army, signer of the Declaration of Independence, Treasurer of the first U.S. Mint, temperance reformer, lecturer, and teacher, as well as the single most influential medical writer of the opening decades of the American republic. Like other medical scholars of the time, Dr. Rush was grappling with new information that undermined traditional assumptions about mental health. For instance, in 1809, a study about madness and the moon established that lunar forces were *not* a major cause of insanity. Another causal factor previously associated with insanity—possession by the devil—had also been largely abandoned by physicians. Many in the scientific community, including Dr. Rush, were trying to identify other factors that might cause insanity.

At the time the moon-and-madness report was released, Dr. Rush was working on what would be America's first medical treatise on psychiatry. When *Medical Inquiries and Observations upon the Diseases of the Mind* was published three years later in 1812, it taught that "what is commonly called madness (is) a disease of the blood-vessels of the brain," and that one of the causes of this disease was masturbation. In support of this conclusion, Dr. Rush cited his

Daniel Cook's
"Self Protector"
No. 104,117 (1870)

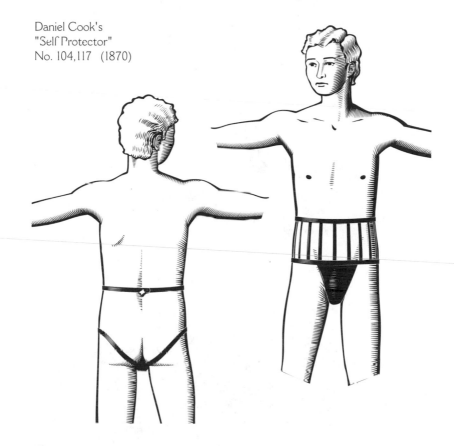

firsthand clinical experience with persons he said had masturbated themselves into insanity.

Dr. Rush's writings established much of what was taken as medical fact for the next century. Throughout the 1800s there emerged many competing schools of medical therapy across America, ranging from mainstream MDs to vegetable-brew Thomsonians, from Seventh-Day Adventist spiritual healers to water-cure hydropaths. But a common link among all of them was the belief that masturbation was not just a morally reprehensible behavior, but a disease in its own right.

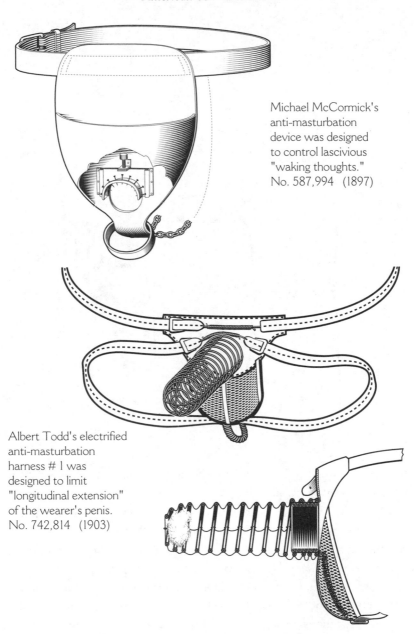

Michael McCormick's anti-masturbation device was designed to control lascivious "waking thoughts." No. 587,994 (1897)

Albert Todd's electrified anti-masturbation harness # 1 was designed to limit "longitudinal extension" of the wearer's penis. No. 742,814 (1903)

Records left by physicians throughout the latter half of the 1800s indicate that medical professionals organized national anti-masturbation movements that urged family members and peers to spy on and expose suspected masturbators. Illinois physician Allen W. Hagenbach wrote that some adults who were unmasked as masturbators were incarcerated against their will in insane asylums. In other cases, local government officials approved forced surgeries to remove the testicles of proven adult masturbators.

Inevitably, the problem of how to prevent masturbation and its attendant commercial possibilities caught the attention of America's inventors. In 1870, Daniel Cook of Connecticut applied for a patent on a device for "covering up the sexual organs of a person addicted to the vice of masturbation. Cook's invention was called a "self protector" and involved a genital pouch which could be fixed around the lower body with a lockable girdle of leather or metal bands. The pouch itself was to be customized so that it was "impossible for the wearer to touch the confined organ." Cook noted that a small hole had to be left in the pouch so that urine could dribble out when necessary.

Along with those who were forcibly restrained from the practice by surgery or devices like Cooks's, many others voluntarily sought treatment to curb their habit. Males and females worried about the long-term effects of solitary sexual activities became a profitable market for highly competitive patent medicine wagoneers, mail-order entrepreneurs, and special storefront "medical institutes" offering therapies, elixirs, and gadgetry for controlling masturbation.

In 1896, entrepreneur Michael McCormick of San Francisco sought a patent for an abdomen-mounted, anti-erection device with sharp metal points that was designed to be worn under the clothing. In the case of an "irresponsible" person who needed to be involuntarily restrained from participating in the solitary vice, McCormick noted that the "appliance can be permanently secured to him . . . (with) a fastening strip of some permanent character, like sticking-plaster."

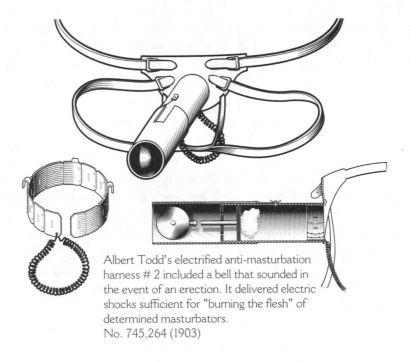

Albert Todd's electrified anti-masturbation harness # 2 included a bell that sounded in the event of an erection. It delivered electric shocks sufficient for "burning the flesh" of determined masturbators.
No. 745,264 (1903)

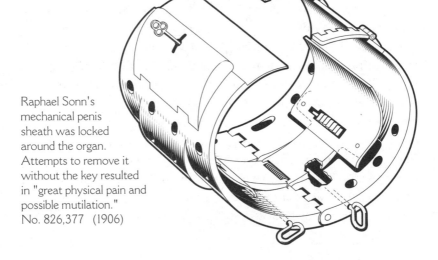

Raphael Sonn's mechanical penis sheath was locked around the organ. Attempts to remove it without the key resulted in "great physical pain and possible mutilation."
No. 826,377 (1906)

In 1903, Albert Todd of Colorado asked the Patent Office to grant him protection on two versions of a device that applied electricity to the task of deterring masturbation. The first was a wire-coil penis-and-testicle cage so fabricated as to "resist any reasonable effort on the part of the wearer in an attempt to break or cut" his way out. The wire cage was designed to physically "limit longitudinal extension" of the organ within. The device also featured a galvanic belt composed of zinc and copper plates that generated a current of electricity when wetted with acids. The current could be generated either by "secretions of the body coming into contact with the belt," or "by dipping the belt into a suitable acid solution for a few minutes" before cinching it around the masturbator. Not insensitive to the potential effect of electricity applied directly to genitals, the inventor noted that the cage and its wire testicle pouch "may be insulated, if desired, in order to protect the patient from the results of a too powerful current of electricity generated by the electric belt."

A month later, the Patent Office examiners granted Todd a second patent for an electrified, solid penile cylinder with an alarm feature. Shaped with a hollow tube and fitted with an internal plunger/detector, the invention could mechanically detect the expansion of the penis and trigger different responses. These included an alarm bell and "a current of electricity strong enough to assist the cure of sexual diseases." Todd again attempted to be sensitive to the potential traumatic effects of the treatment and noted that "if necessary, the inner face of the (electric) belt may be covered with chamois-skin to prevent the belt from burning the flesh." Additional anti-masturbation features were built into a deluxe version, including metal "points and brads," which were "of sufficient length to cause considerable annoyance and pain to the patient should any attempt be made to manipulate the penis by means of the tube." He explained that "in practice the appliance is strapped to the patient" with a band "of sufficient length to be tied in difficult knots to prevent a weak-minded patient from removing the device."

One apparent disadvantage of Todd's approach was that these devices were bulky and difficult to conceal under clothing, thus limiting their utility and sales potential. Three years later, seeking to remedy this deficiency, Raphael A. Sonn presented a miniaturized anti-masturbation device to the Patent Office. His key-locked penile clamp was easily concealed by clothing and well suited for "walk around" use. As brutally ingenious as it was compact, the sheath of intricately machined metal parts featured an internal clamp as well as a lock and key. Sonn explained the best way to use the invention: "In positioning the appliance the sheath members are unlocked and moved to position . . . It is then properly disposed on the organ and locked, after which the holding-pins are withdrawn, thereby allowing the clamping members and gripping elements to resume their operative positions. Once positioned, it will be impossible to remove the appliance without great physical pain and possible mutilation, and if removed it cannot be replaced without the key, so that detection will be inevitable."

The Attack on Asylum Masturbation

Since the early 1800s, when it became accepted that masturbation caused insanity, asylums were compelled to address this problem as a daily concern. Medical textbooks taught that masturbation not only caused—but also progressively worsened—the state of mental derangement. Thus, physically preventing a patient from further masturbation was perceived as a crucial element in the treatment of his or her madness. In his study of the daily practices inside asylums throughout America in 1876, John Charles Bucknill reported that the use of physical restraints was considered justified for four categories of patients: "(1) suicidal patients, (2) persons who will not remain in bed, (3) persons who persistently denude themselves of all clothing, and lastly (4) the inveterate masturbator."

An Australian physician who prepared an extensive government report about his tours of asylums in the United States in the late 1800s noted that "cages, iron chains, handcuffs, hobbles, straps, crib beds, and fixed chairs are common modes of restraint for patients . . . In one institution I saw 215 women in various modes of restraint—camisoles, wristlets, straps, etc.—secured upright to racks around the dayrooms. In another there were forty-three women in box beds, ironed hand and foot, and extended in spread-eagle fashion, at 3 in the afternoon."

Potent pharmaceuticals also became part of this arsenal of asylum restraints. In his account of a typical situation in an Indianapolis institution, Dr. Alexander Robertson reported, "About 100 out of the 330 patients were getting special medical treatment . . . Opium is given in large doses . . . Many are taking bromide of potassium in 30 gr. doses; no medicine like it, in Dr. Lockhart's experience, in its influence over epilepsy and in repressing the habit of masturbation." The general premise was that high levels of nervous tension fueled a person's drive to masturbate. Calming the patient's overall nervous condition with opium was believed to greatly ease the person's tensions.

The link between masturbation and mental health remained a concern among institutional officials well beyond the turn of the century. In 1908, Ellen E. Perkins of Beaver Bay, Minnesota, told the examiners in the U.S. Patent Office, "It is a deplorable but well known fact that one of the most common causes of insanity, imbecility and feeblemindedness, especially in youth, is due to masturbation or self abuse."

"The many melancholy human tragedies of this character," Perkins wrote, "which have transpired before my own eyes, have impressed upon me the great necessity of a device which will aid those concerned in the treatment of such cases (and) in the cure for this disastrous practice."

Perkins then provided the patent examiners with the drawings and descriptions of an invention she called "Sexual Armor." Its central technological feature was a lockable metal compartment that covered the complete crotch area of a male or female. She noted that the leather straps connecting the assembly to the patient should also be secured with padlocks "so that it will be absolutely impossible to remove the garment." The metal crotch portion had a hinged genital "gate" with holes so that "liquid matter may be passed there through." The gate could also be swung open "by the proper person" to permit defecation.

Perkins explained that "in actual practice I have found that an armor or device of the character above described, when properly made and fitted to a patient, may be worn with very little, if any, discomfort, and that when properly covered by garments the fact of its application will not be noticeable." After a review, the patent examiners judged her invention to be novel and potentially useful and granted Ms. Perkins a patent for anti-masturbation armor.

Two years later, in 1910, Jonas Edward Heyser of Philadelphia, Pennsylvania, presented the Patent Office with an application for a less cumbersome genital barrier device "for use on insane patients." He said his metal genital pouch with riveted leather straps and a lockable body harness "cannot be removed by the patient and will absolutely prevent any attempt on the part of the patient to masturbate."

Mindful of competing inventors who might be working along similar lines with different materials, Heyser asked the patent examiners to grant him protection for leather, sheet metal, and chain mail versions of the device. He also described different configurations for use on individual patients with special needs.

In 1915, Alfred M. Jones of Des Moines, Iowa, proposed to the Patent Office that they grant protection to his idea of putting the asylum patient in a suit of rubber, canvas, chain, and iron so bulky it could have been mistaken as part of some underwater diving apparatus. He explained that "the principal object of the invention is to provide an appliance . . . for use in hospitals, sanatoriums, and the like . . . to treat patients for the purpose of protecting them from practicing masturbation or self-abuse."

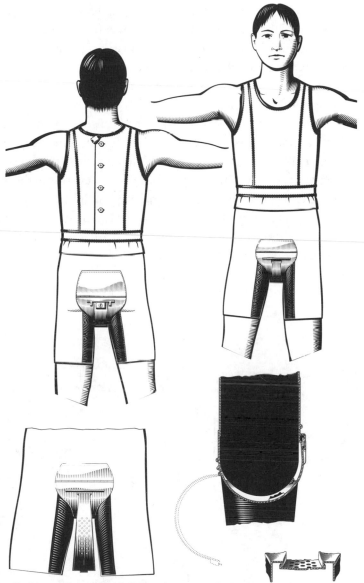

Ellen Perkins told the Patent Office that masturbation was such a serious problem in the insane asylums where she worked that she invented metal "Sexual Armor" to deny patients access to their genitals. No. 875,845 (1908)

Jones pointed out that "the garment is provided with a belt, to which are secured the suspenders engaging over the shoulders of the patient, and provided with a breast strap and a back strap to prevent the patient from pushing the suspenders down from the shoulders. In the seams of the belt are sewed chain . . . The end of the rubber pouch is provided with a stiff ring which produces an opening through which urine is discharged. This ring is of such diameter that the patient cannot get his or her finger therein. On females . . . the rubber pouch may be dispensed with and an open wire mesh pouch substituted through which urine can pass. The lower ends of the legs of the garment are provided with comparatively tight bands . . . to prevent the entrance of the hand by the patient . . . suspender straps are reinforced with woven wire fabric . . . to insure against the possibility of the patient forcing an opening through which to insert the hand."

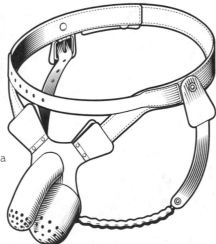

Jonas Edward Heyser received a patent for leather, sheet-metal and chain-mail versions of this anti-masturbation genital pouch for asylum patients.
No. 995,600 (1910)

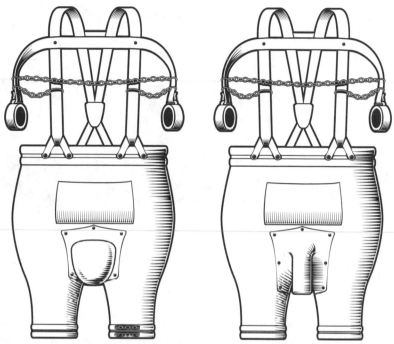

Alfred Jones invented extraordinarily bulky asylum anti-masturbation suits resembling underwater diving gear. Made of rubber, canvas, iron, and chain, they were available in male and female versions. No. 1,215,028 (1917)

Fading Concern

Interest in the invention and commercial protection of anti-masturbation technology appears to have faded in the wake of World War I, although it did not disappear. Some mental institutions continued to classify masturbation as a "functional disturbance" that required treatment up until 1933. A survey of the period detailed in *Sin, Sickness & Sanity: A History of Sexual Attitudes* indicates that reputable medical reference books published up until 1936 continued to recommend the use of mutilating surgical procedures—such as cauterization—to deter masturbators.

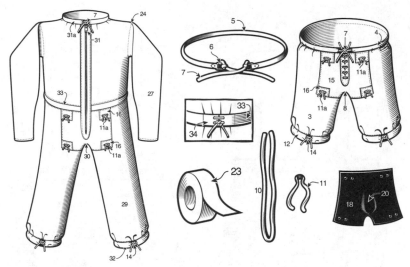

Allan Risley's anti-masturbation night clothing system included special adhesive tape that could be used to glue portions of the garments directly to the skin around the thigh and groin area. No. 1,865,280 (1936)

One final patent application was submitted in 1930 by Allan P. Risley of Indianapolis, Indiana, for a system of restraining clothing. While suitable for some institutional purposes, the invention appears to also have been aimed at a larger consumer market as well. The Risley anti-masturbation system swathed its wearer in layers of barrier clothing held together by webs of laces, zippers, and cords that could tightly cinch off sections of the male or female body. It included special reinforced slots that allowed adhesives to be inserted to cement the interior surface of the garment to the skin of the wearer to ensure the barrier integrity.

Risley told the Patent Office that his invention was "especially adapted to protect and prevent male and female persons from handling certain parts of the anatomy while asleep or partly asleep and thereby prevent masturbation during such time." In the spring of 1932 Risley was granted the Patent Office's last anti-masturbation patent.

Meanwhile, the broad medical establishment was rapidly moving toward the acceptance of a more objective scientific view of human sexuality. This new era was crystallized in the 1948 and 1953 landmark studies by Alfred Kinsey suggesting that masturbation was a common practice among American males and females.

Medically, all the fantastic theories that originally motivated the creation of anti-masturbation machinery have long been recognized as wrong. Psychologically, though, it's a different picture. The concept of masturbation as an unnatural and reprehensible behavior is still inextricably tangled in our culture. Clear evidence of this can be seen in the 1994 *Sex in America* survey that, on the one hand, established that 60 percent of American males and 40 percent of American females between the ages of eighteen and fifty-nine masturbate regularly, but on the other hand, that half of those people feel significant amounts of guilt each time they do so.

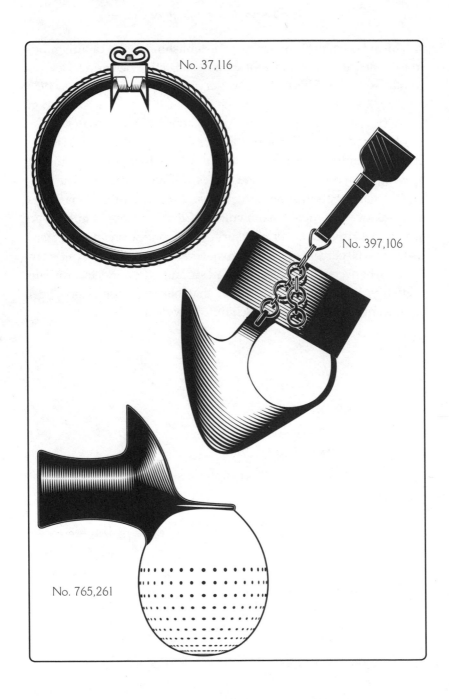

No. 37,116

No. 397,106

No. 765,261

3

The War on Wet Dreams

It is not difficult to understand why ancient cultures viewed human semen as a sacred substance. Knowing the human body only by what could be seen, it would have been obvious that ejaculate contained the very essence of new life and involved mysterious celestial forces that demanded awe and caution.

Records left behind by past civilizations indicate that this liquid life force was believed to be part of a finite reservoir within each male; every expenditure of semen being seen as an irretrievable loss of that person's total energy. Within such a belief system, nocturnal orgasms were understandably a matter of serious concern. In the first century A.D., Pliny the Elder recorded that some Roman men slept with small, flat ingots of lead against their genitals. He explained that the "comparative chilly nature" of the leaden plates helped keep the sleeper from being aroused to "venereal passions and the libidinous dreams that cause spontaneous emissions."

A hundred years later in the second century A. D., Galen, one of the most influential medical writers of the ancient world, also reported that Greek men slept with cold leaden plates at their loins to prevent nocturnal emissions. He noted that males were advised to avoid such emissions by sleeping on their sides, sleeping on a "hard, cold bed," or packing their genitals in sponges dipped in vinegar.

The Theory of Seminal Weakness

By the early 1700s, as the professional disciplines of what would become modern medicine and science were just emerging, they continued to embrace the belief that excessive semen loss could be physically harmful.

By the time of the American Revolution, it was an accepted medical fact that "seminal weakness" caused by excessive loss of semen was a serious disease that could even contribute to dementia. By the 1830s, this area of treatment was deemed sufficiently important to warrant its own medical textbook, *On Involuntary Seminal Discharges*, by Claude-Francois Lallemand. Dr. Lallemand coined a new term—"spermatorrhoea"—to encompass the growing list of aliments attributed to the loss of the body's vital balancing force through nocturnal emissions. This new disease was of particular concern in America because it was believed to sap the physical strength, sense of logic, and intellectual powers required for fruitful business endeavors. Individuals who did poorly at their jobs or seemed overly tired or inattentive to other matters were often suspected by peers and family members of being secret victims of spermatorrhoea.

"Nocturnal Pollutions"

General male anxiety in this area was further heightened by new Victorian medical theories that held that nocturnal emissions were *not* involuntary at all, but rather caused directly by the immoral daily thoughts of the individual. William Acton, a physician specializing in diseases of the urinary and generative organs and author of a number of eminent works on the subject, referred to the problem as "nocturnal pollutions" and taught that men who were "not debased" had the power to keep their "dreaming thoughts pure."

Imagine how males who experienced emissions in their sleep worried about being suspected by their wives of engaging in depraved thoughts or other sexual excesses during the day. They also had to grapple with their own fears about the physical harm such seemingly unstoppable nighttime events might cause.

Many physicians offered cures for spermatorrhoea. Dr. Louis Bauer of St. Louis described a typical patient: "It was evident that his mind was greatly agitated (and) that he lived in constant fear that he might lose his reason." The doctor administered potassium and chloral hydrate to lessen sexual response, and also performed surgery. "I (pierced) the (foreskin) by silk slings, and directed (the patient) to fasten them in front of the glans penis on going to bed," explained the doctor. "The object being to wake the patient by pain when the penis should get in a state of erection. This treatment proved effectual in preventing seminal emissions."

Anti-Nocturnal Emission Technology

A major disadvantage of such surgical procedures was that the foreskin eventually became riddled with holes. Having one's penile parts pierced was also a daunting emotional experience. Not surprisingly, many men sought to devise better ways of preventing nocturnal emissions. Patent medicine companies sold all manner of bottled substances they claimed could save men from the shame and debilitating effects of nocturnal emissions. Religious reformers called on males to adopt ascetic lifestyles organized around bland, meatless diets featuring raw vegetables, coarse-grain breads, and mineral water. And manufacturing entrepreneurs and tinkers in general saw a potentially profitable market for a mechanical product that could inhibit nighttime emissions.

Writing in the *Charleston Medical Journal* in the fall of 1853, South Carolina physician J.A. Mayes excoriated the hucksters who were merchandising miracle cures for spermatorrhoea. He charged that "the unfortunate subjects of this disease have often exhausted their purses by buying nostrums (but) the remedies of the advertising

  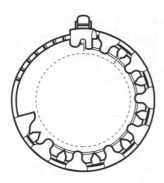

Medical journals indicate that penile pricking rings were first used by Boston physicians in the 1850s. L. D. Sibley, who lived near Boston, received a patent on the device in 1856. No. 14,739 (1856)

quack have failed to do any good, the suffering man remaining weaker in both purse and body." Dr. Mayes announced that he had found a more effective treatment that was, he wrote, "a purely mechanical one . . . I allude to the Spermatorrhoea Rings lately used by the Boston physicians."

Dr. Mayes explained he had used a spermatorrhoea ring successfully on a patient suffering from nocturnal emissions. The man, he said, "had become very much impaired, and his disorder occupied his thoughts so much as to render him almost incompetent to attend to any kind of business." The doctor provided the patient with a penile ring obtained from a mail-order company in Baltimore. He noted that "the first week of its use (the patient) could scarcely sleep at all, being awakened every few minutes by the teeth of the ring piercing his flesh; sometimes waking in fright, dreaming that some serpent had seized him by the organ. The interruption to the seminal discharges, however, was almost complete the first week; and from that time till now, he has been constantly wearing the ring at nights with a complete exemption from the disorder."

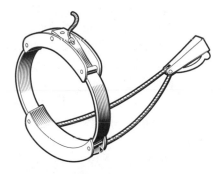

Dwight Gibbons's "Spermatic Ring"
featured a quick release mechanism.
No. 22,796 (1859)

Pricking Ring Patents

Three years later, in 1856, L. D. Sibley of Northampton, Massachusetts, was granted the first patent for an improved version of the nocturnal penile ring. Sibley said that his improved ring was "for the purpose of pricking the penis only sufficiently hard to awaken the patient and warn him of danger, as soon as the organ begins to distend and erect itself and before any evil consequence ensues." Three years later, a Rochester, New York man was granted a patent for a "Spermatic Ring" incorporating features that allowed it to be "more easily adapted to suit organs of various sizes (and which will) bring its point into action upon the organ more suddenly and without previous irritation."

In 1861, the first year of the Civil War, Hiram H. Reynolds received patents for a spiral spring and a pressure-plate-with-abrasive-pricks devices. Each sandwiched the penis between spring-tension pressure-plate assemblies. Reynolds explained the first: "The erection of the penis is prevented by the action of the coiled spring which exerts a pressure upon the glans penis against an increase in length and by the action of pressure against an increase in diameter

... the result is that an erection makes but slow progress and soon dies away." The second version was somewhat more aggressive in its design, incorporating metal spurs around the pressure plates. Reynolds explained that "this pressure and pricking of the roughened surface of the plates, although it will not pierce or wound the flesh, will produce the kind of uncomfortable sensation and counterirritant as will arrest the excitement and wholly prevent an involuntary emission."

A year later, La Roy Sunderland of Boston informed the patent examiners that designs like that of Reynolds were highly suspect. He explained that such direct pressure "served rather to increase than to diminish sexual excitement, thereby tending much more to promote than to prevent the disease which it is desired to cure." Sunderland

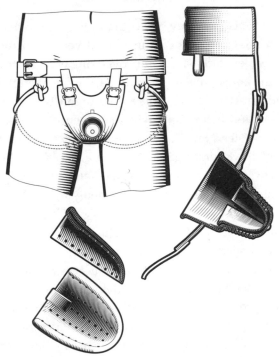

Hiram H. Reynolds's metal-spur penile pressure harness was worn to sleep. It employed abrasive pressure plates to envelop the flaccid penis. An erection caused the plates to dig into the organ, causing pain that would "arrest the excitement." No. 33,162 (1861)

went on to say that his own spartan pricking ring invention was superior because "while it may be secured to the body of the person it will not come in direct contact with the penis when not excited . . . but may be so arranged as to give the necessary alarm . . . I accomplish this result by attaching to a ring . . . an elastic spring-lever armed with teeth or sharp points . . . set at any desired horizontal and vertical angle with regard to the periphery of the ring, whereby it can be regulated so as to conform to

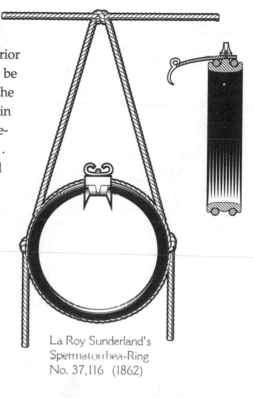

La Roy Sunderland's
Spermatorrhea-Ring
No. 37,116 (1862)

any and all positions and sizes of the penis."

In 1876, Harvey A. Stephenson of Pennsylvania was granted a patent for what he called a "Spermatic Truss." This device was designed for "preventing involuntary erections, and repressing inordinate amative desire, and too frequent emissions." Suitable for wearing beneath clothing, the Stephenson Spermatic Truss was a leather and canvas affair that allowed the user to place his penis in a pouch, secure it with a loop of string, and then stretch the penis down and back between the legs, where it was held in place by a taut buttocks strap. In such a forced position, erections were extremely painful, thereby focusing the mind on the physical discomfort and away from the lascivious thoughts that had started the process. Four

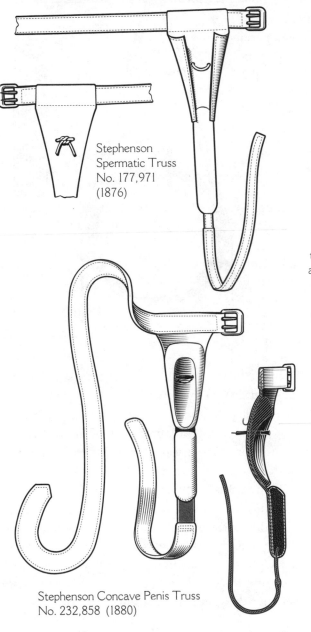

Stephenson
Spermatic Truss
No. 177,971
(1876)

To "prevent involuntary erections" and repress "amative desire" during both day and night, Harvey Stephenson of Pennsylvania invented two varieties of a penile truss. The penis was tied in, then pulled down and back between the legs. Even a partial erection caused significant pain.

Stephenson Concave Penis Truss
No. 232,858 (1880)

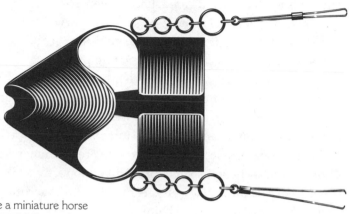

Not unlike a miniature horse bridle, James H. Bowen's invention fit over the head of the penis. The spring clasps at the ends of the chains were then anchored to tufts of pubic hair at the base of the penis. In the event of an erection, the pubic hair was pulled, causing acute pain that awakened the sleeper.
No. 397,106 (1889)

years later Stephenson received another patent for a refinement of his canvas design that, he indicated, had proven insufficiently strong to restrain some penises. His new version was carved from a piece of hard wood. Like the first, it drew the penis down and back so that even a partial erection caused excruciating pain.

In 1889, James H. Bowen of Philadelphia, Pennsylvania, unveiled a nocturnal erection prevention invention that seemed particularly distinctive in its design aesthetics as well as in its creative approach to the use of pain as an anti-erotic force. Bowen appears to have drawn inspiration, at least in part, from the restraining mechanisms of horse bridles. The stylish lines of his invention are visually suggestive of an ornate piece of jewelry. A metal cap was secured over the head of the penis, with small chains on either side dropping down to end in spring-loaded clips. These clips were used to securely grasp tufts of pubic hair at the base of the penis. When an erection began and the penis extended beyond the length of the delicate chains, the pubic hair was pulled, inflicting a kind of pain guaranteed to wake the sleeper who was, according to Bowen, "thereby enabled to prevent or check the discharge."

Penile Coolers

At the other end of the scale from Bowen's minimalist design elegance were the innovations of Frank Orth, an inventor from Astoria, Oregon, who opened what might be thought of as the Rube Goldberg era of nocturnal emissions control technology. In 1893, Orth was granted patents for water-cooled and air-cooled night harness systems, each as bulky and complicated as a major kitchen appliance. One had its own plumbing system, with a water reservoir mounted on the wall and a drainage tub beneath the bed. The other employed the latest technology of the era—a battery-powered electric motor. The motor drove a fan that forced cooling air down a tube into rubber drawers fitted with air circulation bladders.

Each of these thermal harness systems was installed permanently in the bedroom, like a piece of furniture. At night, the user would fit his body into the device and then, along with the trailing straps, wires, and flexible pipes, slide under the covers.

In the case of the gravity-powered water system, Orth explained that "the penis is inserted in the hole and between the levers . . . (so that) if during the night, an erection occurs, the dilation of the penis spreads the levers, thus separating the jaws, and permitting the cold water to flow through the tube to the sack or envelope. The cold water fills the hollow walls of the sack or envelope, and cools the organs of generation, so that the erection subsides and no discharge occurs."

Orth's electrically powered air-cooled apparatus was based on the common belief that as the body heated up beneath comfortable bed covers, it became more sexually responsive. He explained to the U.S. Patent Office examiners that "in the event the organ should become heated and an erection should take place, the enlargement of the organ will cause . . . the spring rods to engage with the terminal wires of the circuit and close same; at this time the fan will be set in motion and the organ will be subjected to a current of cool air until its expansion is overcome." The same circuit provided for "the sounding of an alarm bell prior to the critical period being reached."

This idea of linking the penis to an audible alarm system had also caught the imagination of other inventors who, at the turn of the century, were also working in the erection detection and prevention field. In 1899, George E. Dudley of California received a patent for a metal tube device that fit over the penis, to be strapped in place by a waist band. An intricate, clock-like mechanism inside the tube used a light piston to detect penile movement. A ratchet wheel, springs, and elastic band power were used to trigger a bell at the top of the tube when an erection occurred. This, according to Dudley, "will awake the sleeper to that self-control which will relieve him from the consequences which would otherwise occur."

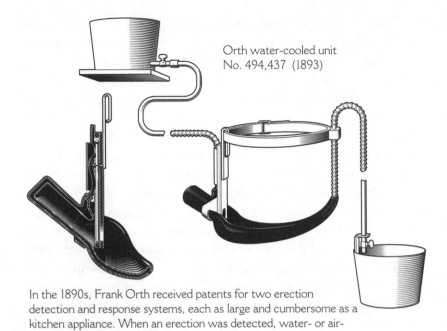

Orth water-cooled unit
No. 494,437 (1893)

In the 1890s, Frank Orth received patents for two erection detection and response systems, each as large and cumbersome as a kitchen appliance. When an erection was detected, water- or air-cooling systems were triggered to chill the sleeper's penis.

Orth air-cooled unit
No. 494,436 (1893)

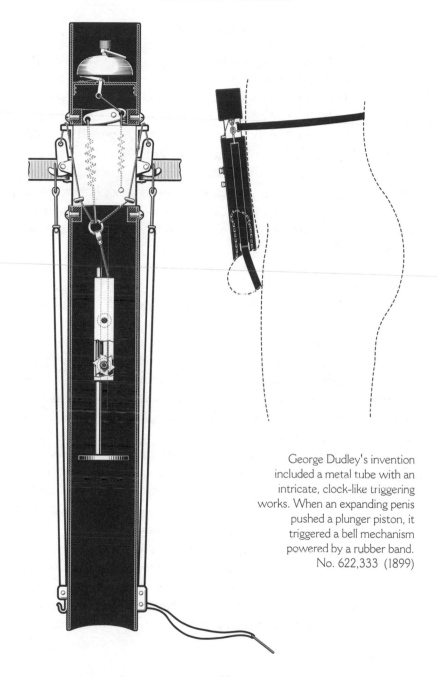

George Dudley's invention included a metal tube with an intricate, clock-like triggering works. When an expanding penis pushed a plunger piston, it triggered a bell mechanism powered by a rubber band. No. 622,333 (1899)

The Electric Age

At the turn of the century, electricity had become a craze as the nation's newspapers lionized a new national hero in the person of the "Wizard of Menlo Park"—Thomas Edison. In 1878, Edison, who had made a modest fortune inventing improvements to Samuel Morse's telegraph system, received a patent for, and was catapulted to world fame by what would be his single most original invention—the talking machine. By the 1890s Edison's own phonograph, as well as competing devices called "gramophones" and "graphophones," were being sold throughout the United States. Inevitably, retailers, advertising firms, and a host of other commercial interests sought to exploit the lure of the Edison mystique.

One of those inspired entrepreneurs was Joseph Lees of Summit Hill, Pennsylvania, who in 1899 presented the U.S. Patent Office with a nocturnal emission prevention harness utilizing electrical-control mechanisms modeled after the most advanced equipment from Menlo Park. An expensively crafted apparatus, Lees's invention was aimed at discerning and cultured males. He wrote: "The object of my invention is to provide a device which in the event of an erection will automatically sound an alarm sufficient to awaken even a heavy sleeper." He took careful account of the psychological sensibilities as well as the urbane musical tastes of his intended customers. "The nerves of persons having need of a device of the character described are usually weak and are more or less injuriously affected by sharp, loud and especially unexpected sounds," he wrote. "Therefore it is desirable to awake the sleeper by gentle means, so as not to startle him, and this may be attained by strains of music."

Lees's device had an electrical alarm circuit that could be wired to a standard bell or connected to activate "any form of motor used to operate a graphophone, phonograph, or other instrument." In his drawings of the preferred configuration of his invention, Lees showed the connection for the Edison phonograph. Thus, persons wearing the

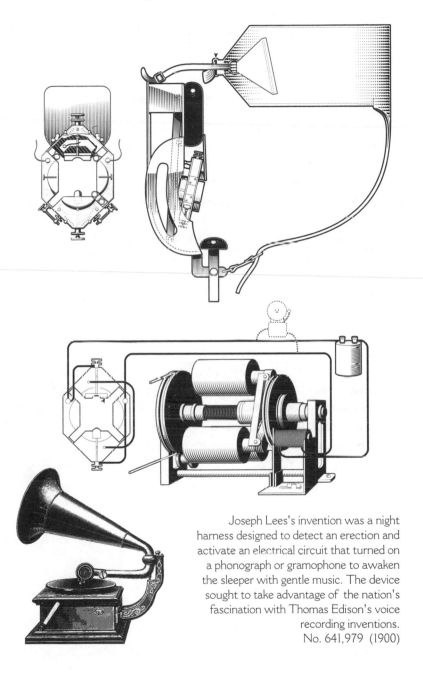

Joseph Lees's invention was a night harness designed to detect an erection and activate an electrical circuit that turned on a phonograph or gramophone to awaken the sleeper with gentle music. The device sought to take advantage of the nation's fascination with Thomas Edison's voice recording inventions.
No. 641,979 (1900)

apparatus who experienced an erection would wake to find the darkness filled with the tinny strains of their favorite opera or piano solo.

The Twentieth Century

For the next twenty years inventors continued to seek—and the Patent Office continued to grant—patents for additional nocturnal erection detection and prevention devices. In all, twenty-one patents were granted over a period of sixty-two years to individual inventors from Massachusetts to Oregon and across time from the Civil War to World War I.

In retrospect, this protracted effort appears all the more heinous because it was based on medical theories that were not only inaccurate but ridiculous. In the post-Kinsey era after World War II, it became recognized as a basic fact of science that nocturnal erections and emissions are a normal part of male physiology. In fact, so important are these as signs of essential *well being*, that the *absence* of nocturnal erections is itself now recognized as a symptom of potentially serious health problems. As outlandish as they appear today, these devices were only one part of a larger, coordinated arsenal of admonitions, public denouncements, repressive laws, drugs, surgery, and brutal punishments used by a society to wage an irrational—but very real—American war against wet dreams.

4

The Evolution of Vaginal Machinery

Despite popular illusions fostered by modern-day movies, the greatest danger faced by early American women was not rattlesnake bites or attacks by native tribesmen or blizzards or starvation or yellow fever. The single most widespread threat to the life and health of females was an act of sexual intercourse that resulted in pregnancy, a condition that often ended in death or debility. High mortality rates were the result of the limited medical knowledge of the period, as well as surgical tools as crude as barnyard implements. During the most difficult deliveries, a doctor or midwife might use an iron kettle hook to break a hole in a lodged infant's skull and wrest the mangled corpse from the mother's body. Unstoppable hemorrhage was a commonplace occurrence.

The existence of bacteria was unknown and infections were rampant. Thus, a woman could experience an easy delivery and produce a healthy baby, and yet both could die weeks later from mysterious raging fevers. Even a "normal" delivery could damage muscles, ligaments, and internal organs in a manner that physicians of the time could not repair.

Small wonder, then, that pregnancy was a matter of constant anguish in a culture of women who, in 1800, were bearing an average of more than seven children each. And of all the "benign" complications women routinely faced as a result of pregnancy, none was quite as dreaded as the condition generally known as "prolapsed," or fallen womb. This was caused by traumatic or repeated birthings that weakened, stretched, or tore the supporting web of muscles and ligaments that held the uterus in place above the vagina. Once the pear-shaped womb was loose of its supports, it fell downward, often pulling the vagina behind it like a sock turned inside out. In some cases, it fell only a short distance into the vaginal cavity. In other cases, the detachment was so severe it allowed the organ to actually hang outside the body, a situation called "procidentia." In his vivid history of women's medical care through the ages, Edward Shorter explained that when suffering from this condition, "the woman looks as though she has an elephant's trunk between her legs."

Prolapse Pessaries

Fallen wombs have plagued women throughout history. The most common early method of treatment takes its name from the Greek word for "oval stone": pessary. Smooth, oiled stones were probably among the first sorts of blunt objects used by women in an attempt to force and hold the vagina and uterus back in their proper place.

Although prolapsed uterus was commonplace among North American women in the eighteenth and nineteenth centuries, it was not something often discussed or written about in a population that generally viewed *any* acknowledgment of the female genitals as a strict taboo. This taboo was so encompassing that some medical students of the 1800s were trained to make gynecological diagnoses and even provide bedside assistance at births without ever making eye contact with the female patient's genitals. This reticence to discuss "female problems" such as prolapse also resulted in a sparse public record about how women coped with a condition that crippled their bodies as well as their sense of sexuality and self-worth.

Early Patent Office Pessaries

However, the files of the U.S. Patent Office indicate that in the 1840s, as the new adherents of mechanical improvement began studying every aspect of daily life to identify those that could be enhanced by proprietary inventions, they quickly recognized the potential market for a better pessary device. A flurry of patents were granted for simple devices made of wood, bone, glass, various sorts of metal, crude rubber, and porcelain.

One functional consideration of many of the new designs was the manner in which the device affected the wearer's ability to engage in sexual intercourse. The most desirable pessary would have been one that held the vagina in place, that was itself not externally visible, and that was constructed in a manner that did not present a physical barrier to the penis. This challenge was taken up by a number of inventors.

In February of 1856, Dr. F. Roesler, a New York City physician, was granted a patent for a spring-hinge pessary designed to clamp itself in place at the top of the vagina, leaving the rest of that cavity free of mechanical obstructions. In the oblique language of the day, he explained that "this instrument enables the female to perform every function of nature as wife and mother without removing it." This metal version meant that the male would have to be careful about the power and range of his stroke during intercourse so as to prevent potential laceration by hard edges and spring assemblies. Several months later, William Provines of Missouri, received a patent for a ring-shaped inflatable pessary that also left the lower vagina clear. The deflated device was inserted

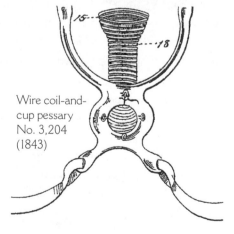

Wire coil-and-cup pessary No. 3,204 (1843)

high in the vagina and inflated by a detachable tube long enough to reach the wearer's mouth. Once wedged into place, it theoretically supported the organs at the same it facilitated vaginal entry by the male. This inflatable approach would have offered an advantage over Dr. Roesler's metal model in that a penile stroke extending to the top of the vagina would have struck only a soft rubber object.

Stem-and-Ball Pessaries

However, the predominant form of pessary that evolved in the latter 1800s was a much bulkier "stem-and-ball" or "stem-and-cup" version that made sexual relations impossible. These pessaries were complex pieces of machinery, incorporating body harnesses with support arms, hinges, springs, levers, extenders, ball sockets, and webs of elastic straps and bands. Their overall function was not unlike that of a carriage suspension system, holding a ball-and-stem pessary in place internally even as a woman flexed and bent her body vigorously as she went about household chores or sweatshop labor.

Inventors vied with each other to claim greater comfort and reliability for these lower-body mechanisms. James A. Morrell's 1868 patent shows a typical harness and pivot hinge device. It featured a chain of interconnected mechanical actions, each being spring- or lever-loaded against the other, from elastic straps anchored to a waist belt to a pivot lever. This lever curved around the belly and into the vagina to a central stem, which was loaded with an internal spiral spring that hefted a ball cup at its top against the mouth of the womb.

Perhaps the most unusual mechanical approach to the prolapse problem was taken by Charles C. Fredigke of Chicago who patented a hollow, pear-shaped pessary with ribs. This fruit-sized corrugated device had to be inserted with the body "in the knee-chest position." Fredigke wrote that it was designed to remain inside the vagina under virtually all conditions because its sheer size assured that it would not be dislodged "in spite of respiration, coughing, or straining."

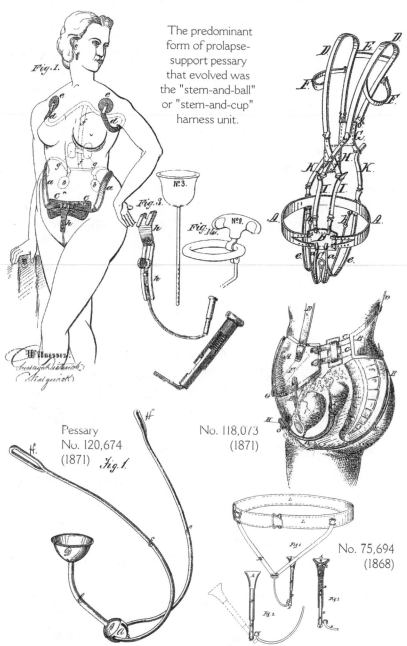

The predominant form of prolapse-support pessary that evolved was the "stem-and-ball" or "stem-and-cup" harness unit.

No. 118,073
(1871)

Pessary
No. 120,674
(1871)

No. 75,694
(1868)

Electric Pessaries

In the years immediately after the Civil War, electricity became a subject of intense public curiosity. During the war, the telegraph became a critical asset for the military, and the industrial economy, greatly expanded by the war effort, had also come to rely on the device. Cities such as Philadelphia, New York, and Boston had their rooftops spider-webbed with telegraph wire connecting the banks and stock exchanges, which now relied on rapid telegraphic communications. Legions of telegraph workers and assorted electric tinkers were obsessed with the idea of inventing new applications for the electrical forces they only partially understood. Across the country, freewheeling marketers attempted to harness the perceived "magic" of electricity to all manner of products and services. Corps of self-proclaimed "doctors of electricity" began practicing in the unregulated new field of "electric medicine" that would flourish into the early twentieth century. In his chronicle of the era, James H. Young notes that newspaper and magazine advertising routinely offered therapies and products such as "Magnetic Fluids and Galvanic Belts, Electric Insoles and Electro-Magnetic Wrist Bands, plus an infinite variety of cravats, pillows, anklets, elbow pads, necklaces, head-caps, corsets, combs, and infernal machines by which magnetic entrepreneurs have tried to transmit healing potency to the ailing human frame."

Among the earliest medical devices to incorporate these curious electric theories was the electric pessary. In 1867, Albert J. Steele of New York City filed the first patent application for an electrode pessary and girdle powered by a bulky collection of open acid battery cells of the type then used in telegraph stations. Mr. Steele explained to the patent examiners that "this invention . . . consists of insulated wires bent in suitable shapes for providing a medium of conduction to the diseased part."

Three years later, in 1870, James S. Shannon of Illinois received a patent for a galvanic harness that utilized a zinc and silver stem-and-ball pessary. Aside from holding the internal organs in place, Shan-

non explained that "the zinc ball with
the silver cap forms a combination of metals,
which, when acted
upon by the secretions
of the skin or bladder,
creates an electrical ac-
tion." Dr. Leland A.
Babcock of Illinois assured
the patent examiners that
such electrical current delivered directly to the womb
"is believed to aid in the

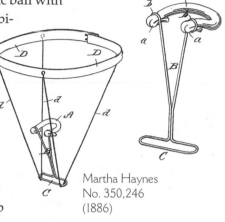

Martha Haynes
No. 350,246
(1886)

speedy restoration of the parts to a normal condition."

Another practitioner of the electric medicine school, Dr. Emily A.
Tefft of East Otto, New York, explained in her patent for an electro-
magnetic ball pessary and galvanic body harness that "the treatment of
disease by galvanism, voltaic electricity, and electro-magnetism is a
recognized branch in the medical profession (and) when it is desirable
to convey a constant current through the part affected, my (portable)

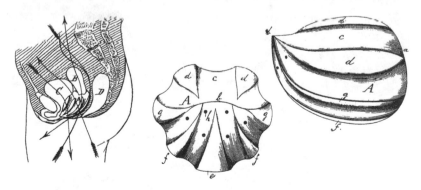

The size of a small grapefruit, Charles Fredigke's unusual pessary design required
considerable strength for its insertion and removal. No. 435,491

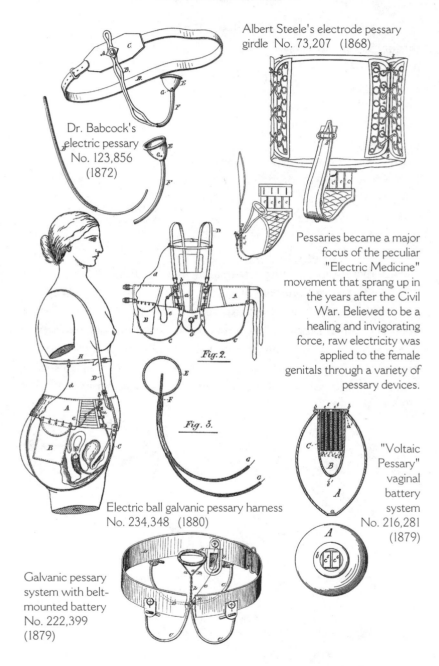

Albert Steele's electrode pessary girdle No. 73,207 (1868)

Dr. Babcock's electric pessary No. 123,856 (1872)

Pessaries became a major focus of the peculiar "Electric Medicine" movement that sprang up in the years after the Civil War. Believed to be a healing and invigorating force, raw electricity was applied to the female genitals through a variety of pessary devices.

Fig. 2.

Fig. 3.

"Voltaic Pessary" vaginal battery system No. 216,281 (1879)

Electric ball galvanic pessary harness No. 234,348 (1880)

Galvanic pessary system with belt-mounted battery No. 222,399 (1879)

appliances permit the application in cases when it would not otherwise be possible." Dr. Tefft's device sent current "from the battery in the pocket, through the insulated flexible wire stem or shank, to the metal ball, which distributes the electricity within the womb."

Another inventor, John Jay Looney of Pennsylvania, ridiculed inventors of such harness-mounted galvanic pessary systems. He explained to the Patent Office that "I am aware that portable batteries are applied to the human body for hygienic purposes; but they are worn around the body, generally at the waist, and special conductors are used to connect the battery with the suffering parts. These batteries are an inconvenience to the wearer, liable to derangement, and have to be frequently artificially moistened when the perspiration of the body is not sufficient to keep them in operation. By applying the poles of my improved battery directly to the suffering parts I avoid the use of intermediate conductors, and I am enabled to use a smaller battery than otherwise." Looney's invention was a rubber spheroid of battery parts inserted directly into the vagina to be constantly moistened and "powered" by vaginal secretions. He said his "Voltaic Pessary" invention eliminated the voltage loss of waist-mounted units and significantly increased the power applied directly to the vagina.

Parallel Pessary Developments

At the same time that inventors continued to create such increasingly baroque prolapse pessaries, another branch of vaginal technology was also evolving. This one viewed the pessary as a convenient tool for the prevention or termination of pregnancies. By the second half of the nineteenth century, such new devices would play a major role in decreasing the nation's birth rate at the same time they sparked a raucous national debate that continues to reverberate today.

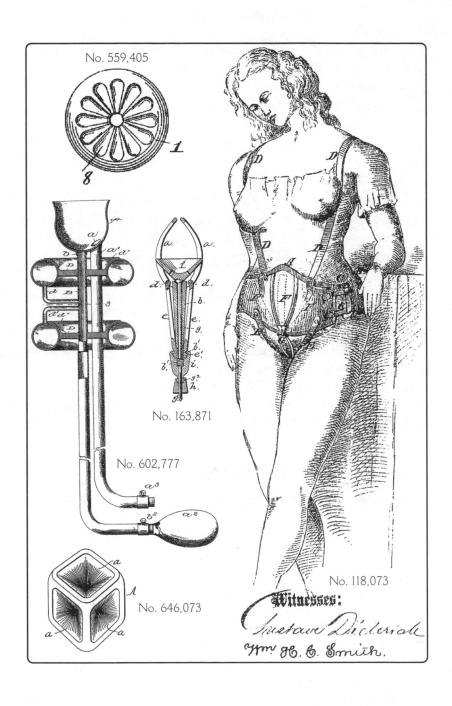

No. 559,405

No. 163,871

No. 602,777

No. 646,073

No. 118,073

Witnesses:

Gustave Dieterich

Wm. H. E. Smith.

5

The Victorian Era of Contraception

In an 1866 address to the New Hampshire State Medical Society, Dr. W. D. Buck decried the widespread use of pessaries of all sorts. He noted that the official publication of the National Medical Association for 1864 "has figured one hundred and twenty-three different kinds of pessaries, embracing every variety, from a simple plug to a patent threshing machine, which can only be worn with the largest (dress) hoop." The medical society president went on to say, "Pessaries, I suppose, are sometimes useful, but there are more than there is any necessity for. I do think that this filling the vagina with such traps, making a Chinese toy-shop of it, is outrageous." He also notes "if there were fewer pessaries there would be fewer abortions."

Dr. Buck's remarks have often been quoted by historians as one of the rare published accounts providing information about the intravaginal birth control devices used in the nineteenth century. While it is generally known that instruments of abortion and contraception were sold as "pessaries" during this period, little documentation about these individual mechanisms has survived. Advertisements of the era used artfully vague euphemisms. After 1873, when Congress outlawed the distribution of information or goods related to the performance of abortions or prevention of pregnancies, public references to such products became even more cryptic.

However, filed away in the archives of the U.S. Patent Office, under "Pessary," "Apparatus for Treating Diseased Cervix," "Spinal Supporter and Uterine Regulator," "Pherysteron," "Uterine Supporter," "Womb Battery," and other similarly oblique titles, are more than five dozen patents containing detailed drawings and descriptions of birth control implements registered by doctors and other inventors throughout the Victorian era.

Syringe Pessaries

In late 1846, the Patent Office granted a patent to Joel B. Merriman of Sheffield, Massachusetts, for a hollow-stemmed glass "pessary" that allowed the user to "inject medicated solutions" directly at the mouth of the uterus. At that time, it was believed that spraying hot water or various sorts of caustic mixtures directly at the mouth of the uterus was the most effective method for producing the uterine contractions that could expel a fetus.

Hollow-stem pessary No. 4,825 (1846)

This abortion-inducing potential was only one of the reasons that syringe-like devices had become such ubiquitous items in American households by the late 1840s. The medical community originally promoted their use for douching for purely hygienic reasons. Bathing was then a sporadic practice and the natural results of this— frequent vaginal infections—were routinely treated with a regime of vaginal douching. Limited numbers of women were known to have used douching to prevent pregnancies in the late 1700s, but it was not until the publication of some of the first "marital handbooks" in the 1830s that contraceptive douching became a widespread practice. James Reed explained, "Douching reduced the risk of conception by over 80 percent of those who used it faithfully . . . The persistence of douching as a contraceptive means (by) women who denied any contraceptive intent in the practice reflected the attractiveness of a birth control method that could be disguised as simple personal cleanliness and involved the purchase of no overtly contraceptive devices."

In this era, the syringes available to midwives and physicians for abortion purposes were crude affairs of brass and pewter, lacking the long thin nozzles needed to extend up through the vagina to the mouth of the uterus. An illustration of one of these early syringes is included in a patent granted to L. Anthony Gescheidt of New York in 1848. Mr. Gescheidt's invention, called a "pherysteron," facilitated "injections upon the suffering parts" at the upper reaches of the vagina. The crude rubber device was inflated by mouth to plug the upper vagina. A hollow channel through the pherysteron allowed a syringe to force liquids into the blocked space, forcing them into the uterus as well.

Two years later, in 1850, Jonathan Hovey Robinson of Massachusetts devised a silver stem-and-cup pessary whose stem featured a hollow-tube core. He explained: "The directing pipe of a small syringe can at any time be introduced into it, and when so applied any liquid or medicament with which the syringe may be charged, may be readily injected into and through the said stem, and from there through the supporting cup" that pressed tightly against the opening to the uterus.

"Pherysteron" with syringe No. 5,556 (1848)

Syringes became ever more sophisticated in their fabrication and function as time went by, and, in many cases, the simple term "syringe" was commonly used to disguise what were actually highly specialized abortion instruments. For instance, in 1878, Anna L.

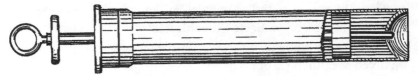

Anna Palmer's syringe was actually an all-purpose abortion tool.
No. 213,588 (1879)

Palmer of Chariton, Iowa, applied for a patent on what she told the commissioners was a "Combined Aspirator, Concealed Uterine Cauterizer, and Vaginal Syringe." The invention was shaped like a heavy-duty syringe plunger mechanism and featured a thin probe that could be inserted and manipulated through the center of the plunger piston. The piston head itself was curved in a mirror image of the protruding mouth of the womb. The device could be used to create a vigorous suction "to extract morbid accumulations from the uterus." Pushed firmly in place against the uterine entrance, the piston also served as a targeting device that allowed the thin probe to be inserted to abrade the organ's walls, causing fetus-expelling contractions. The probe could also be adapted to either insert small wads of absorbent material or quantities of "crystallized caustic" into the uterus.

Among others who received patents for similar devices was Horatio E. Cook, whose syringe nozzle featured a miniature spoon-shaped opening particularly suited for scraping the walls of the uterus; and Andrew L. Henry of Ladoga, Indiana, whose syringe invention involved a long, thin, hollow tip bent to an angle that maximized its usefulness as an intrauterine irrigation and suction device. But the most elaborate entry in this field appears to have been the "Return-Flow Syringe" invention submitted to the patent office by Denwood N. L. Newbury of New York City. It was an ergonomically contoured wire cage device that filled and dilated the vagina and supported itself with a superstructure that hugged the external genitalia. Running up its middle was a water tube. Not unlike a fire hose precisely held in place

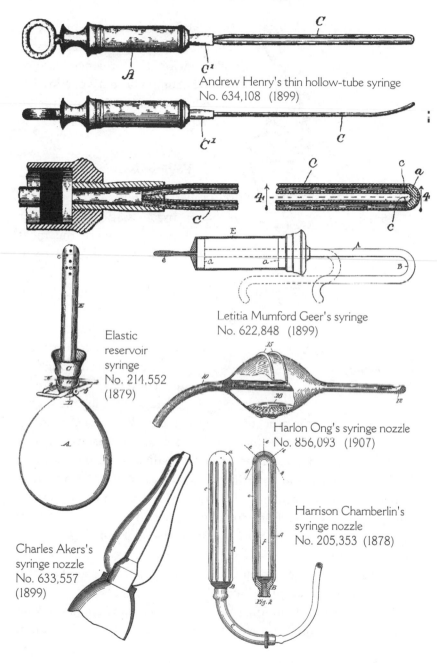

Andrew Henry's thin hollow-tube syringe
No. 634,108 (1899)

Letitia Mumford Geer's syringe
No. 622,848 (1899)

Elastic
reservoir
syringe
No. 214,552
(1879)

Harlon Ong's syringe nozzle
No. 856,093 (1907)

Harrison Chamberlin's
syringe nozzle
No. 205,353 (1878)

Charles Akers's
syringe nozzle
No. 633,557
(1899)

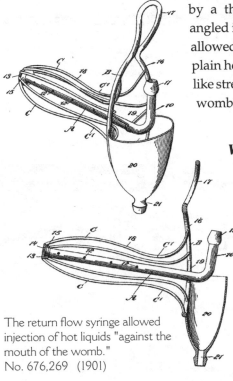

by a three-dimensional matrix of angled iron, the Newbury apparatus allowed for the "prolonged use of plain hot or medicated water in a jet-like stream "against the mouth of the womb."

Vaginal Barrier Pessaries

Along with syringe douching, vaginal barrier pessaries were the most commonly used contraceptive devices of the 1800s. While the technology of such barriers evolved significantly during the century, the basic concept was ancient. Women throughout the world have used various substances to plug the vagina

The return flow syringe allowed injection of hot liquids "against the mouth of the womb."
No. 676,269 (1901)

during intercourse in order to avoid pregnancy. While early cultures may not have understood the exact biomechanical reasons why this worked, they appreciated the practical results. These old methods involved making and inserting vaginal plugs of local materials ranging from honey and crocodile dung in Egypt; tufts of wool mixed with cedar gum in old Rome; oiled wads of bamboo paper in Japan; and putty-like globs of beeswax in medieval Europe. American whalers and other sailors of the square-rigger age returned from South Pacific voyages to tell of island women who used wads of seaweed as a contraceptive vaginal plug.

By the early 1800s in America, the use of a natural sponge or wad of cotton for this purpose was common. Tied with a trailing bit of

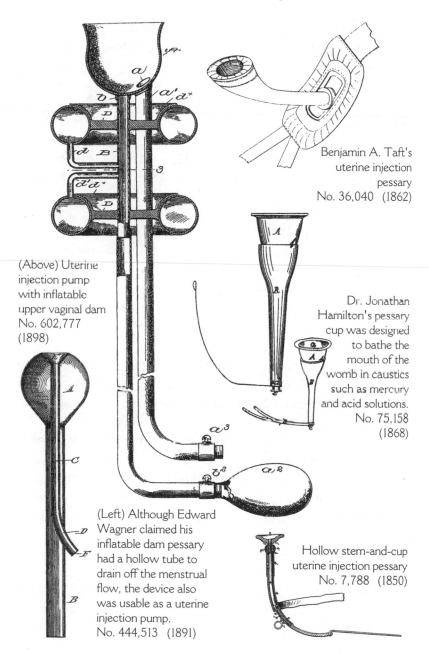

Benjamin A. Taft's
uterine injection
pessary
No. 36,040 (1862)

(Above) Uterine
injection pump
with inflatable
upper vaginal dam
No. 602,777
(1898)

Dr. Jonathan
Hamilton's pessary
cup was designed
to bathe the
mouth of the
womb in caustics
such as mercury
and acid solutions.
No. 75,158
(1868)

(Left) Although Edward
Wagner claimed his
inflatable dam pessary
had a hollow tube to
drain off the menstrual
flow, the device also
was usable as a uterine
injection pump.
No. 444,513 (1891)

Hollow stem-and-cup
uterine injection pessary
No. 7,788 (1850)

string or ribbon, the sponge or cotton wad was saturated with lemon juice or other acidic substances and pushed high into the vagina prior to intercourse. There, it acted as a physical barrier to impede semen from entering the uterus. It was believed that acidic juices and astringent brews were effective in somehow thwarting the fertilizing qualities of semen. However, using the fingers to insert a wet sponge high in one's vagina was a somewhat messy process in an era when there was no indoor plumbing. In 1849 Russell Caulkins applied for a patent on an invention that appears to address this inconvenience by using the mechanical plunger functions of a syringe to deliver a wet sponge to the top of the vagina.

The contraceptive sponge itself—cut and hollowed to a bell shape forming a tight cervical cap—was patented in 1867 by W. G. Grant of Clyde, Ohio. His patent notes that his vaginal sponge was designed to make it "more easily inserted or withdrawn" and included an "inserter" to facilitate ease of placement. A string threaded through the closed end of the bell shape allows the sponge to be easily withdrawn after use.

In the 1864 revision of his previously published marital advice manual, *Medical Common Sense*, Philadelphia doctor Edward Bliss Foote reported to his readers that a new invention—a "womb veil"— was the best contraceptive device. He wrote that it "spreads a thin tissue of the rubber before the mouth of the womb so as to prevent the seminal aura from entering . . . Its application is easy and accomplished in a moment, without the aid of a light. It places conception entirely under the control of the wife, to whom it naturally belongs." One of the best-selling publications of its time, Dr. Foote's book was instrumental in making the concept of the diaphragm, which he claimed to have invented, widely known in America. While Dr. Foote was a superb promoter, he was not the original inventor of the device. The use of thin, impermeable barriers to cover the cervical opening to prevent the entry of semen was first described in Germany in the 1830s by Dr. Friedrich Adolphe Wilde. In 1842 another German

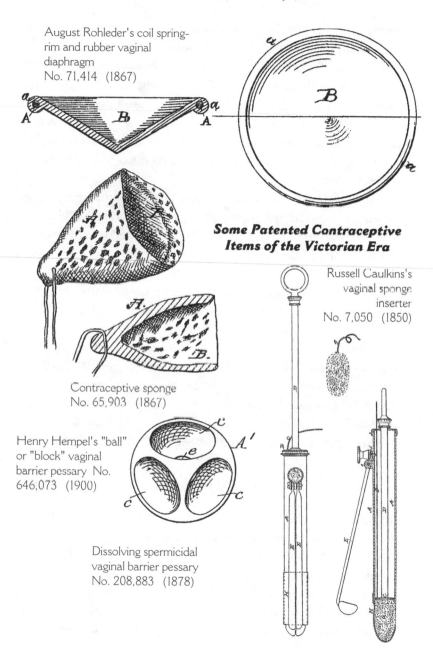

August Rohleder's coil spring-
rim and rubber vaginal
diaphragm
No. 71,414 (1867)

**Some Patented Contraceptive
Items of the Victorian Era**

Russell Caulkins's
vaginal sponge
inserter
No. 7,050 (1850)

Contraceptive sponge
No. 65,903 (1867)

Henry Hempel's "ball"
or "block" vaginal
barrier pessary No.
646,073 (1900)

Dissolving spermicidal
vaginal barrier pessary
No. 208,883 (1878)

doctor—W. P. J. Mensinga of Breslau—described and provided patients with vaginal diaphragms made of the earliest crudely vulcanized rubber. As noted earlier, Rochester dentist John B. Beers had filed for and received the first U.S. sex patent in 1846 for his own version of a vaginal diaphragm device that used oiled silk as the barrier material. By 1864, when Dr. Foote began writing about, as well as selling, his own brand of diaphragm, the device had benefited from the significant strides made in the process of vulcanizing and forming rubber.

In 1867, August C. Rohleder of New York received a patent for a thin rubber vaginal diaphragm with a steel coil spring embedded in its rim. The diaphragm could be easily compressed with the fingers as it was inserted into the vagina. Once in place, its spring pushed outward to create a rim seal against the surrounding walls of the vagina. By the turn of the century, interest in the inventive improvement of this basic device appears to have quickened and several more inventors received patents for variations on soft rubber, cup-like diaphragms.

By 1914, when the term "birth control," coined by Margaret Sanger, had become a political battle cry, another round of diaphragm designs was submitted to the Patent Office. These demonstrated the new levels of sophistication achieved by manufacturers in constructing thin, spring-loaded rubber barrier diaphragms.

"Block" Pessaries

A peculiar—and ultimately dead-end—design offshoot in this barrier contraceptive concept was the "block pessary," an idea that appears to have been plucked from literature of the 1700s and presented to the U.S. Patent Office as a "new" invention in 1900. That year, Henry A. Hempel of Gotha, Florida, applied for and received a patent for both square and round versions of a vaginal barrier device with six concave indentations around its surface. The mechanical concept was this: when inserted in the vagina, lubricated by body fluids and pressed upon (as by the tip of a penis), one of the block's concave indentations naturally tended to seat itself over the cervix, creating a sperm-blocking barrier. The patent examiners who granted Mr. Hempel a patent apparently were not familiar with the writings of Giovanni Giacomo Casanova, the Italian author, military adventurer, and sexual libertine who had recorded his own use of block pessaries made of pure gold more than a century earlier.

Intrauterine Stem Pessaries

A much more important and far-reaching branch of pessary innovation emerged in 1864 when James Lee of Stevens Point, Wisconsin, combined the idea of a diaphragm-like vaginal barrier with a new kind of uterine anchoring device. Mr. Lee explained that he had invented a pessary device with "a peculiarly-constructed sound or stem" that could be inserted directly into the uterus. His rigid intrauterine stem pessary could, he wrote, be made of ivory, metal, hard rubber or other substances. One of its uses was to straighten a

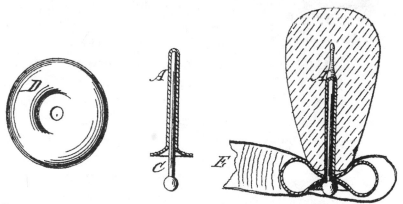

James Lee combined the concepts of a diaphragm with a "peculiarly-constructed stem" anchoring device. It began a new line of patents that became infamous. No. 45,506 (1864)

womb. He also pointed out that other "advantages of my invention will be obvious to physicians and others familiar with the use of such implements, and need not be enumerated here." Ironically, one of those unenumerated purposes was to increase a woman's chances of pregnancy. It was then believed that mechanically widening the mouth of the uterus could make a woman more fertile, the idea being that a perforated intrauterine stem might function something like a fish ladder for sperm migrating up from the vagina.

A fourth mechanical possibility was exploited in 1871 by Dr. William S. Van Cleve of Centralia, Illinois, who applied for a patent on an apparatus that combined the concept of the intrauterine stem with that of the abortion syringe. Called the "Abdominal and Spinal Supporter and Uterine Regulator," it seemed like just another in a long line of ornate systems. But the tip of its hollow vaginal stem came through its uterine cup and continued upward, like the stamen of a flower, as an intrauterine stem. Dr. Van Cleve explained to the patent examiners that this "uterus-holder and injector" accepted "nozzles of different sizes" that allowed for unusually well-controlled injections of fluids directly into the uterus.

Between 1887 and 1920, at least eighteen other patents for intrauterine stem pessaries were granted by the Patent Office. Several included quick-disconnect handle attachments that allowed plug-like pessaries to be quickly put in place or removed. Design and visual appeal appear to have become important considerations by the turn of the century. For instance, Herman M. Ryman's two patents resemble nothing so much as the face and stem of a fancy earring or half of an ornate cufflink.

Dr. Van Cleve's intra-uterine injection stem No. 118,073 (1871)

Four of the intrauterine stem pessary patents involve devices made of disparate metals to generate galvanic currents directly into the walls of the uterus as an apparent means of abortion. The first trendsetter in this evolution of birth control and electric medicine was the 1894 "Womb Battery" of Julius C. Petit. Employing a widely used euphemism for abortion, Petit explained that the device would "regulate menstruation and promote the cure of the many diseases peculiar to the female." Similarly, Martha Ellen Keller said that her galvanic intrauterine stem pessary design was for the treatment of "abnormal conditions of the uterus." And Charles Souder wrote with equal semantic aplomb that his intrauterine stem pessary "will ensure the passage of the current through the walls of the womb" and that the advantages of such a device "will suggest themselves" to readers.

In 1912 Richard Jentzsch of Chicago patented an intrauterine stem design that would become infamous as a "wishbone" pessary. Shaped like a "Y" at the far end, the device forcibly dilated the uterus in a manner that was particularly efficient in causing the expulsion of a fetus. Jentzsch explained that the hollow core of his device also allowed the uterus to "continuously drain thus permitting effete and noxious matters to continually pass out of the womb." This wishbone technology became popular and continued to evolve, as can be seen in the 1920 patent of Leon Martocci-Pisculli of New York, who created a uterine stem pessary with a reservoir that allowed the device to both dilate, and emit caustic formaldehyde vapors into the uterus.

The Dissolving Chemical Pessary

A final avenue of contraceptive pessary development involved the use of purely chemical barriers to prevent pregnancy. In 1878, Trevanion N. Berlin established a new category of registered pessaries when he received a patent for a bullet-shaped pessary made of gummy chemicals that dissolved as a result of body heat and moisture in the vagina. The functions of the pessary involved both the

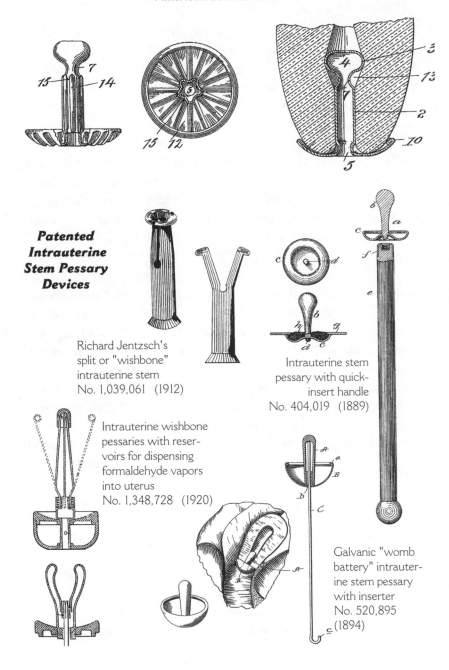

Patented Intrauterine Stem Pessary Devices

Richard Jentzsch's split or "wishbone" intrauterine stem No. 1,039,061 (1912)

Intrauterine stem pessary with quick-insert handle No. 404,019 (1889)

Intrauterine wishbone pessaries with reservoirs for dispensing formaldehyde vapors into uterus No. 1,348,728 (1920)

Galvanic "womb battery" intrauterine stem pessary with inserter No. 520,895 (1894)

barrier it created as it melted around the contours of the cervical opening and the action of the chemicals released throughout the vagina as it slowly disintegrated. While he officially notes that the purpose of the chemical release is to "act as a curative agent medicinally," it seems more likely that the "cure" involved the chemical neutralization of deposited semen.

Modern Pessary Trends

By the 1930s, surgical procedures for repairing a prolapsed uterus had been perfected, eliminating the need that had given rise to the original nineteenth-century designs for vaginal machinery. But the pessary lived on, now so mechanically mutated that the term itself has come to describe virtually *any* implement placed in the vagina for medicinal, therapeutic, or birth control purposes. And that meaning is expanding still as new categories of vaginal devices are envisioned and patented by today's inventors.

Without question, the most noteworthy class of these new mechanisms—items so extraordinary they demand their own chapter later in this book—were created in response to a growing national militancy against sexual assault. Shaped like tampons, but fitted out with barbs and internal blades, they are designed to mutilate the sexual organs of rapists. One can only imagine how Dr. Buck, who so eloquently decried the dehumanizing aspects of needless vaginal gadgetry more than a century ago, would have responded to such a diabolically modern concept: the use of proprietary machinery to convert the vagina into a deadly weapon.

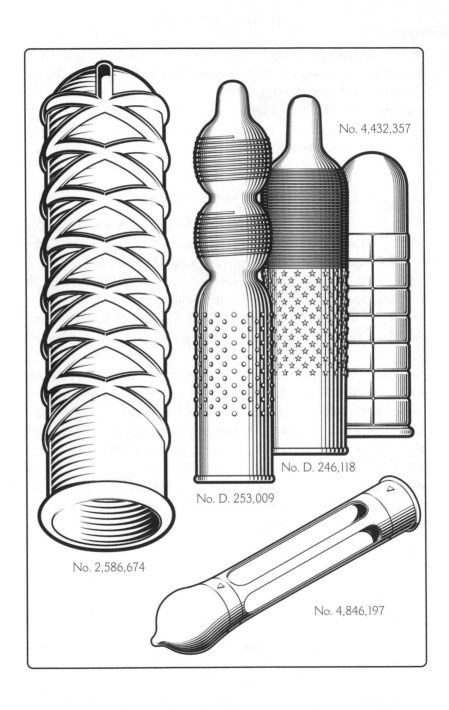

No. 4,432,357

No. D. 246,118

No. D. 253,009

No. 2,586,674

No. 4,846,197

6

The Rubber Revolution

Mechanically speaking, the civilization that emerged from the American Revolution was one of bad seams and pervasive ooze. The machinery of daily life that had to contain or function in contact with fluids was constructed of materials poorly suited for the purpose. The same culture that carved its pessaries from walrus ivory and cut its condoms from lamb gut also made its water pipes from hollowed-out logs, its hoses from sewn leather, and its rain gear from tar-smeared canvas. Almost everything used to hold or repel fluids, except costly glass and ceramics, leaked. Sodden feet were a fact of life during the opening decades of the 1800s. Even boots coated in varnish or impregnated with wax quickly became water-saturated along muddy streets and river walks in summer. In snow and ice, individuals could safely travel only short distances before the inevitable freezing wetness resulted in crippling and potentially deadly frostbite. Thus, the lack of an adequate waterproofing substance seriously limited the physical mobility of the population. It also dramatically impacted commerce. Brewers of beer, for instance, watched helplessly as a good percentage of their product seeped away through porous hoses and bad vat seals.

This was a society that sorely craved some new material as easy to form as wood, but as flexible as leather and totally impervious to moisture. In 1820, a ship returning from Caribbean trading ports put into Boston harbor with a product that appeared to have these very qualities: a pair of crudely-shaped shoes made from a substance whose name was pronounced "ko-chook." The shoes were solid, yet pliant; firm, yet strangely soft. When placed in a rain barrel, they floated like boats. Splashed water beaded up and rolled off their surface.

The arrival of this lumpy, ill-formed footgear made from a jungle gum that could not be penetrated by water was a thunderbolt event. That first pair of truly waterproof shoes is reported to have sold for $5—a sum of money equivalent to more than $300 today. And ko-chook soon captured the imagination of the New England mercantile community like few other commodities in its history. Ultimately, the substance would revolutionize the mechanical matrix of American civilization and play a central role in the daily sexual—and even political—practices of that society.

The History of a Jungle Gum

Long before Europeans first clamored ashore with their fire sticks and metal armor, tribal societies throughout what is now Mexico, Central America, and South America cut gashes in the bark of certain trees to make ko-chook ooze. Aztecs coated their capes and war shields with it. In the 1730s, a French scientific expedition recorded that Amazon tribes dipped loose clay molds into the milky ko-chook sap to create various sorts of goods for trade. Built up layer by layer on the mold, like a hand-dipped candle around a wick, the items were dried by a brief exposure to smoke after each layer. The finished results were awkwardly shaped but serviceable objects that were flexible and waterproof. The two most common items produced by the tribes were shoes and tear-shaped hand bulbs. When the necks of the bulbs were left open, they held liquids, like bottles. When closed around a hollow reed, they became crude syringes.

This strange new material did not seize the attention of America until that first pair of waterproof shoes arrived in 1820. Within a few years, rubber shoes made by Amazon tribesmen were being offloaded at Boston docks in lots of 30,000 and sold at profit margins of more than 800 percent. Meanwhile, apothecary shops were soon doing a brisk business in imported "bottles" sold under brand names like "Brown's Self-Injecting India Rubber Instruments."

Although wildly popular, these crude rubber products rarely remained serviceable for more than a year. While they were initially impervious to moisture, they were dramatically affected by temperature, turning hard and brittle in cold weather and soft and runny in warm. Their vulnerability to heat was notorious, and it became common knowledge that rubber items should *never* be worn or placed near fireplaces, stoves, or candles. Even more of a problem was the natural decomposition of the rubber gum itself. Despite an initial solid feel, the material rotted from the inside out, causing items like shoes or syringes to ultimately collapse in upon themselves in an odoriferous, gelatinous mass.

The Rubber Boom and Bust

In the early years of the 1830s, a sudden rubber "boom" erupted across Connecticut, Massachusetts, and Rhode Island, as various parties claimed to have found secret ways to "cure" rubber, thereby eliminating its tendency to rot, melt, or freeze stiff. Investors and entrepreneurs appreciated that the discovery of a method for stabilizing rubber would give birth to a major new industry. In a frenzy that gathered momentum through 1834, corporations were formed and large, barn-like factories were erected to spew forth rubber goods. Their production techniques were the same: blocks of kochook gum were dissolved in turpentine to form a reconstituted liquid rubber. The most valuable product—waterproof cloth—was created by dipping fabric into this mix. Once dry, the rubberized fabric could be sewn into useful objects, one of the most important of which was the inflatable life preserver.

In 1834, a thirty-five-year-old New Haven inventor and tool merchant walked into an office of the India Rubber Company of Roxbury, Massachusetts, to purchase one of the firm's recently advertised inflatable life preservers. Intensely mechanical-minded, Charles Goodyear had already received patents on manufacturing methods for buttons and spoons as well as a new spring-lever faucet mechanism for molasses crocks. Although good at inventing, he was bad at business. The string of hardware stores he and his father had opened in multiple cities had just collapsed. Goodyear was nearly out of money and increasingly desperate to identify some new business opportunity.

He found it in the rubber goods shop.

Goodyear learned that the life preserver he had just purchased would soon rot away. The rubber "boom" was based on fraudulent claims. The processes that were supposed to stabilize crude rubber didn't really work. Tons of rubber goods then being sold by the new factories across New England were coagulating into fetid, useless lumps.

Goodyear recognized a simple fact: The person who *did* invent an effective method for stabilizing rubber would make enormous amounts of money. He became obsessed with becoming that person.

His subsequent story is as colorful and poignant as any Charles Dickens novel. It was the tale of a sickly man who repeatedly lost all, was beset by incredible bouts of bad luck, endured debtors prison, a pauper's burial of his son, widespread ridicule, chemical poisoning as his own experiments went awry, and near-starvation that forced his family to subsist on half-grown potatoes in a blizzard-wracked hovel. All the while, he struggled on, a creature possessed with the gobs of raw jungle gum he constantly kneaded in his hands.

Finally, by accident, he did what was never supposed to be done: He touched a wad of crude rubber mixed through with powdered sulfur to the surface of a roaring hot wood stove in his kitchen. The sulfur-impregnated blob charred rather than melted. Outside in the cold, it retained its resilience without hardening. It would also prove impervious to heat and internal rot. The process of mixing raw rubber gum with sulfur and exposing it to certain levels of heat "cured" the material, making it long-lasting and stable. In 1844, Goodyear received patent number 3,633 for the process he called "vulcanization," after the ancient Roman god of fire.

It is not an exaggeration to say that the invention of vulcanization was one of the single most important events of the industrial age. It made possible revolutionary advances in machine design and operation by the time Goodyear died in 1860.

A Sexual Revolution Wrought by Rubber

Far less publicized, but no less important, was the sweeping sexual revolution wrought by Goodyear's discovery. Vulcanized rubber provided the first material truly suited for a safe and effective interface between machinery and internal human organs. Moisture-proof rubber devices were as light as they were strong, as pliable as they were resilient, and as inert as they were durable. Cheap rubber bulbs, hoses, nozzles, catheters, condoms, vaginal barriers, and similar implements offered the potential for previously unthinkable levels of intervention in, and control over, certain bodily functions. And even as they were still perfecting their basic production techniques in the late 1840s, New England's rubber manufacturers offered rapidly expanding lines of sex-related rubber items. Medical historians note that the appearance of the rubber tube in the form of a catheter made abortions available and popular by the late 1850s. As we have seen in the last chapter, a variety of rubber barrier pessaries began appearing in the 1850s, and the rubber douche syringe became one of the best-selling items for pharmacists and mail-order merchants. The first thick and awkward rubber condoms soon became available and are believed to have been used—in limited quantities— among the prostitutes who appeared in growing legions throughout the cities and military staging areas of a nation suddenly overrun with war.

But a young Union soldier who tramped through that conflict would soon take personal umbrage with public sales of such "damnable" new products as "Dr. Power's French Preventives" for gentlemen or "Goodyear Ring" diaphragms for ladies. Shortly after he mustered out of the Seventeenth Connecticut, Anthony Comstock would launch an extraordinary forty-two-year battle against that substance he perceived threatened the virtue of women, the sanctity of the family, and all else that was good and holy in America: rubber.

Comstock's War on Rubber

Born the same year rubber vulcanization was patented, Anthony Comstock grew up in New Canaan, Connecticut, just thirty miles from Charles Goodyear's home in New Haven. Headed by a farmer and sawyer, the Comstock family belonged to a fundamentalist Christian sect that lived in accordance with the beliefs of the original Puritan settlers. An austere, ascetic group, they worshipped in a stark wooden structure without paint or internal ornamentation and, likewise, eschewed the consumption of alcohol, the playing of cards, the wearing of bright colors, and participation in any sexual activity except that necessary between husband and wife to produce offspring.

They were also a frugal, hardworking people who taught their children to aggressively declare the righteousness of God's will to the surrounding sinful world. In 1862, when he was eighteen years old and working as a grocery clerk, burly Anthony Comstock broke into his first saloon, spilled all the liquor kegs on the floor and left an anonymous note threatening the proprietor with further action if he did not close his establishment.

The following year, after his brother died in the battle of Gettysburg, Comstock enlisted in the Union Army. In his diary, he wrote of his shock as he was forced to live in tents where "the air resounded with the oaths of wicked men." The army routinely issued daily rations of whiskey to its members. Comstock not only wouldn't drink his ration, but each day ceremonially spilled it on the ground rather than give it to others who asked for it.

When the bone-tired soldiers of the Union and Confederacy ceased fighting and peacefully trudged away from Appomattox in the spring of 1865, they wandered home across a landscape of physical ruin, economic chaos, and emotional dislocation. The war had literally ripped America apart, leaving postwar society convulsed by street crime, openly tainted by debauchery, and riven with political corruption. Heywood Broun and Margaret Leech would write of the period: "Social behavior, notoriously lax in the years succeeding war, dissolved in the easy warmth of plentiful money. All that was vulgar in the republic, all that was raw and crude, rose to the surface and floated there."

For instance, the continuing revolution in printing technology during the war era had made it possible to print vast numbers of cheap books, the most profitable of which were the erotic pulp novels favored by young males. By 1865, the widespread availability of such ribald publications was perceived to be enough of a threat to the public decency that Congress, lobbied by a growing "moral reform" movement, passed a law making it illegal to send obscene materials through the mails. However, the law was weakly written, narrowly focused, and widely ignored in the free-wheeling atmosphere of bribery and kickbacks endemic to cities such as New York, where Anthony Comstock settled in 1867.

Comstock had originally come to New York to seek his fortune in the dry goods business but was appalled by what he found. He wrote that being in the city was like being "stationed in a swamp at the mouth of a sewer." To combat the decadence, depravity, and vice he saw in every direction, he joined one of the leading organizations in the city's growing "social purity" reform movement: the Young

Men's Christian Association. The YMCA of this era was a vibrant and powerful political organization backed by the money, connections, and prestige of some of New York's wealthiest industrialists. There, Comstock's zeal, charisma, pithy speaking skills, and careful cultivation of friendships with reporters at leading newspapers catapulted him to celebrity. First acting as an agent of the YMCA and then as the head of his own "New York Society for the Suppression of Vice," Comstock took reporters along with him as he conducted his own raids on street-corner book dealers, girlie dance shows, gambling halls, and patent medicine stores.

When Comstock went to Washington in 1872 to lobby for a greatly expanded federal anti-obscenity law, he was already a hero to a large audience of people frustrated and angered by the general lack of order and decorum in postwar society. Under pressure from his potent political allies, the Congress passed, and President Ulysses S. Grant signed, what came to be known as the "Comstock Law" in the opening months of 1873. Along with prohibiting the production and sale of virtually any printed materials that contained depictions or references to sexual subjects, the new law also prohibited "every article or thing designed, adapted, or intended for preventing conception or producing an abortion, or for any indecent or immoral use; and every article, instrument, substance, drug, medicine, or thing which is advertised or described in a manner calculated to lead another to use or apply it for preventing conception or producing abortion, or for any indecent or immoral purpose." In short, Comstock, now a federal law enforcement agent, intended to halt the production, sale, and availability of all the "damnable rubber goods" he believed had facilitated the national sexual revolution he was determined to thwart.

Doctors were arrested for writing books and pamphlets instructing women on such basic matters of hygiene as how to douche or insert a rubber diaphragm. Druggists were arrested for selling syringes; barbers for selling condoms. During the first twelve months of enforcement of the new law, Comstock's New York group seized more than 60,300 "immoral rubber articles" and 3,150 cases of patent medicine substances intended for "immoral purposes."

They also struck at the rubber fabricating industry. One of Comstock's operational reports read thus: "Three factories, where abominations that would put to shame Sodom and Gomorrah were made, have been raided and closed, while molds and stock have been seized and destroyed."

The Condom Underground

Throughout the Comstock era, inventors applied for many patents for improvements to syringes, contraceptive pessaries, and abortion implements, but not for condoms. Condoms, however, were widely perceived as being designed for only one use—the prevention of pregnancy, while the other devices had alternate medical and health uses that allowed them to be legally sold.

As a symbol, the condom had been targeted by Comstock-led reformers as the most infamous kind of "immoral rubber article." While patents were granted for various manufacturing processes used to produce thin-walled rubber goods, no attempts were made to register inventions for the improvement of the condom itself. There was, after all, no incentive for innovation. Condom manufacture was an

Inventors had no incentive to devise or register improvements on a product that was illegal to sell.

underground business whose products were furtively distributed by bartenders and barbers.

In the 1920s, as enforcement of the Comstock Law slackened and a national movement in favor of birth control gained political momentum, the newly formed Youngs Rubber Company, headed by Merrill Youngs, launched the first national condom sales campaign. Youngs made arrangements to sell his "Trojan" brand condoms only through drug stores, adding a new aura of respectability to the product. He convinced druggists to cooperate by pricing Trojans so that they were the single most profitable item in the store. More importantly, he focused his marketing on the disease-prevention attributes of condoms and avoided mention of any other use.

By the end of the decade, Youngs's sales were mushrooming when another competitor copied the Trojan logo and packaging. The underground industry had routinely ignored patents, trademarks, and other regulations because manufacturers engaged in an illegal business would not sue each other. However, Youngs filed a lawsuit that took on both his competitor and portions of the Comstock Law. Ultimately, Judge Thomas Swan of the U.S. Court of Appeals not only upheld Youngs's trademark rights, but neutralized the Comstock Law as it pertained to condoms.

Meanwhile, throughout the 1930s, Margaret Sanger and her birth control coalition initiated their own legal challenges to the remaining sections of the Comstock statute. In a 1936 landmark ruling on a case that involved the importation of contraceptive pessaries seized as immoral contraband by U.S. Customs agents, the Second Circuit Court of Appeals nullified the rest of the Comstock prohibitions.

The American government's war on immoral rubber goods was over. Ninety-two years after Charles Goodyear patented the process that made possible revolutionary advances in technology related to human sexuality, it finally became legal for this unique material to be openly used for such purposes. By the end of the 1930s, Youngs

Rubber and Schmid Laboratories, Inc., were conducting vigorous and rapidly expanding national marketing campaigns for the brand names that became synonymous with the product: Trojan, Sheik, and Ramses. Sales volume rose to about 1.5 million condoms daily.

The New Era of Condom Invention

The establishment of an open and orderly condom market in the 1940s fostered a new atmosphere of innovation. Lured by the potential for patent-protected royalties, inventors began studying and working on improving the mechanical interface between condoms and genitalia.

Two nearly legendary deficiencies of the devices were their tendency to fail and the medical problems that could result from their use. In order to successfully function as a contraceptive and disease-preventive sheath, a condom had to remain in place and intact throughout all stages of intercourse. The traditional blunt rubber tube necessarily fit tightly around the penis and, during the normal action of intercourse, was pulled even more tautly across the tip of the organ. During orgasm, pressurized jets of semen often could not exit the penis because of this tight rubber seal and, hence, generated damaging back pressure on the prostate gland. When semen *did* exit into the tight space between skin and condom, it exerted considerable force as it suddenly increased the total volume of matter pressing outward against the thin membrane. It was believed this force was the most common cause of burst condoms. And such bursting occurred with distressing frequency. While manufacturers in the 1940s developed better quality controls and stronger grades of latex rubber, they did not succeed in eliminating either of these two problems.

In 1948, Stanley Penksa of Yonkers, New York, filed for a patent on a condom with a "reservoir" tip—a semen-collecting bulb that extended beyond the usually blunt end of the device. This initial

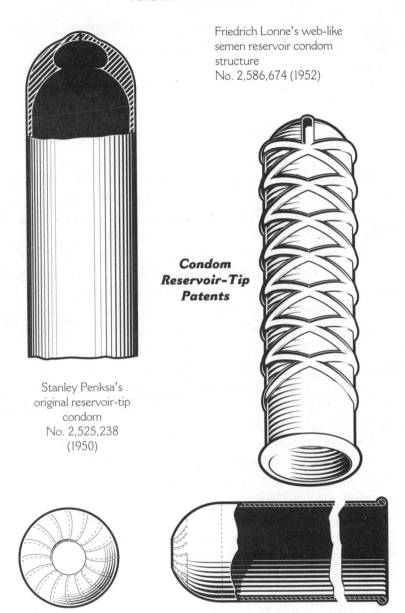

Friedrich Lonne's web-like
semen reservoir condom
structure
No. 2,586,674 (1952)

**Condom
Reservoir-Tip
Patents**

Stanley Penksa's
original reservoir-tip
condom
No. 2,525,238
(1950)

Stanley Penksa's iris-folds reservoir-tip condom No. 3,085,570 (1963)

design actually included a tiny air hole at the very tip of the reservoir. Penksa explained: "It will be apparent that when the semen is discharged . . . under pressure (it will) force air out of the opening but the opening is so small that fluid may not pass there through." However, any opening large enough to pass air tended to also pass minute quantities of fluid. The air hole was eliminated in the design that ultimately went to market in the 1950s.

Friedrich Lonne criticized Penksa's reservoir tip design and sought his own patent for a different approach to the problem of semen pressure dispersion. He told patent examiners that in the Penksa design, the reservoir actually became so compacted by the stress of intercourse that it either didn't function, or did so very inefficiently. Lonne's idea was to criss-cross the rubber condom membrane—or pellicle—with thicker rubber ribs. He explained that this allowed ejaculated semen to disperse into the expandable reservoirs of thin membrane within each criss-cross of the thicker ribs. In effect, the internal body of the condom became a honeycomb of semen reservoirs.

Twelve years after he received his original reservoir tip patent, Penksa was back at the Patent Office with a new reservoir mechanism that featured expanding iris-like folds. Generally, his new design operated something like the self-contained foil popcorn poppers that expand as the corn puffs exert an upward pressure.

In 1975, after conducting what appears to have been a comprehensive engineering study of the forces at work on condoms during intercourse, Clayton H. Allen of Cambridge, Massachusetts, explained to the Patent Office that previous inventors had inaccurately understood the primary reasons for prophylactic bursting. He wrote: "It is well known that the thin rubber tubular sheath type of condom occasionally ruptures during coitus. This usually happens at the height of coital movement after ejaculation. The reason for rupture . . . has been attributed to the stretching of the rubber material due to the added volume of the seminal fluid issued from the penis. New shapes of such prophylactics now being sold are formed from a small reservoir at the forward end advertised to receive fluid without stretching the condom member itself. These forms with the reservoir are no less likely to rupture than the more conventional form with the simple rounded end, and in fact, under the usual conditions existing after ejaculation the reservoir design is more likely to rupture. The reasons for this seeming paradox are simple. The conventional rubber condom has an elastic limit order of magnitude greater than needed to accommodate the increased volume of the ejaculated semen. If this were not so, one size of condom would not be as universally usable as it is, since the variation in the size of the erect human penis is far greater than the 2 to 5 cc of semen normally issued during ejaculation. As a demonstration it can be shown that such a condom may be stretched repeatedly from a relaxed length near 7 1/2 inches to a length of 48 inches without damage. Further, it may be blown up with air to a size of 8 inches in diameter and over 30 inches long and relaxed repeatedly without rupture. Therefore it is not the small increase in volume due to semen that contributes to the rupture of a condom after ejaculation."

Allen continued: "After the emission of semen the pressure of the forward walls of the vagina against the condom transports the semen along the penis toward the open end of the condom and thereby lubricates the penis so that the condom slips more freely on the penis than against the walls of the vagina. This is especially true if the penis is withdrawn totally or to such an extent that the lubricated portion of the penis extends outside the relatively dryer lips of the vagina. The movement of the condom into the vagina is further inhibited occasionally by resistance against pubic hair. During a subsequent deep penetration of the penis, the closed end of the condom can be stretched beyond its elastic limit. A normal thrust can easily exceed the few pounds of force needed to push through and rupture the thin wall of the rubber membrane."

In addition, Allen indicated that when the penis suddenly became more slippery against the internal surface of the condom than

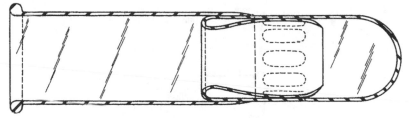

Clayton H. Allen's double-walled cul-de-sac condom No. 4,009,717

the exterior condom was against the walls of the vagina, the base of the condom tended to move up the penile shaft during the final movements of intercourse. This obviously exposed the vaginal wall to direct contact with semen.

Allen presented his own design for a new kind of condom structure that better addressed these problems: a doubled-layered device that formed its own internal cul-de-sac to capture all semen in the front half. In this manner, dry contact could be maintained between the rubber surface and the skin along the base of the penis.

Condom Slippage

Upward slippage of the condom along the penile shaft has been widely recognized as a major deficiency and inventors have focused on it in many different ways. Two individuals received patents for condom retention straps. One was an integral part of the condom and slipped over the scrotum to provide a secure anchor. The other utilized the concept of an elastic hip strap with a snap that could quickly be attached to the trailing edge of any standard condom.

Yet others have taken a chemical approach and devised systems that made tip-mounted spermicidal release systems part of the condom structure. James P. Robinson created a condom with a special pouch for exuding spermicidal chemicals into the vagina. Albert L. Brown patented the concept of condom that released drugs to its *interior*. Even as semen was being ejaculated, it would be mixed

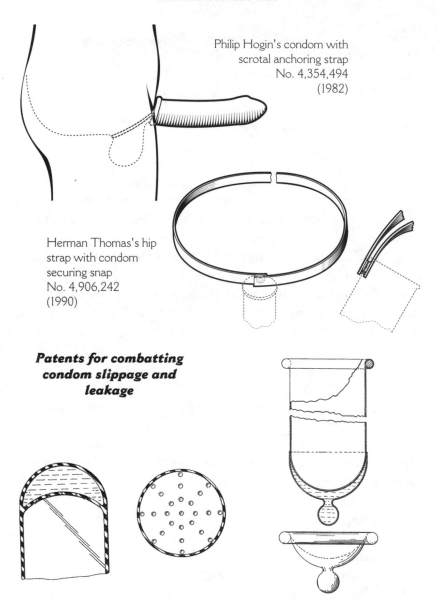

Philip Hogin's condom with
scrotal anchoring strap
No. 4,354,494
(1982)

Herman Thomas's hip
strap with condom
securing snap
No. 4,906,242
(1990)

**Patents for combatting
condom slippage and
leakage**

Albert Brown's system released
spermicide to the interior of the
condom. No. 2,904,041 (1952)

James Robinson's system released
spermicide to the exterior of the
condom. No. 2,410,460 (1941)

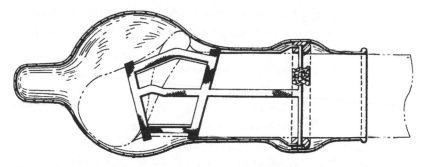

Edward Meldhal's condom system included an internal semen barrier ring, a spermicide release system, and a "sensitivity harness." No. 2,586,674 (1952)

with a spermicide to render it inert before it had a chance to leak. Morton Gutnick envisioned a condom and chemical dispensing system that could be used as part of geographically focused health campaigns. His 1984 concept utilizes an external chemical release system that could be loaded with spermicide and other drugs appropriate for the types of venereal disease known to be most prevalent in a given region. Edward N. Meldhal patented a condom with a spongy internal ring that acted as both a physical barrier against the movement of semen down the penile shaft and an internal release reservoir for spermicidal agents. He also included a "sensitivity harness" in the interior of his condom to make it more pleasurable for males to use. The contour of the whole affair was so bulky that Meldhal received a separate design patent for the unusual shape of the special double-bulbed condom shape required to cover the whole apparatus.

The Truncated, or "Minimal," Condom

The "sensitivity" issue addressed by Meldhal had long been a critical one for the industry. No matter how thin the condom material, it inevitably affected the sensations felt by both partners. From the earliest days of rubber condom manufacture, it was recognized that large numbers of males and females refused to buy or use the product because of the sensation-deadening effects, which were particularly acute for males.

Among the first condom improvement patents filed in the 1940s was Harold Warner's radically new concept for a truncated, or minimal, version. This condom was actually little more than a "semen reservoir" that fit on the very tip of the penis like a cap. Thus, the rest of the organ remained exposed to the normal sensations of intercourse. It was the first of a dozen patents that would be issued during the next forty years for what might be thought of as "minimal" condoms. In 1971, when he filed for a patent for an improvement on his original 1947 idea, Warner noted that abbreviated condom designs registered to date suffered the common problem of being "somewhat prone to inadvertent detachment." Julius Czirely received a patent for a minimal condom that sought to remedy this problem with glue. Before engaging in sexual intercourse, the male used a skin-bonding adhesive to fasten the tiny "seminal container" around the very tip of the penis. After intercourse, the abbreviated condom had to be removed with a special solvent.

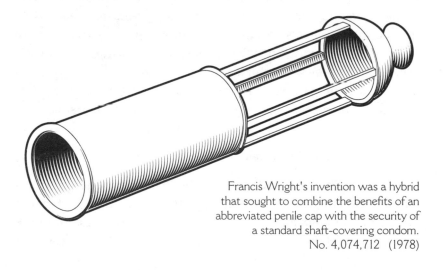

Francis Wright's invention was a hybrid that sought to combine the benefits of an abbreviated penile cap with the security of a standard shaft-covering condom.
No. 4,074,712 (1978)

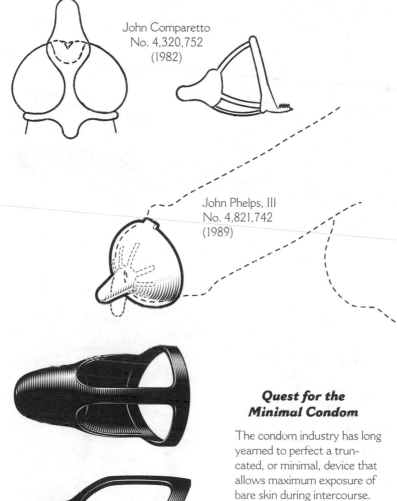

John Comparetto
No. 4,320,752
(1982)

John Phelps, III
No. 4,821,742
(1989)

Quest for the Minimal Condom

The condom industry has long yearned to perfect a truncated, or minimal, device that allows maximum exposure of bare skin during intercourse. A dozen patents have been granted for abbreviated condoms that attach to the very tip of the penis.

Harold Warner
No. 2,433,538 (1947)

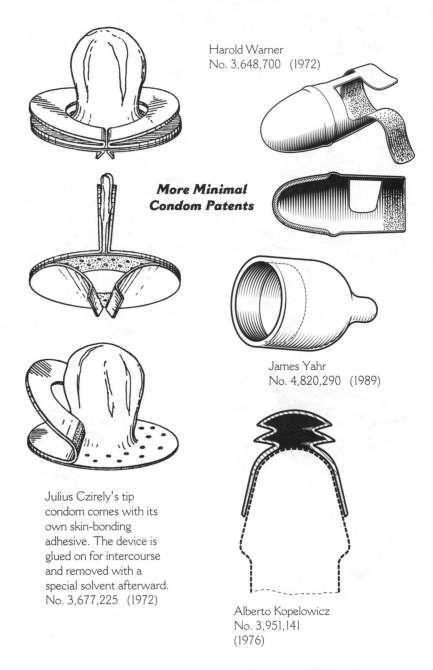

Harold Warner
No. 3,648,700 (1972)

**More Minimal
Condom Patents**

James Yahr
No. 4,820,290 (1989)

Julius Czirely's tip
condom comes with its
own skin-bonding
adhesive. The device is
glued on for intercourse
and removed with a
special solvent afterward.
No. 3,677,225 (1972)

Alberto Kopelowicz
No. 3,951,141
(1976)

Others, like A. Francis Wright of Ohio, sought to construct a hybrid that resembled a standard condom with large sections of its sides cut out to expose broad expanses of the shaft and tip to direct stimulation. This theoretically allowed increased sensation at the same time it provided for a more secure fit of the semen retaining section of the device.

Female-Sensitive Condoms

In the 1970s inventors began to engineer new condoms that took into account the genital sensitivities—and potential purchasing influence—of females. The idea was that a penile barrier sheath could also serve to stimulate the clitoris. In 1974 two Alabama men received a patent for a condom surfaced with dot-and-dash ridges designed to provide such direct stimulation. Between 1977 and 1979, Tadao Okamoto of Japan received four design patents for specific exterior condom configurations of spiral lines, nubs, dots, and stars that served the same purpose.

Sensation-Deadening Condoms

Other inventors working with the sensitivity issue realized the need for improvement at the other end of the spectrum: a condom that actually deadened or impeded male sexual sensitivity. The target market for such a device was males plagued by premature ejaculation. In 1950 three Mississippi men applied for a patent on a condom with a thick-walled tip which, they said, "effectively cushions the nerve centers in the male organ to increase the period of copulation prior to spermatic emission." Richard B. Freeman of Ohio told the Patent Office that the Mississippians' tip-enveloping device was deficient because it cut off too much sensation. He explained: "The entire penis has a general tactile sensibility but the area of the penis comprising the lower edge of the glans is critically sensitive to tactile

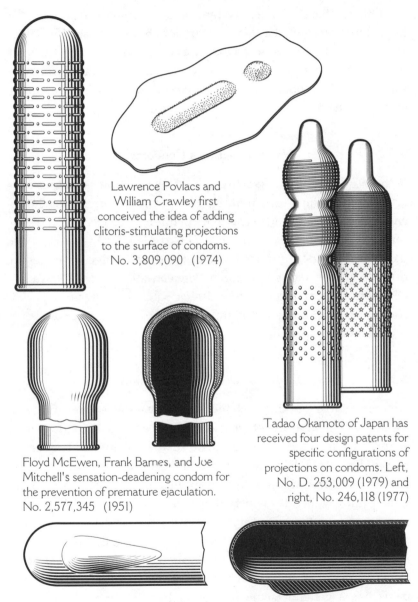

Lawrence Povlacs and
William Crawley first
conceived the idea of adding
clitoris-stimulating projections
to the surface of condoms.
No. 3,809,090 (1974)

Floyd McEwen, Frank Barnes, and Joe
Mitchell's sensation-deadening condom for
the prevention of premature ejaculation.
No. 2,577,345 (1951)

Tadao Okamoto of Japan has
received four design patents for
specific configurations of
projections on condoms. Left,
No. D. 253,009 (1979) and
right, No. 246,118 (1977)

Richard Freeman's sensation-deadening condom for the prevention
of premature ejaculation No. 2,816,542 (1957)

stimulation. The control of stimulation in this critical area can effectively delay orgasm without minimizing the general sensation of sexual intercourse." To achieve this, Freeman's patented condom was fabricated with a tear-shaped thickening that fit over the penile cleft area. This sensation barrier area was twelve times the thickness of the surrounding rubber membrane.

Other Condom Innovations

Beyond the issues of barrier integrity and tactile sensitivity, inventors in the postwar years studied and sought to improve other mechanical aspects of condoms. For instance, Kunitami Asaka of Tokyo pointed out to the Patent Office that "wasted rubber condoms frequently float on the water in city sewerage systems and may be viewed at exposed places." Mr. Asaka revealed a new chemical formula that would produce an elastic membrane "which is decomposable by contact with cold water within a short time period, yet durable in contact with warm aqueous liquid." In 1971 he received a patent for the first biodegradable condom.

For others, the condom offered a potential means to enhance sexual performance, particularly for males who felt their organ was deficient in size or rigidity. An interest in making the condom a performance-boosting device as well seems to have emerged strongly at the end of the 1970s after years of incessant publicity about the country's ongoing sexual revolution. It was also a time when medical authorities were beginning to acknowledge that impotence appeared to be far more a common male problem than was previously known.

In 1981 M. Maurice Rogers of Downsville, Louisiana, was granted a patent for an inflatable condom "which serves to enlarge the male sex organ and which can be adjusted in size during coition by either partner to achieve a desired degree of satisfaction." The double-walled condom had an attached rubber bulb that could be squeezed by hand to further inflate the device. Rogers noted that it came "in

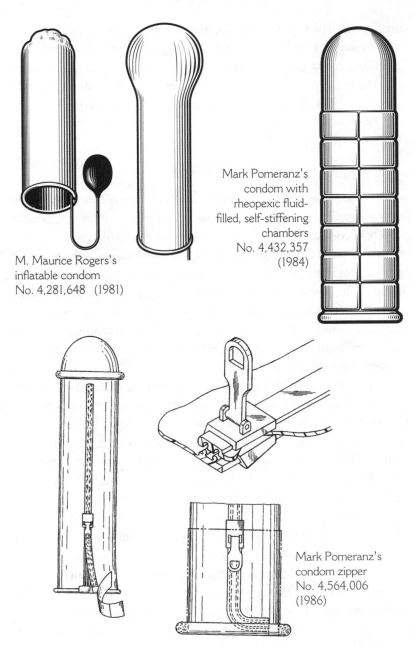

M. Maurice Rogers's
inflatable condom
No. 4,281,648 (1981)

Mark Pomeranz's
condom with
rheopexic fluid-
filled, self-stiffening
chambers
No. 4,432,357
(1984)

Mark Pomeranz's
condom zipper
No. 4,564,006
(1986)

both [a] lubricated and non-lubricated design" and that it could be fabricated with "beads or ridges projecting from the surface of the sheath for greater stimulation."

Self-Stiffening Condoms

Mark L. Pomeranz of Jacksonville, Florida, in a particularly high-tech example of prophylactic enhancement, exploited the peculiar characteristics of a new class of "rheopexic" chemical fluids to create a self-stiffening condom. Rheopexic fluids are peculiar chemical compounds that thicken in consistency or viscosity as they are subjected to shear stress. Mr. Pomeranz created a condom comprised of a thin membrane of chambers filled with these fluids. He explained, "in use, shear stress is applied to the rheopexic fluid chambers . . . under the effect of repeated movements carried out during sexual intercourse. As a result . . . the rheopexic fluid increases its consistency and becomes stiff, thereby simulating an erection." Two years later, he received another patent for a condom with rheopexic panels and a zipper up the side. He explained that standard condoms "are suitable for use only when the penis is erect. If the penis is flaccid, for example as would be the case with an impotent male, it is extremely difficult, if not impossible, to place the condom on the penis." With his new invention, the condom was unzipped, placed around the full length of the organ, and then zipped closed.

Condoms: The Modern Controversy

The use of such high-tech chemical technologies to make the condom a performance enhancer for ailing males is an interested exercise in innovative thinking, but not something you're likely to see on your drug store shelf very soon. This is because the condom, whose structure fascinates inventors with endless possibilities, is also one of our society's most politically sensitive personal hygiene products.

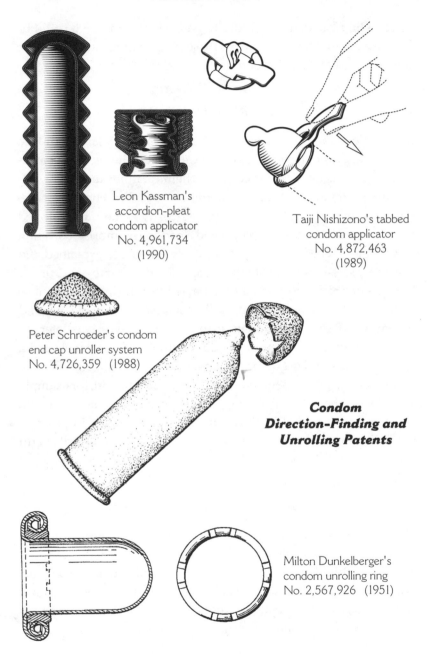

Leon Kassman's
accordion-pleat
condom applicator
No. 4,961,734
(1990)

Taiji Nishizono's tabbed
condom applicator
No. 4,872,463
(1989)

Peter Schroeder's condom
end cap unroller system
No. 4,726,359   (1988)

***Condom
Direction-Finding and
Unrolling Patents***

Milton Dunkelberger's
condom unrolling ring
No. 2,567,926   (1951)

Despite quantum leaps in technology; revolutions in communications; breakthroughs in the understanding of psychology and sociology; and miraculous medical developments that have allowed us to study and understand the most elemental functions of the human organism, we are, as a nation, still unable to deal with sexuality in an open and rational manner. The strident nature of today's debates about such things as, for example, whether or not sexually active teenagers should be provided with condoms, clearly demonstrates the schizophrenia of our social customs that, in part, remain anchored in the philosophies championed by Anthony Comstock.

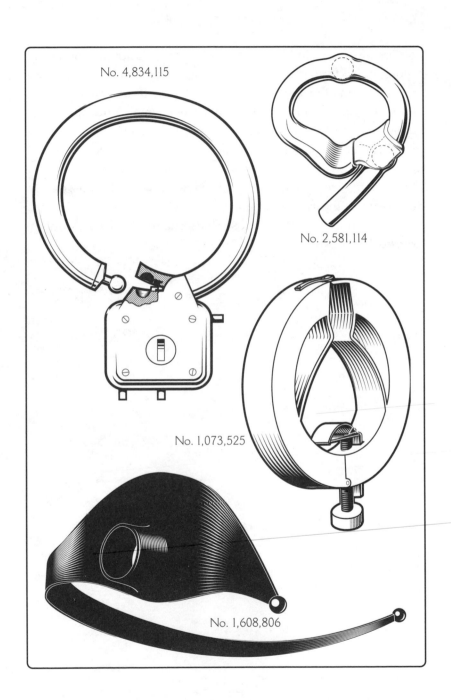

No. 4,834,115

No. 2,581,114

No. 1,073,525

No. 1,608,806

7

Erector Rings

Throughout the nineteenth century, impotence—the inability of a male to have or sustain an erection—was widely viewed by the medical community as just another of the many crippling diseases caused by masturbation. The general belief was that masturbators had "used up" excessive amounts of nervous energy and permanently damaged their systems in a manner that rendered them unable to support normal adult sexual functions. Thus, seeking treatment for impotence was a tacit admission by the patient that he had previously engaged in what was widely viewed as a sexual perversion.

Not surprisingly, most males were less than eager to bring such a problem to their physicians. Nor were physicians generally eager to be confronted with such distasteful matters. Even medical reference books avoided the topic. For instance, in his landmark 267-page reference book on disorders of the human reproductive systems, Dr. William Acton, one the era's leading authorities, devoted fewer than seven pages to the subject of impotence. In a typical anecdote, he explained how he dealt with a college student who sought treatment because he was unable to achieve an erection. Dr. Acton wrote, "My reply to such a (patient) is, 'Be thankful that your studies are not interfered with by sensual thoughts.'"

Although there are no hard statistics on impotence in the 1800s, it seems likely that the numbers were even greater than those of today.

That period's poor nutrition, often-abominable hygiene standards, rampant infectious diseases, and crude medicine, as well as an over-whelming burden of institutionalized sexual guilt and anxiety surely guaranteed high levels of organic and psychological impotence. Authorities currently estimate that about 24 percent of modern-day adult males suffer impotence at any given time. It seems likely that the Victorian era's number would have been greater. Nor could individuals with the problem reach out to a library or bookstore for information because laws made it a federal and state crime to publish, sell, or possess books and pamphlets on virtually any sexual subject.

One nineteenth-century physician's account suggests the extent of anguish experienced by afflicted males. "Large towns harbor crowds of persons suffering from a diseased nervous system, who, in the different stages of life, are afflicted with sexual infirmities which throw a gloom over their existence . . . All this aggravated by self-reproaches of the worst kind, for almost every one believes he has himself caused his misfortune."

However, while the official medical community declined to acknowledge impotence as a legitimate concern, a burgeoning "alternative" community of self-proclaimed healers, wagon board hucksters, and advertising entrepreneurs made it a major focus of a wild and woolly medicine-show culture that emerged as a national institution in the second half of the 1800s.

These traveling road shows featured such persons as Violet McNeal, who appeared in silken mandarin robes as "Princess Lotus Blossom." The Princess sold "Vital Sparks," which, she told the nightly crowds, was an ancient Chinese cure for impotence made from the brain matter of a rare Oriental turtle. Later in life, in a book about her road years, McNeal explained that "Vital Sparks" was actually made from a kind of rock candy crushed, dampened, and rolled around in colored aloe powders.

In addition to these traveling medicine shows, American cities and towns sprouted a new kind of street-corner "medical institute" that specialized in "the Secret Diseases of Men." In his history of this peculiar industry, Stewart Holbrook wrote, "the institute was almost certain to maintain a front called a Museum of Anatomy, advertised as Educational and Free . . . leading back into the building was a short corridor lined with glass cases of human figures to show the early stages of various diseases of men. After ten or twenty feet, the corridor opened into the museum proper, and the prospective patient suddenly found himself in a large room facing approximately one hundred wax effigies. These displayed the later stages of the more or less Secret Diseases of Men . . . As the museum visitor moved from one exhibit to another, he eventually came to a glass cabinet completely dark inside. If he paused a moment, the inside automatically and instantly came ablaze with electric light, and the fearsome face of an idiot boy leered out hideously at him. Above this terrible apparition was the warning: LOST MANHOOD."

These "medical institutes" and anatomical museums were the front end of a hard-sell operation geared to marketing various sorts of products for impotence and venereal disease. In his book on the subject, James H. Young explained, "The New York Museum of Anatomy issued a catalog in 1868 listing its 2,167 exhibits . . . Along with the exhibits of sickness went samples of sin, sadism, and sex to lure the curious to the waxworks show . . . the main stress was upon gruesome renditions of all parts of the

Joseph Cheever
No. 14,085
(1856)

body ruined by disease, especially private parts ravaged by unmentionable maladies. Agents haunted the gallery to watch the spectators and exhort those who appeared shamed and stricken back behind scenes where the 'doctor' waited with his high priced 'cures.'"

Along with pills, powders, potions, and salves, the medicine men, mail-order advertisers, and waxworks hawkers also offered various mechanical products. Some sense of what these were like can be seen in the patent issued to Joseph Cheever of Boston, Massachusetts, for a galvanic testicle pouch. He assured the patent examiners that his device cured "impotency and other diseases of the genital organs." Powered by rows of buttons of disparate metals moistened by perspiration, the device consisted of a chain-mail pouch that delivered a constant flow of electric current to the testicles. Cheever indicated to the Patent Office that electricity sent into the testicles would naturally flow through the penis and that, in some manner, this electrical flow would "produce curative and useful results."

The Gross Clinic

Throughout the second half of the nineteenth century, this sort of hucksterism existed in direct competition with mainstream doctors. Perceived as a serious commercial threat to those medical professionals, it became the subject of heated debate and forced some members of the medical establishment to reconsider and address areas of patient complaints, such as impotence, that they had previously ignored. For instance, it was a major event for the national medical community when, in 1877, the renowned Dr. Samuel W. Gross of Philadelphia made impotence a topic of a lecture to the Philadelphia County Medical Society. At the time, Dr. Gross was the nation's most renowned surgeon, and his clinic at Philadelphia's Jefferson Medical Hospital was world-famous even before it was immortalized by the painter Thomas Eakins.

In a groundbreaking address, Dr. Gross explained that "reduced sexual power, from whatever cause it may arise, is one of the most distressing of maladies, and is, therefore, entitled to the deepest sympathy and consideration on the part of the honest practitioner, by whom, unfortunately, it is rarely discussed." He noted that the pathology of impotence was "imperfectly understood," but that his own observations and patient studies had caused him to conclude that impotence was "traceable, in the larger proportion of instances, to masturbation." He detailed in his lecture how "masturbation affects the sexual powers by inducing a state of constant congestion and undue excitability of the urethra." This excitability, he believed, caused internal strictures to eventually form inside the urethra. These strictures, he indicated, caused "morbid sensibility," which, in some manner, disabled the ability of the penis to erect itself.

Dr. Gross advised his colleagues that there were three ways to deal with a patient's complaints of impotence: give him bromide of potassium to "blunt the venereal appetite" and make the impotence more bearable; counsel the patient about the importance of "chastity in thought and action"; and ream out the patient's urethra with a "steel bougie" or blunt instrument once each day. The doctor believed the passage of the steel bougie rod up and down the length of the urethra broke up the strictures that were the cause of the impotence.

Hydraulic Principles of Erection

During the next decade, mainstream physicians began formulating their own theories and treatment therapies for impotence. In his address to the Baltimore Medical and Surgical Society in 1879, Dr. John J. Caldwell outlined the relatively simple hydraulic principles that actually made erections happen. He emphasized that the muscular constrictions crucial to the erection of a penis were controlled by nerve impulses vulnerable to influence by nervous states, physical problems, and age. He reported that some doctors were using various sorts of electrical shock treatments, wiring their impotent patients' penises and testicles to Leyden jars and faradization machines.

Caldwell himself favored a more subtle approach to the impotence problem aimed at soothing the nerves and calming the emotions. He recommended "tonics, malt, beef-steak, exercise, mountain air or sea bathing." He explained that "one of the finest restoratives . . . is the shower bath poured upon the lower part of the spine; vigorous friction with flesh brush or coarse towel must follow its use. This is most excellent for old men . . . who are gradually losing power which is generally lost before desire."

The First Rubber-Band Therapy

Still others began to focus on the possibility of direct intervention with the bio-hydraulics of the penis itself. In an 1885 journal article, Dr. James H. Dunn wrote, "the frequency of (impotence), the great agony of mind and body caused to the ignorant sufferers, the frequency with which they fall into the hands of a class of charlatans most vile, the crying need of a better understanding of the physiology and hygiene of the generative apparatus, shall be my apology for asking your attention to the subject. Nor can it be denied that the more deserving of these patients have in the past received scant satisfaction from the profession, but of late, thanks to a rapid increase of scientific knowledge in nearly all branches of medicine, new light is being thrown upon this class of affections, and the profession at large is taking a greater interest in their scientific management." A key tool in Dr. Dunn's scientific management of such patients was a rubber band. He explained: "Occasionally a case in which the erection subsides as soon as intercourse is attempted, is helped by placing a light rubber band about the root of the penis to prevent the discharge through the veins. I supposed this to be a little invention of my own, but of late, I find many patients and physicians have used the same plan."

This general idea—of artificially constricting the dorsal vein in a manner that mechanically caused an erection—was an attractive one to patients and physicians alike. Some doctors saw in it the potential for new surgical procedures. Dr. G. R. Phillips wrote that he had performed an operation on an impotent railroad manager, partially tying off the dorsal vein in the man's penis. This permanently restricted the outflow of blood from the penis, maintaining the organ in a permanent state of semi-tumescence. While it may have fascinated Dr. Phillips's surgical colleagues, the approach of slicing and suturing the penis at a time when even minor surgery regularly resulted in massive infection was not one that generated a great deal of enthusiasm among impotent males.

The Mechanical Pressure Ring

Inevitably, gadgeteers and entrepreneurs sought to create a simple, exterior mechanical device that could accomplish the same vessel-constricting result without dangerous surgery, pain, or inconvenience. Mechanically, the device would have to fit securely around the penis and be able to exert clamping pressure on the outflowing veins along the top of the organ. It was equally important, however, that this pressure not be such that it would constrict the arteries at the center of the penis which had to supply blood in order to inflate the erection-sustaining spongy chambers. Such a product could have a

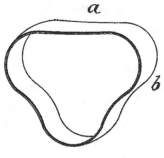

Horace Taggart
No. 594,815 (1897)

potential market as large and endless as the ongoing problem of male impotence itself.

In 1897, the first penile dorsal vein clamp patent application arrived at the Patent Office in Washington. Horace D. Taggart of Akron, Ohio, told the commissioners that his triangular device was "a simple and efficient device for use on the male generative organ during sexual intercourse and adapted to produce elastic compression of the dorsal vein when the generative organs shall have become so inactive as to refuse to perform their natural duties."

Within months of Taggart's grant in November of 1897, the examiners received another application from James Doty of Syracuse, New York, who proposed adding galvanic electrical current to the basic penile constrictor concept. His invention consisted of a waistband with a rear strap that passed down and under the buttocks to loop around the penis. This strap was somewhat elastic at the same time it contained wires for carrying electrical current from the cells of galvanic metals built into the waist belt. The strap was adjustable so that one could increase or decrease the strain it exerted on the "electromagnetic" loop that pulled downward on the dorsal vein at the base of the penis.

Penile Ring Marketing

The often florid tone of the back-street marketing for such devices at the turn of the century can be seen in the documented activities of Coryell Bartholomew of Jackson, Michigan. In 1900, Bartholomew, a medicine show trooper who referred to himself as "Professor Bartholomew," was granted a design patent for a tubular "bandage." Design patents differ from device patents because the applicant is asking the Patent Office for protection for the "look" rather than the function of a thing. After receiving his design patent, the professor began promoting the device as "A Boon to Men." It was, he told the public, "Nature's Cure for Loss of Manly Power Without Drugs." And, he pointed out "the United States Government has unhesitatingly granted a patent for it, which speaks for itself." In fact, the Patent Office was never informed about any specific use for Mr. Bartholomew's "bandage" design. In his ads, the patentee exclaimed of his invention: "It stands alone. It excels over all other treatments. It is only a matter of time when the Appliance will be universally used for the relief of Impotency." In effect, it was little more than an expansion of the original rubber-band idea publicized in medical journals fifteen years earlier.

By 1909, external penile vein clamp designs had evolved to resemble intricate surgical implements such as that patented by Silas T. Yount of Chicago. Designed to be made of 25-gauge tempered steel covered with rubber, silk, or leather, Yount's clamp was relatively simple to operate. The padded spring steel arms were pulled apart, the penis inserted, and then the arms were clicked close in an action not unlike that of a safety pin.

From World War I through World War II, numerous inventors filed patents for new and more ingenious configurations of penile constriction devices. However, it was difficult to advertise or sell such instruments throughout mainstream society, which continued to avoid discussion of impotence or allow public mention of the male genitals. After World War II, as American society's sexual restrictions continued to loosen, interest in the engineering and use of new kinds of penile constriction ring technology increased. Between 1950 and 1990, more than twenty new penile constriction ring patents were issued, many involving increasingly clever and sophisticated new mechanical features.

The Hazards of Penile Rings

However, at the same time, health authorities and some inventors themselves cautioned that such penile tourniquets can cause grave injuries. Repeated use can harm or break down both the walls of the veins and the body of the erectile tissue sacs themselves. Such devices also partially or fully block the urethra, often damming the flow of semen and setting up conditions that can cause other sorts of internal harm. Perhaps most importantly, tourniquet devices essentially strangle the penis and can be kept in place for only very brief periods of time. Males who leave them on or fall asleep with them on after

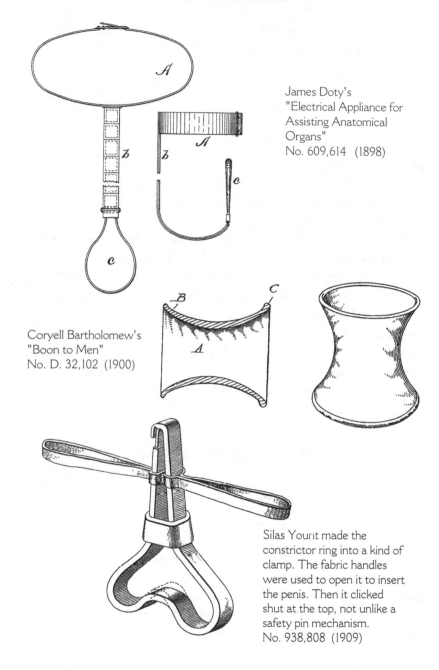

James Doty's
"Electrical Appliance for
Assisting Anatomical
Organs"
No. 609,614 (1898)

Coryell Bartholomew's
"Boon to Men"
No. D. 32,102 (1900)

Silas Yount made the
constrictor ring into a kind of
clamp. The fabric handles
were used to open it to insert
the penis. Then it clicked
shut at the top, not unlike a
safety pin mechanism.
No. 938,808 (1909)

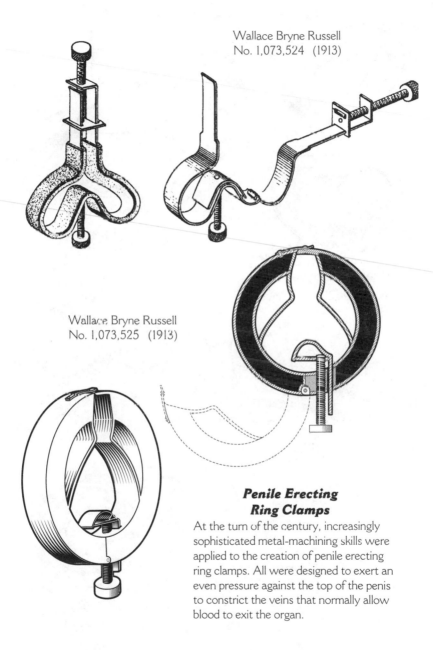

Wallace Bryne Russell
No. 1,073,524 (1913)

Wallace Bryne Russell
No. 1,073,525 (1913)

Penile Erecting Ring Clamps

At the turn of the century, increasingly sophisticated metal-machining skills were applied to the creation of penile erecting ring clamps. All were designed to exert an even pressure against the top of the penis to constrict the veins that normally allow blood to exit the organ.

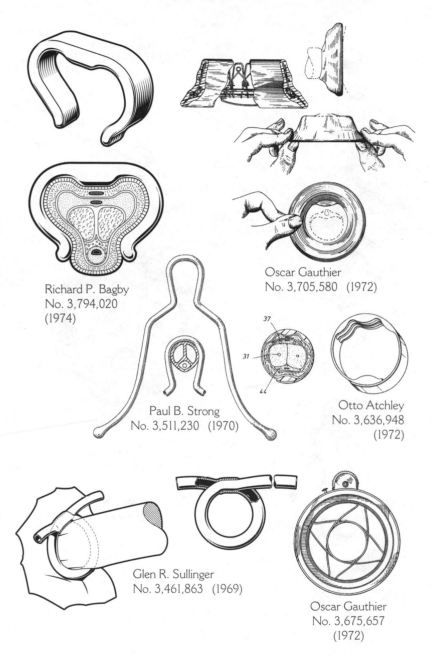

Richard P. Bagby
No. 3,794,020
(1974)

Oscar Gauthier
No. 3,705,580 (1972)

Paul B. Strong
No. 3,511,230 (1970)

Otto Atchley
No. 3,636,948
(1972)

Glen R. Sullinger
No. 3,461,863 (1969)

Oscar Gauthier
No. 3,675,657
(1972)

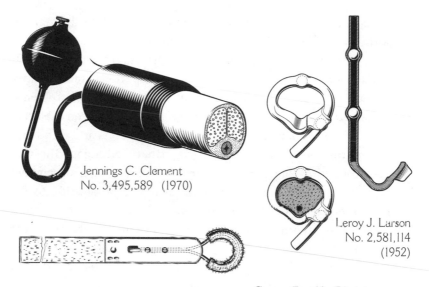

Jennings C. Clement
No. 3,495,589 (1970)

Leroy J. Larson
No. 2,581,114
(1952)

Some Penile Ring Clamp Patents of the Post-WWII Years

These two pages contain illustrations of just some of the penile vein constriction devices that have been granted patents since the end of World War II.

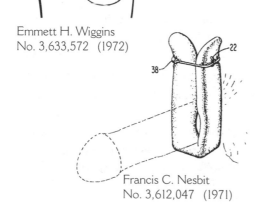

Emmett H. Wiggins
No. 3,633,572 (1972)

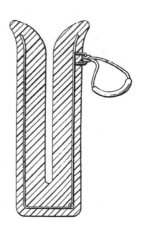

Francis C. Nesbit
No. 3,612,047 (1971)

intercourse can sustain necrosis—death of the tissues—throughout all portions of the penis forward of the constriction.

One of the most recent penile ring patents—granted to Edward T. Stewart of Dodge City, Kansas—incorporates space-age radio control and computer concepts to help avoid some of these potential problems. He explained: "Penile constrictor rings have in the past been subject to certain well-known and even rather notorious defects and disadvantages. First, they may be dangerous to use, in that if left engaged around the penis for unduly long periods of time, they may result in permanent damage to and modification of the flesh of the organ, due to the artificially induced lack of blood circulation therein . . . If applied and fully operative at the moment of orgasm and ejaculation, they interfere with normal ejaculation, and also reduce the pleasurable sensations of orgasm and ejaculation. It is normally almost impossible to interrupt the sex act for removal of the constrictor ring at the moment of orgasm."

Stewart's unit had a built-in electronic latch-release mechanism controlled by a radio signal generated by a small, hand-held button device similar to those used for the remote opening of electronic car door locks. At the appropriate moment during the sexual act, the user pressed the button to open the ring and allow it to fall away.

Pneumatics

Through the years, other inventors have sought to manipulate the penis's internal hydraulic system by externally applied pneumatic pressures and suction systems. Mechanically, this had the inverse effect of a constrictor ring. Instead of pressing inward in a narrow band to constrict the veins, outward-pulling pressure was applied across the entire surface of the organ to expand it. The goal, however, was the same: to force more blood to suddenly flow into the erectile tissue sacs in a manner that began the process of erection.

One of the first such systems was a hand-cranked suction tube apparatus introduced in 1914 by Dr. Alwin Ach. The user inserted his

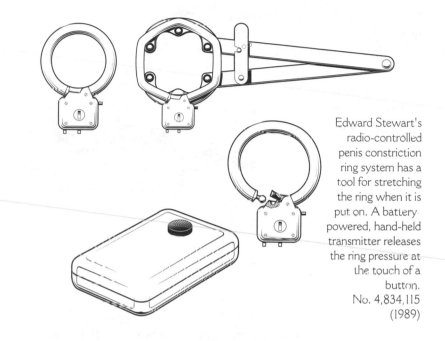

Edward Stewart's radio-controlled penis constriction ring system has a tool for stretching the ring when it is put on. A battery powered, hand-held transmitter releases the ring pressure at the touch of a button.
No. 4,834,115 (1989)

penis into a metal tube where a pressure plate squeezed the penis flat as air was pumped out, exerting a suction force around the compressed organ.

In 1917, Otto Lederer was granted a patent for a rubber chamber that fit completely over the penis with a pressure bulb at the top and a constriction band built into the base. The bulb was used to create a negative pressure in the chamber while the constriction band prevented blood from exiting the organ. Once an erection was achieved, the upper section of the suction chamber or sleeve was detached, leaving only the constriction ring around the penis. Lederer explained that, "the erection caused by the sleeve in this manner lasts at least from fifteen to twenty minutes."

By the 1970s, plastics and miniaturized control mechanisms allowed far more efficient external suction devices to be created at a

time when a small but growing number of
health professionals were beginning to
openly address the widespread, but still
largely invisible, problem of male impotence. The general structure of these modern
instruments can be seen in the pneumatic tube "Genital Erec-
tor" patent granted to
Marvin A. Burdette, Jr.
in 1972.

Dr. Alwin Ach
Penis pressure pump
No. 1,117,618 (1914)

Several types of pneumatic
"vacuum constriction" devices are
currently used in a limited fashion by
some clinics offering treatment for
impotence. In a 1993 report, the National Institutes of Health (NIH)
noted that some of these devices are relatively
safe and can be effective, but "are difficult for
some patients to use." It also noted that "patients
and their partners sometimes are bothered by the
lack of spontaneity" that results when an assembly of hoses, tubes, and a portable air pump must
be used to prepare the penis immediately prior to
intercourse.

Otto Lederer
No. 1,225,341
(1917)

Other Fields of Erection Technology

While constriction rings and pneumatic erectors
may seem strange to many, these categories of
devices actually constitute the *tamer* end of a
surprising wide spectrum of additional penile
erection machines registered at the Patent Office.

Throughout American history, male insecurity about the size and staying power of the

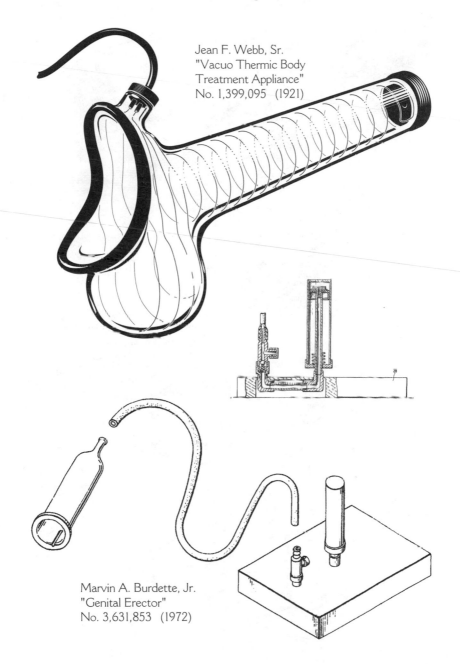

Jean F. Webb, Sr.
"Vacuo Thermic Body
Treatment Appliance"
No. 1,399,095 (1921)

Marvin A. Burdette, Jr.
"Genital Erector"
No. 3,631,853 (1972)

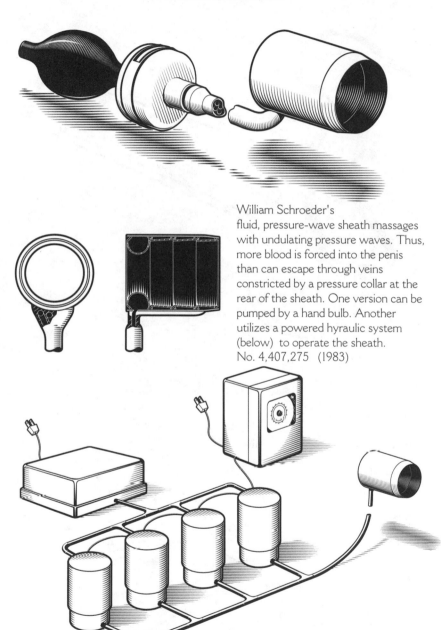

William Schroeder's fluid, pressure-wave sheath massages with undulating pressure waves. Thus, more blood is forced into the penis than can escape through veins constricted by a pressure collar at the rear of the sheath. One version can be pumped by a hand bulb. Another utilizes a powered hyraulic system (below) to operate the sheath. No. 4,407,275 (1983)

reproductive organ has been as common and enduring a part of daily life as society's inexorable emphasis on sexual performance. Male insecurity in this regard has also exerted a sort of siren call on generations of entrepreneurs who view human weakness as the strongest and most lucrative kind of market force. For instance, by the 1890s, one of America's largest industries was organized around the concocting and selling of bogus elixirs purchased by millions of American males seeking a quick cure for real and perceived penile dysfunction.

At the turn of the century, when Congress passed laws to curtail this snake oil trade, it inadvertently opened another field of mechanical penile erection invention. This new school of innovation sought to perfect the ultimate penile splint—a concept that would evolve into some of the oddest contrivances ever to pass across a patent examiner's desk.

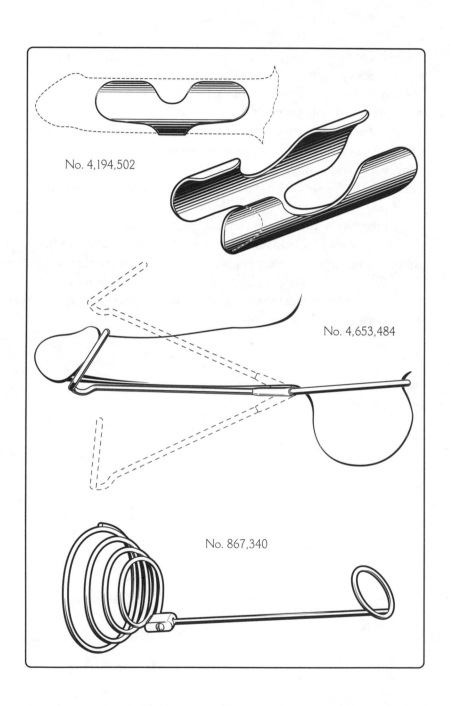

No. 4,194,502

No. 4,653,484

No. 867,340

8

Penile Splints

By the year 1900, the sale of patent medicines had become one of America's largest revenue-producing industries, generating an estimated $80 million in annual sales. At the same time, the fields of science and professional medicine had entered a new era of discovery and biological understanding that underscored the dangers posed by the home-brewed cure-alls and magical mechanical treatments hawked by legions of unregulated quacks.

In 1905, free-lance writer and former *New York Sun* reporter Samuel Hopkins Adams authored the first comprehensive investigative report exposing the pervasive extent and often bizarre nature of medical quackery throughout the country. His lengthy series, "The Great American Fraud," was published in the national weekly, *Colliers*, and became one of those landmark journalistic events that forever altered the national consciousness about a given subject. Adams took on the whole pantheon of medical hucksters, whose large-scale newspaper advertising activities had previously made them immune to scrutiny by most newspaper companies.

Adams's expose resulted in a rush of state and federal legislation aimed at imposing the first regulatory controls and standards on the sale and advertising of medicinal goods. In 1906 the Federal Pure Food and Drug Act was passed, requiring makers and sellers of medicines to list ingredients on the labels and substantiate the alleged benefits of the nostrums. This had an immediate impact on many patent medicine companies, with some simply going out of business and others drastically changing their product lines and pitches. There was a sudden drop in the market supply of bottled elixirs and pills being offered for the cure of impotence. Patent Office files show there was a simultaneous burst of efforts to perfect, and commercially protect, a variety of mechanical devices for the treatment of impotence. Instead of potions and pills—now regulated by the federal government—mail-order and other marketing operations were more likely to be urging customers to purchase mechanical penile splints, which were not regulated.

T. Williams
No. 837,993
(1906)

For instance, in December of 1906, Thaddeus W. Williams was granted a patent for a tubular rubber splint device that functioned like an artificial penis. Mounted on a base that fit against the body, the conical shape was angled at the same general tilt as an erect penis. The user simply inserted his own flaccid organ inside the device.

Within weeks of that grant, Louis B. Hawley filed for a patent for a slightly different tubular penile stiffener with larger side openings. He explained to the Patent Office that his invention "performs a beneficial service in a manner quite

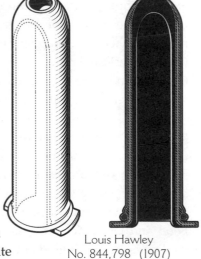

Louis Hawley
No. 844,798 (1907)

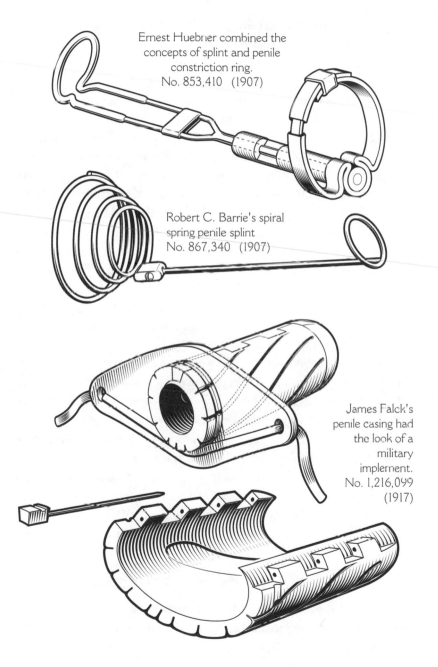

Ernest Huebner combined the
concepts of splint and penile
constriction ring.
No. 853,410 (1907)

Robert C. Barrie's spiral
spring penile splint
No. 867,340 (1907)

James Falck's
penile casing had
the look of a
military
implement.
No. 1,216,099
(1917)

within the rules of morality and in violation of no law or public policy (because it) favors procreation and its use for other than legitimate and lawful purposes is a thing impossible to accomplish." In an era when the Comstock law was still being vigorously enforced, Mr. Hawley was delicately assuring the Patent Office examiners that his device was not suitable for contraceptive purposes. His was the first of three penile stiffener patents that would be issued in rapid succession in 1907. The second went for a wire frame structure that ran along the shaft of the penis and included an anchoring ring that also served to constrict the blood flow. The third patent, to a Philadelphia man, was a device not unlike a slightly reconstituted bedspring, with a spiral section that fit around the base of the penis and a single support rod ending in a loop that fit over the organ's head. In this manner, the flaccid organ was stretched out straight. The inventor pointed out that the loop could be hidden under the foreskin and that the "rod and spring being veiled by the hirsute covering presents a seemingly natural and inoffensive appearance to allay suspicion and fear of the opposite sex."

During the next twenty-eight years, as ten more penile stiffener patents were granted, the concept of a thick-walled penis-stiffening tube remained a dominant one, improved or varied in accordance with the new materials and production techniques that were evolving in that World War I period. A good example of this was the patent issued to James Stanley Falck of Washington, D.C. in 1917. It was an intricately fabricated wrap-and-lock rubber penile casing secured firmly in place with a small strap that could be tied around the waist. Exterior rifling and a tread-like interlock mechanism gave the apparatus the vague look of some new military implement.

The Age of New Propriety

Throughout the 1920s, tumultuous changes in America's sexual customs were evident in increasingly bold dressing, dancing, acting,

Jean Marshall's harness and splint was designed to stiffen and increase the caliber of the wearer's organ. No. 1,511,572 (1924)

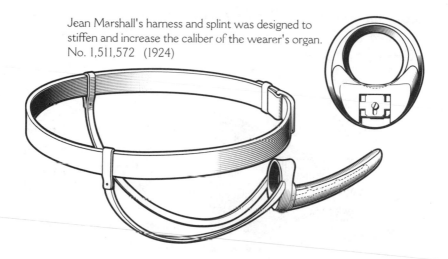

writing, and the public discussion of issues that challenged or ignored previous taboos. By the 1930s, most of the remaining public vestiges of the national Victorian morality had tumbled away. Even conservative medical circles were formally recognizing sexuality as a legitimate health consideration and an integral part of the whole human experience addressed by their disciplines.

The files of the Patent Office also document a sea change in attitudes during this decade. Previous generations of applicants often apologized to the Patent Office for addressing sexual functions and took great care to allude to procreation as the only thinkable goal of the sexual act. And they had often written and titled their documents to semantically obscure the actual purpose of their devices. But in his 1933 application for a patent on a new type of penile stiffener, Lawrence M. Smith of Chicago broke with this tradition and was as openly sympathetic of sexual pleasure as was his invention itself. That device was a penile stiffener and clitoral stimulator. Based on the rubber-tube stiffener idea, it was shaped with an arched outer contour designed to press upward against the clitoris with each stroke during intercourse. His explanation of the background of his invention was one of the longest ever submitted in its field and mirrored the changes occurring in the larger world beyond the examiners' desks.

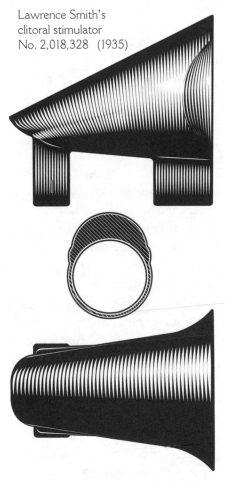

Lawrence Smith's clitoral stimulator No. 2,018,328 (1935)

Smith wrote, in part: "The present invention is highly desirable for use in intimate association with the male organ of generation during the natural performance of the sexual act, and contributes in no mean manner to the general health and well-being of both the male and female. While the sexual act itself, and mechanical devices to aid in the proper performance of this act, are not infrequently frowned upon by some for various reasons, nevertheless it is indisputable that the leading physicians, psychiatrists, and sexologists are unanimous in their assertion that the proper and natural performance of the sexual act, especially when consummated with mutual satisfaction, is not only highly beneficial, but in some cases essential, to the general health and well-being of the individuals concerned. The converse is equally true, namely that sexual excitation at frequent intervals without culmination is injurious to the human being, often times resulting in neurotic, neurasthenic or even, in some cases, in psychiatric or paranoiac disorders. Frequently, coition results in excitation or over-excitation without proper culmination to one of the parties, and in most instances this party is the female, the cause of which is, in normal cases, lack of knowledge or regard on the part of the male, which can only be compensated for by the use of the present invention in the absence of proper education, or a natural incongruity residing in a misfit of the male and female genitalia, which can be cured by mechanical means, such as the present invention, except in those rare instances where the female genitalia is too small to accommodate that of the male."

"With the foregoing in mind," he continued, "it is accordingly an object of this invention to provide an appliance which, while capable of aiding greatly in the sustainment of an enfeebled congested organ, is also highly desirable for use as an aid to normal and healthy male organs in performing the act of coition with the proper culmination."

The patent examiners kept Mr. Smith's application in review for twenty-nine months before issuing him a patent in 1935.

Penile Splints after World War II

After World War II, new chemicals, new metals, new manufacturing techniques, and new consumer marketing possibilities came together to again change the nature of American civilization. This era's dual spirits of sexual freedom and fast-paced technological innovation are demonstrated by the patent applications for the more than two dozen additional penile splint patents that were granted from the end of the war to the present day. Inventors dropped all pretense about the purpose of their products, and splints for impotent males began to look like the organs they were designed to augment. This is nowhere more apparent than in the patent application filed by John J. Briggs of Indianapolis in 1957. His invention was a larger-than-life, solid rubber, penis-shaped device that could be fit over an impotent male's

John Briggs
No. 2,899,957
(1959)

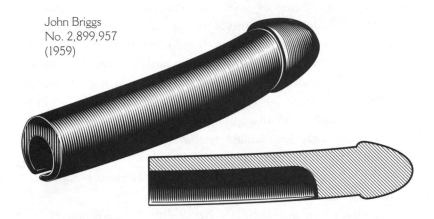

organ during intercourse. Briggs wrote to the Patent Office: "This invention relates to human relations including the promotion of peace and harmony between the sexes and particularly within the marital status, as well as to the welfare and happiness of mankind, including the propagation of the species."

"I have found from experience," he said, "that difficulties between husband and wife frequently are because of tensions resulting from unhappiness caused by frayed nerves brought on by failure of one or the other to maintain a calmness notwithstanding a lack of satisfaction. It is an object of the invention to overcome deficiencies as to size and weaknesses. Another object of the invention is to bridge the chasm between the sexes, particularly husbands and wives suffering from a malevolent lack of mental, spiritual and physical complementation, and to promote the marital relations and the mutual enjoyment of the beautiful of life." The Patent Office granted him a patent on a solid rubber penis in 1959.

In 1978, Joseph W. Reiling of Battle Creek, Michigan, filed an application for a patent on a device that combined and improved a number of diverse characteristics previously established in the field. The invention, which Reiling called a "Sexual Stabilizer and

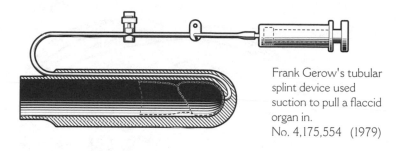

Frank Gerow's tubular
splint device used
suction to pull a flaccid
organ in.
No. 4,175,554 (1979)

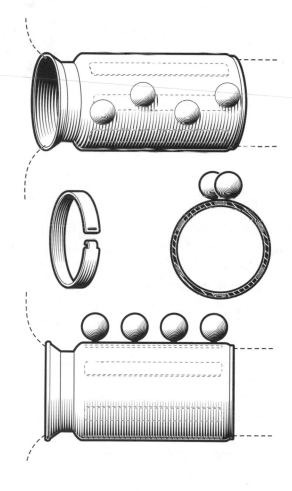

Joseph Reiling's
"stabilizer and
stimulator"
featured clitoral
roller balls.
No. 4,224,933
(1980)

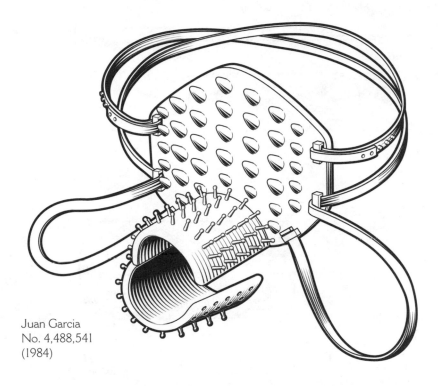

Juan Garcia
No. 4,488,541
(1984)

Stimulator," was a dorsal vein constrictor, a penis-stiffening, sheath and a clitoral stimulator all in one. A particularly novel and visually memorable feature was the row of clitoris-stimulating roller balls running along the top of the sheath.

Reiling told the patent examiners: "It is generally well known that a great percentage of women do not find fulfillment during a sex act. Also, men often find themselves hard-pressed to maintain an erection during the act. Thus, many married couples, in time, feel that they are sexually incompatible, and it is a proven fact, from surveys made, that the greater percentage of divorces stem directly from a lack of sexual compatibility. This serious situation is, accordingly, in want of a solution."

Thinking along generally similar lines in 1982, Juan A. S. Garcia of

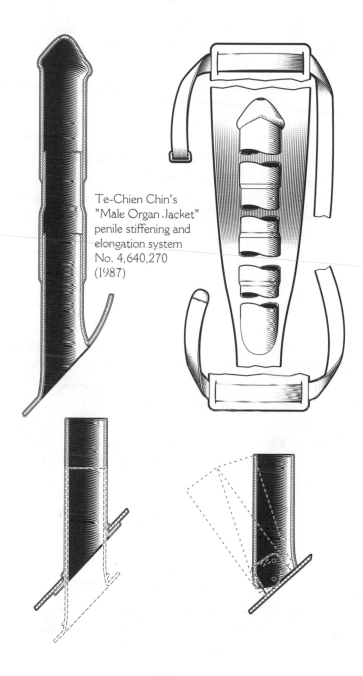

Te-Chien Chin's
"Male Organ Jacket"
penile stiffening and
elongation system
No. 4,640,270
(1987)

Houston, Texas, filed for a patent on a penile stiffening sheath apparatus with an unusual pubic plate studded with hard rubber nubs.

Another application filed in May of 1985 by Te-Chien Chin of Hercules, California, took umbrage with the past seventy-nine years of penile stiffening patents because, he told the examiners, the length of these devices could not be adjusted "to satisfy different needs at different times." Chin submitted documentation of a multi-sectional, penis-shaped tube with sliding joints that allowed it to be extended to different lengths. Called a "Male Organ Jacket," it was worn over the penis and secured to the body with a waist strap. Chin said it was designed for "supporting and/or strengthening the penis, especially the imperfect ones," and to "provide stability and strengthen the wedlock in many families in which inharmonious sexual relations may become a serious factor between the husband and the wife . . . (and) to make up the deficiencies on many men who cannot successfully satisfy their wife's sexual needs."

He explained that "sexual harmony plays an important role in the maintenance of happy marriage. Unfortunately, many husbands will sooner or later find that their male organs are inadequate or unable to satisfy their wives because the male organs are easy to contract and become weaker owning to aging, sickness, injuries, hard work, excessive sexual activities, psychological factors, etc., while their partner's female organs become loose due to childbirth and long years of sexual activity." His device was, he said, "a new and efficient prosthetic penile device which can support an impotent male organ or make up an undersized penis to provide a versatile male organ casing with separable sections to meet the different needs of different people on different occasions."

The Internal Penile Splint

A totally new technological approach to the penile splint was unveiled in a patent application filed by John Friedmann in 1988 for a

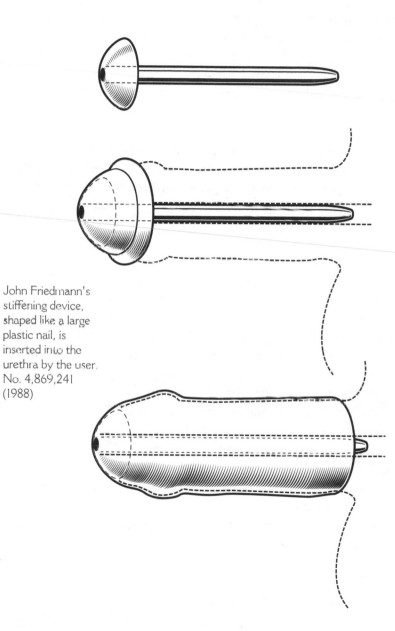

John Friedmann's stiffening device, shaped like a large plastic nail, is inserted into the urethra by the user. No. 4,869,241 (1988)

"Disposable Internally Applied Penile Erector." A device guaranteed to send shivers down the spine of all but the most intrepid—and desperate—males, it was shaped somewhat like a large plastic nail and designed to be inserted down the length of the penis to stiffen it from the inside. Friedmann explained, "To use the device, one merely slides the support tubing down the urethra of the user's penis until the concave disc at the end of the hollow support tube touches the head of the penis . . . The use of the urethra as an area of support offers a perfect open area inside of the penis in which to place a splint, which in turn provides rigidity to the penis. Further, the use of the urethra for insertion of the splint in conjunction with the anatomically correct disc 'mooring' and condom-like latex or rubber sleeve also assures that there will be no injury to the male or female involved in sexual intercourse."

While it seems unlikely that such a concept would ever be taken seriously by consumers, Friedman's patent did demonstrate the new willingness of inventors to focus their creative efforts on the interior of the penis. In the post-World War II age, medical advances made it feasible for the first time to consider direct surgical intervention into the biomechanical systems that control penile erection. Thus, yet another branch of penile erection technology evolved.

At first, these pioneering surgical endeavors had a crude—even Frankensteinian—feel about them. Later the level of sophistication steadily increased as growing numbers of reputable surgeons, institutions, and medical equipment manufacturers saw market possibilities in the frustration of America's large population of impotent men. With corporate zeal, new technologies, solid financing, and legions of consulting engineers, these enterprises set out to create and patent nothing less than a true bionic penis.

9

The Bionic Penis

The explosion of new scientific discoveries, mechanical inventions, and organizational advancements that revolutionized the American manufacturing industry during World War II had an equally dramatic effect on the business of medicine. In fact, the very sense of what surgery *was* changed during the war years. For one thing, the discovery and widespread use of penicillin and other infection-fighting drugs suddenly allowed for the routine performance of surgical procedures that were previously life-threatening. For another, the vast numbers of severe military mutilations provided unprecedented opportunities for experimentation and innovation by a globe-straddling corps of military surgeons supported by new drugs, instruments, materials, and knowledge.

These armies of military physicians and technicians re-entered the civilian world of the 1950s with a radically changed sense of what was—or might be—possible through surgery. Their efforts and continuing innovations spawned the new age of biomedical engineering and bionics, the science that sought to integrate manmade mechanical devices and controls into the internal systems of the human body. By the late 1960s, this high-tech medical industry had, in many ways, become symbiotically linked with the new space program, where rapid advances in plastics, metallurgy, and miniaturized power and control systems directly supported improvements in the design and durability of artificial limbs, organs, and biomedical support systems.

The most publicized breakthroughs of this era involved the heart. The first crude external heart machine was used successfully in the 1950s, followed by implantation of the first manmade heart valves and, soon after that, implantation of the first completely manmade heart. Although they received somewhat lesser press coverage, equally impressive results were being achieved by corporations and physicians inventing and implanting electronic pacemakers, artificial joints, and ophthalmic lenses.

One organ, the penis, was the subject of significant surgical experimentation but virtually no popular publicity during this same period. In the 1950s various surgeons had attempted to stiffen the penis internally by implanting sections of bone or cartilage taken from other parts of the body. However, this approach failed because the living material was eventually partially or totally reabsorbed. In the 1960s, other doctors experimented with lengths of acrylic and polyethylene rods.

The first U.S. patent for a surgically implanted penile stiffening device was issued on September 3, 1974, to Viktor Konstantinovich Kalnberz of Riga, then part of the Soviet Union. In that immediate post-Sputnik period of intense technological competition between the United States and the Soviet Union, it seems something of a coup for the U.S.S.R. that a Soviet citizen was granted the first patent in this high-tech field. Kalnberz provided the Patent Office with details about the successful use of his invention in the Soviet Union. In one case he described a seventy-year-old man who had been impotent for thirty years and was subjected to another new Soviet surgical intervention for impotence: transplant of testicular tissue from a bull into the human patient. When this failed, Kalnberz's yoke-like plastic implant, made of polyethylene rods and shaped like two prongs of a fork, was tried and within "four months after the operation, the patient got married and performed a successful coitus."

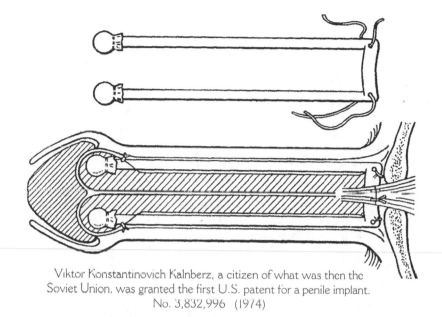

Viktor Konstantinovich Kalnberz, a citizen of what was then the Soviet Union, was granted the first U.S. patent for a penile implant. No. 3,832,996 (1974)

Kalnberz explained that a stiffening device implanted inside the penis had a number of advantages over external support methods, not the least of which is that it "ensures a good cosmetic concealment of the fact of the prosthesis."

Semirigid Penile Implants

In rapid succession over the next two years, Americans working in the same field received patents for improved versions of rod-type penile implants. Michael P. Small of Miami Lakes, Florida, and James E. Cox of Goleta, California, patented a double semirigid rod implant. Frank J. Gerow of Houston, Texas, invented a semirigid silicone rod implant that was malleable to the point where it could bend. Gerald W. Timm and John H. Burton of Minneapolis, Minnesota, created another variety of double semi-rigid malleable rod implant. Timm and Burton explained: "The malleable rod portion enables the pros-

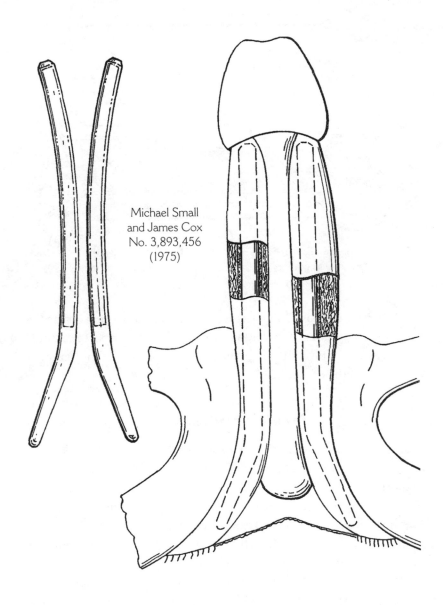

Michael Small
and James Cox
No. 3,893,456
(1975)

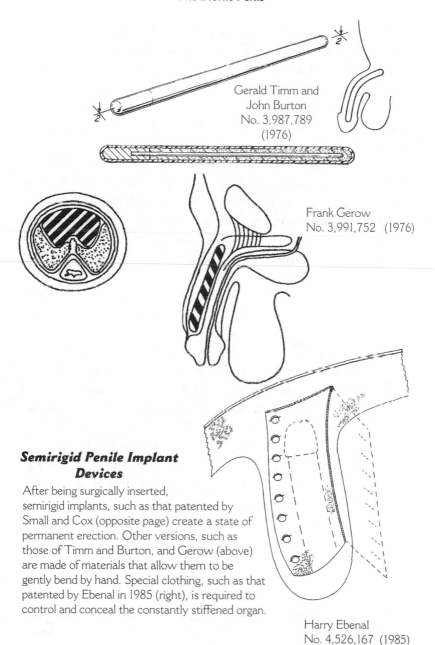

Gerald Timm and
John Burton
No. 3,987,789
(1976)

Frank Gerow
No. 3,991,752 (1976)

Semirigid Penile Implant Devices

After being surgically inserted, semirigid implants, such as that patented by Small and Cox (opposite page) create a state of permanent erection. Other versions, such as those of Timm and Burton, and Gerow (above) are made of materials that allow them to be gently bend by hand. Special clothing, such as that patented by Ebenal in 1985 (right), is required to control and conceal the constantly stiffened organ.

Harry Ebenal
No. 4,526,167 (1985)

thesis to be conformed to a variety of shapes by bending or twisting same. During intercourse the prosthesis will maintain the penis in an erectile state, and afterwards the penis may be positioned and maintained by the prosthesis in a convenient comfortable position."

Perhaps the chief drawback of this general concept of permanent penile stiffness is best illustrated by the patent granted to Harry R. Ebenal of Daly City, California, for special underwear to restrain a penis rendered permanently erect by implant surgery. Ebenal's invention looked something like an athletic supporter, except for the "non-pinch enclosure compartment" at the front designed to "immobilize the male organ in its upright position, so that its state of erection is not readily visible when the user is wearing outer garments." Later inventors informed the Patent Office that persons implanted with permanently erect devices tended to find that state "physically uncomfortable or emotionally disconcerting." At the same time, they noted that the semi-rigid rod had "in a number of instances eroded through the skin and fallen out of the penis" as a result of the stresses imposed on the organ and implant by vigorous sexual activity.

In 1978, Roy P. Finney of Tampa, Florida and Henry Wilfred Lynch of Racine, Wisconsin, received a patent for a semirigid rod implant that was hinged. Although the greater length of the device remained permanently stiff, the hinge allowed the penis to be manually dropped so it did not protrude when not in sexual use. The hinge was not a mechanical one, like that of a door, but rather a clever "soft hinge" made by replacing one section of the semirigid silicone rod with much softer silicone that was easily bent.

Inflatable Penile Implants

In December of 1974, three months after Victor Kalnberz received his patent for a semirigid penile implant, Berish Strauch, Allan E. Bloomberg, and Selwyn Z. Freed of New York City received the first patent for an entirely different class of penile prosthesis: multicom-

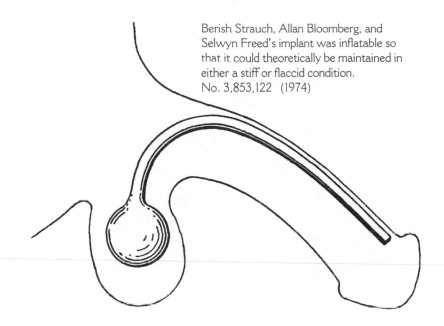

Berish Strauch, Allan Bloomberg, and Selwyn Freed's implant was inflatable so that it could theoretically be maintained in either a stiff or flaccid condition. No. 3,853,122 (1974)

ponent inflatables. Mechanically more complicated and requiring a more extensive surgical procedure to insert, these systems generally consisted of an inflatable tube or bladder implanted along the length of the penis and a reservoir for a stiffening liquid that was implanted most often in the scrotum. The Strauch-Bloomberg-Freed device theoretically allowed the patient to squeeze the reservoir, forcing pressurized fluid through a valve and into the tube. This hydraulic pressure stiffened the tube, causing the penis to assume a semirigid state.

During the next twelve years, a succession of increasingly intricate inflatable implant systems received patents, many of them involving the latest advances in materials and miniaturized control technology. However, significant problems were encountered with some types of these devices and alluded to by other inventors who sought to overcome the shortcomings. In his 1976 patent for a

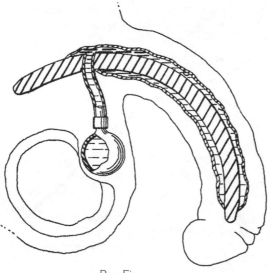

Roy Finney
No. 4,201,202 (1980)

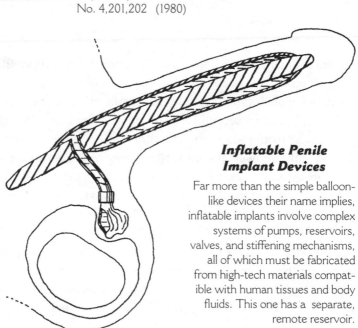

Inflatable Penile Implant Devices

Far more than the simple balloon-like devices their name implies, inflatable implants involve complex systems of pumps, reservoirs, valves, and stiffening mechanisms, all of which must be fabricated from high-tech materials compatible with human tissues and body fluids. This one has a separate, remote reservoir.

hydraulic inflatable implant system, Robert E. Buuck of Golden Valley, Minnesota, noted that his system utilized a dye-containing hydraulic fluid that would show on subsequent x-rays and was "also compatible with the body tissues and organs should a leak occur." In his 1977 patent for an improved inflatable implant system, Aurelio C. Uson of Englewood, New Jersey, reported that the mechanical complexity of the valve and tubing systems of previous devices caused them to jam and otherwise malfunction and that the repair or replacement of such faulty implants could only be accomplished through more surgery. Uson's system used semirigid materials at the base of the prosthesis to minimize the quantity of hydraulic fluid required for inflation of the forward tubular portions. It also featured a simplified valve system. In another patent, Roy P. Finney and Henry W. Lynch pointed out that "inflatable implants currently available must be inflated periodically to prevent scar tissue capsule which forms about the implant from bridging folds in the fabric of the

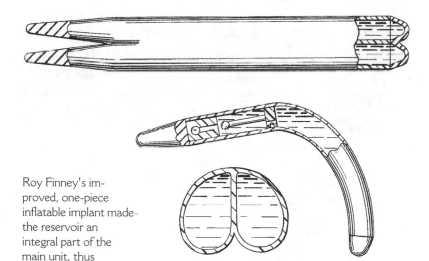

Roy Finney's improved, one-piece inflatable implant made the reservoir an integral part of the main unit, thus simplifying surgical insertion.
No. 4,378,792 (1983)

inflatable or distensible portion and preventing the implant from becoming fully inflated."

Two years later, in 1982, Finney and Lynch received another patent for a revolutionary self-contained inflatable implant that contained the fluid reservoir within the main penile shaft mechanism. This one-piece approach greatly simplified the process of insertion because it eliminated the need to perform a separate surgical procedure to implant a remote fluid reservoir in either the scrotum or abdomen and run the lengths of tubing necessary to connect the remote reservoir to the main penile device. Finney received another patent on an improved version in 1983.

In 1985, Gerald W. Timm, Donald L. Sandford, and Timothy J. Claude invented a new hybrid implant that utilized a wire-tensioned "articulated joint" mechanism combining some aspects of hinged semirigid implants with those of inflatables. A spring-loaded cable ran down the center of the unit through a set of special plastic joints that functioned as a self-stiffening hinge. The articulated joints could be made to assume either a stiff or flaccid state by bending the penis in certain directions to alter the cable tension.

The AMA Penile Implant Evaluation

Gerald Timm,
Donald Sandford,
and Timothy Claude's
"articulated joint" implant
No. 4,517,967 (1985)

In 1988, the American Medical Association convened a panel of twenty-one urologists to evaluate several kinds of semirigid, hinged, and inflatable penile implants. In a report published in its journal that year, the AMA said: "Three semirigid penile prostheses and a multicompo- nent inflatable penile pros- thesis were considered safe and effective treatment for impotence unre- sponsive to medical management. Each of these prosthesis has its own advantages and disadvantages. The en- tire semirigid prosthe- sis group is surgically easier to implant than the inflatable models ... However, the semirigid

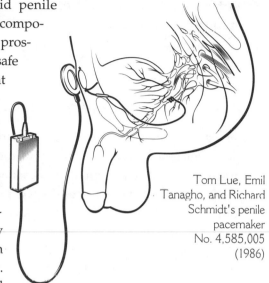

Tom Lue, Emil Tanagho, and Richard Schmidt's penile pacemaker No. 4,585,005 (1986)

models are not as aesthetically pleasing or as sexually satisfying to both partners as are inflatable devices. Multicomponent inflatable penile prostheses have had a history of mechanical failure; however, im- proved design and materials have reduced this problem."

The AMA noted the existence of the new self-contained inflatable prosthesis as well as the "articulated joint" concept, but said that at that time, "there are not yet enough long-term data available to evaluate these single-component devices."

The Penile Pacemaker

Another approach was taken in 1984 by Tom F. Lue, Emil A. Tanagho, and Richard A. Schmidt of California. Their system was based around the idea of a penile pacemaker, which functioned very much like a cardiac pacemaker. Electrodes were surgically implanted near the nerves in the vicinity of the prostate gland. These nerves initiated the penile erection process. A small, hand-held radio control box, similar in size to those used to automatically open car door locks, sent an activating signal to the implanted electrodes when the impotent user wanted to engage in sexual activity. Electric stimulation was sent into the nerve bundles, causing a natural erection by remote control.

Chemical Penile Splints

Perhaps the single most unique departure from the traditional mechanical principles of artificial erection supports has been that involving what might be thought of as a chemical penile splint. In the late 1960s, experiments were conducted to determine the actual amount of blood that had to pass through the penis each minute to cause an erection. By the early 1970s, these studies had established that, on average, blood flow through the penis had to increase to about 90 milliliters per minute to sustain an erection. In healthy males, arteries naturally widened to produce this flow rate during periods of sexual excitement. In some impotent males, however, it was found that damage or deterioration of the arteries had rendered those vessels incapable of supplying the minimum level of blood flow required to initiate the erection process.

In 1973, a three-year program of experimental operations was conducted on specially selected impotent males in an attempt to surgically increase blood flow in their penises. Generally, the procedure was not unlike the now-common surgery used to bypass clogged coronary arteries in older patients. It is common for physicians to use "vasoactive" drugs during such surgery. These are drugs that directly affect the smooth muscle structure of veins and arteries, causing those muscles to dilate or constrict. During one experimental penile surgery, a vasodilator drug was mistakenly injected into the sac of erectile tissue of the patient's penis. Within minutes, and to the surprise of the doctors, this produced "a prolonged fully rigid erection of two hours' duration." Thus was the concept of a chemical penile stiffener accidentally discovered.

In March of 1977, Alvaro Latorre of El Paso, Texas, applied for a patent on the process of using vasodilator drugs to achieve an erection. His application also included a design for a dual hypodermic needle especially designed for injecting drugs into the penis. Latorre told the Patent Office: "The injections are made on any area of the (top) side of the penis where both corpora cavernosa are accessible. The needles of the syringe should be placed equidistant from the subcutaneous dorsal vein, which is easily visible. The needles are preferably inserted all the way into the corpora cavernosa, thus resulting in an intra-corpora cavernosa injection... Ideally, the syringe is available pre-loaded for use, which is quite easy as the needles are simply inserted up to the curved stop."

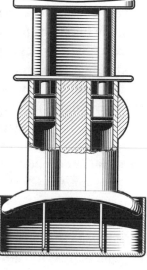

Since the mid-1980s, various drugs have been tested and prescribed by physicians for such self-injection programs. In 1990, the American Medical Association convened a panel to assess this method of impotence treatment. Overall, a panel of twenty-eight urologists and endocrinologists concluded that papaverine hydrochloride, alone or in combination with phentolamine mesylate, "is safe and effective treatment for organic impotence. These drugs, when injected into the penis, are able to induce partial or full erections in the majority of men with organic impotence and to date have been used in more than two thousand patients."

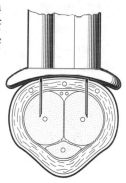

Alvaro Latorre's
self injection
system
No. 4,127,118 (1978)

However, the panel also sounded a number of warnings about the possible side effects of this procedure. Sometimes the drugs cause erections that won't go away for eight hours or more. This condition, known medically as "priapism," can cause serious damage to the internal tissues of the penis. In tests, up to about 8 percent of the men who were injected experienced such prolonged erections. After using the injections for more than a year, some patients were also found to have developed a kind of fibrosis, or inner scarring, of the blood-filling, erection-creating penile cavities affected by the drugs.

The panel also noted that the method was only useful for patients who were "highly motivated" and willing to regularly push surgical steel needles half an inch deep into their penises. Predictably, a 1993 report by the National Institutes of Health noted that "there is a high rate of patient dropout, often early in the treatment."

This same sentiment was expressed by Robert F. Boeck of Racine, Wisconsin, in the patent application he filed in 1987 for a different method of applying vasoactive drugs to the penis. He said that Latorre's double-needle injector system was "uncomfortable or painful, as well as frightening." Boeck presented the patent examiners with a design for a condom with a special interior structure comprised of cells of vasoactive drugs that were absorbed through the skin of the penis. The drug release mechanisms were not unlike the fast-acting transdermal patches now used to administer other kinds of drugs through the skin.

Boeck explained: "As the condom is fitted onto the penis, the friction between the penis and the condom results in a breaking of the surface tension of the transdermal nitroglycerin coating. The transdermal nitro coating thus makes contact with the penile skin resulting in the gradual development of an erectile condition which facilitates a more complete insertion of the penis into the condom . . . (and) enables the individual to obtain and sustain an erection sufficient to achieve intercourse."

Increasing varieties of such high-tech treatments should continue to evolve as the American health and medical communities

Robert F. Boeck's condom with interior transdermal drug patches that release
vasoactive agents into the skin of the penis to cause an erection.
No. 4,829,991 (1989)

increase their attempts to address this previously neglected affliction.
Pharmaceutical and medical instrument companies are likely to
expand their efforts in this area simply because recent studies document that impotence is even more widespread than originally thought.

The largest federally funded study of erectile dysfunction in
America was completed in 1993. It found that about half of all men in
America over the age of 40 suffer intermittent or permanent impotence. Earlier studies previously cited—indicating that about 24
percent of all American men experience occasional or permanent
impotence—relate to the entire population of men.

This study sought to quantify the actual scope of what was
already a generally well-recognized fact: that the incidence of impotence increases with age and that it is a far greater problem for older
men than younger men. The findings showed that on any given day
in contemporary America, about nineteen million men between the
ages of forty and seventy suffer from the inability to achieve or sustain
an erection.

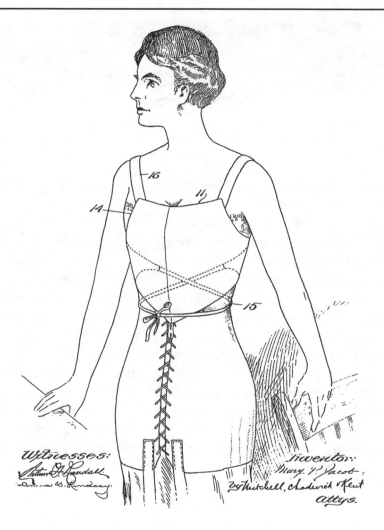

Mary Phelps Jacobs was granted a patent for this garment in 1914 and later successfully promoted herself as "inventor of the bra." However, the actual patent description is for a chest compression device rather than a modern bra. At the same time, Patent Office records show that numerous other inventors registered more modern bra-like devices as early as the 1850s. No. 1,115,674.

10

Who Really Invented the Bra?

Like the light bulb or telephone or computer chip, the bra is now so common an item that we no longer remember it as the epochal mechanical invention it was.

The quest to achieve control over unruly, pendulous breasts—for reasons of basic comfort as well as efficient mobility and social decorum—has been an enduring concern for American females since the early colonial years. Then, the most common breast containment strategy seems to have been a wrap approach aimed at limiting movement by holding breasts firmly to the body with any convenient swath of cloth. In many communities—from the original Pilgrims to the pioneer women of the western plains—a good measure of breast control was naturally imposed by the simple weight of the many layers of heavy clothing women wore. Meanwhile, throughout these same periods, affluent women of fashion favored the ornately ribbed upper-body corsets originally made popular in the courts of European royalty.

The acceptance and commercial popularization of the bra in the early twentieth century ended three hundred years of female clothing traditions largely organized around the concept of upper body-binding. The custom of compressing and generally hiding the breasts gave way to the dramatically different practice of commonly displaying them. By the mid-1900s, innovative bra structures had not only made breasts the dominant focus of almost all female apparel, but an emotionally charged statement about feminine identity as well. When it was popularized in the 1920s, the brassiere was generally hailed by women as a symbol of the new physical and social freedoms enjoyed by a generation rebelling against the spiritual claustrophobia of the fading Victorian era. But by the 1960s, the bra had become reviled by many as a symbol of all that confined and distorted the self-image and opportunity of modern American women.

No other garment in our age has been invested with quite the same sensual, psychological, or political meanings as has the bra. Yet even now—seventy years after the bra became *the* defining women's undergarment—the identity of the inventor of the device remains a point of some confusion. Most standard contemporary reference works unequivocally credit Mary Phelps Jacobs. For instance, *The New York Public Library's Book of Chronologies* flatly states the "first modern bra (was) designed by New York socialite Mary Phelps Jacobs out of handkerchiefs, ribbon, and cord. She patent(ed) her design in 1914." Other writers have credited the invention to French fashion designer Charles R. Debevoise in 1902 or Frenchman Phillipe de Brassière in the early 1920s.

In a major statement on this controversy in 1989, *Life* magazine ran a cover story announcing it had determined the bra was first created by French corset maker Herminie Cadolle in 1889. As a result, *Life* declared June, 1989, to be the one hundredth anniversary of that invention and celebrated the event with nine pages of fleshy photo spreads.

These conflicting claims suggest that the world was a place of bony corsets until, suddenly, in a burst of inspiration, an individual created a revolutionary garment for supporting, separating, padding, and displaying the female breasts. However, the archives of the U.S. Patent Office suggest a different scenario: a steady evolution of garment structure that began before the Civil War and reflected the inevitable convergence of the mechanical components of what we today recognize as the modern bra.

A World of Corsets

During the centuries that corsets were essential foundation garments, their contour and structure changed frequently in relation to the fashion, available materials, and sewing technology of the time. In the 1840s, for example, the short corsets worn for informal or "day" purposes came to feature a new breast treatment. Rows of flattening corset stays stopped at the top of the abdomen. Above that was a special fabric section for the breasts. This included individual cup-shaped fabric pockets supported by light shoulder straps. If one were to snip away the rest of this type of corset below the bust line, the remaining structure would resemble the modern bra. Thus, the essential mechanical components of what we now think of as a bra were well-established concepts in the shops of seamstresses, corset makers, and fabric merchants 150 years ago. It was obviously only a matter of time before one of these enterprising minds actually came up with the idea of dropping away the rest of the corset and working with the breast-supporting structure as its own separate garment.

Corset makers were among the more mechanically curious craftsmen of their day because new improvements—sturdier hooks and latches, lighter and stronger stay assemblies, and more efficient lacing configurations—were often a key to selling such intimate products to status-conscious women. In the failed rubber boom of the 1830s before vulcanization was invented, corset makers were among the most avid clients for elastic rubber goods, which promised not only new forms of closure devices, but revolutionary new forms of what were discreetly called "bust improvers" as well. It was then common for women to stuff their corset tops with pieces of rounded fruit, tufts of quilt, and other sorts of padding. The inadequacies of these items were notorious, from the troublesome weight of the fruit to the often lumpy and uneven nature of stuffings made from dried grass, animal hair, or feathers. The rubberized fabric that was first sewn into inflatable life preservers in the 1830s was immediately recognized as a material of potentially great value to corset makers. Writers of the period claimed that "this novel application of India-rubber is by far the most extraordinary improvement that has ever been effected" in the corset business. However, it was not until the 1850s, when Goodyear's process made possible the production of stabilized rubber fabric, that corset makers began incorporating the elastic material into their products.

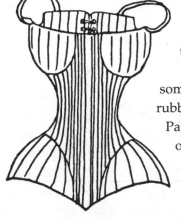

This trend can be seen in the bosom gear, made of double-walled thin rubber fabric, registered with the U.S. Patent Office in 1859 by Henry S. Lesher of Brooklyn, New York. The fabric was shaped into two cup-like pockets that held each breast. The cups were connected to each other in the middle by a thin bridge of fabric. Elastic fabric shoulder and back straps held the garment in place on the woman's upper torso. The double-walled rubber fabric of the

Corset makers in the 1840s created individually-cupped, bra-like structures as the tops of "day corsets."

breast-holding cups could be slightly inflated with air to increase their apparent size. In addition, two wing-like rubber attachments were provided for protecting the wearer's dress from underarm moisture. Lesher wrote that the device provided "a symmetrical rotundity" and was of use "in giving support to the breasts."

In its abbreviated structural lines, its independent breast cups, and its shoulder and back strap assemblies, Lesher's 1859 invention would seem to be the mechanical equivalent of the modern bra.

The Post-Civil War Era

Throughout the Civil War years and into the 1870s, corsets became lighter and smaller and routinely incorporated the concept of indi-

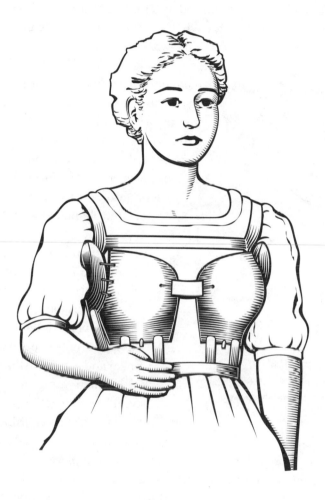

On the eve of the Civil War, Henry S. Lesher of Brooklyn, New York, was granted a patent for this device for "giving support to the breasts." In its structural lines, independent cups, and shoulder and back strap assemblies, it is the mechanical equivalent of the modern bra.
No. 24,033 (1859)

vidual breast pockets supported by shoulder straps. In 1874 Clara P. Clark received a patent for what she called an "improved corset," which was the structural equivalent of today's long-line bra. The fundamental element of her design was the pattern for a fabric breast pocket system held up by a shoulder straps that criss-crossed the back. She wrote: "My improvements consist in a corset having its busts or bosoms formed of such pattern . . . so as to retain its desired shape without the use of bones, wires, or other ordinary stiffening material heretofore required, thus allowing the natural or artificial breasts to be comfortably supported."

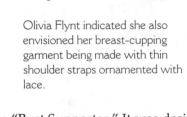

Olivia Flynt indicated she also envisioned her breast-cupping garment being made with thin shoulder straps ornamented with lace.

Two years later, in 1876, Olivia P. Flynt, a Boston dressmaker and activist in the political reform movement that sought to change the accepted norms of female clothing, patented a new garment she called a "Bust Supporter." It was designed to take the place of the corsets Ms. Flynt felt were as uncomfortable as they were physically damaging. She designed a fabric garment that fit around the upper half of the torso, covering the breasts. Each breast was held in a fabric pocket supported by shoulder straps. In her illustration, she showed broad shoulder straps, but she wrote that the straps might also be made more narrow and ornamented with lace. She explained that her invention was "a garment for ladies and misses . . . specially designed as a bust supporter and improver (which) prevents the bust from

descending uncomfortably low, or below
that position on the body requisite to conform the outline of the bust to the true
artistic outline of the human frame...This
garment is specially adapted to ladies having large busts, and will be used instead,
and take the place of, a corset, thereby
enabling beauty of form to be preserved
without lacing or otherwise injuriously
pressing or binding the body."

Mrs. Flynt's bust supporter also came
in a double-walled version that allowed

Charles L. Morehouse
No. 326,915 (1885)

layers of padding to be inserted. Breast size augmentation was an
increasingly important factor in the marketing of clothing which,
while discreetly enveloping the figure from neck to ankles, often
emphasized the contours of the bosom. This, in turn, gave rise to new
types of breast-related inventions such as that registered by Charles
L. Morehouse of Brooklyn, New York, in 1885. His breast-enlarging
garment featured air-filled rubber cups that held each breast at the
same time they added the illusion of increased size. These breast cups
were attached in the middle and held about the upper body by elastic
shoulder and back straps. Mechanically, Morehouse's device, which
individually cupped, supported, separated, shaped, and augmented
the individual breasts, also had the same structural lines and mechanical components of what we now call a bra.

Herminie Cadolle's Soutien-Gorge

Four years later in 1889, the "bust bodice" came into fashion in
France. The device resembled the full-cut, bandeau top of a contemporary two-piece bathing suit, and was originally designed by Pari-
sian corsetmaker Herminie Cadolle to take the place of the upper half
of a corset. It was called a *soutien-gorge*, the French term still used

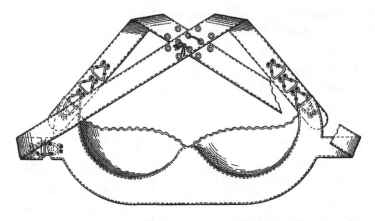

Marie Tucek's patented "breast supporter" above would not be out of place even in today's lingerie shops. No.494,397 (1893).

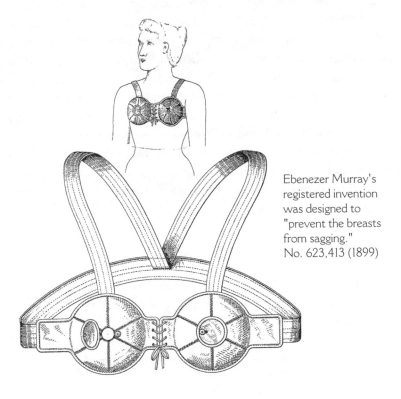

Ebenezer Murray's registered invention was designed to "prevent the breasts from sagging." No. 623,413 (1899)

today to describe a bra. Some corsets at this time had become greatly abbreviated in size and were actually more similar to what is now known as a girdle than the traditional corset. They stopped at the top of the abdomen. Above that, the soutien-gorge covered and supported the breasts. Inevitably, some women—particularly those who favored the diaphanous gowns and figure-hugging casual wear of the "Gay 90s"—dispensed with the lower half of the soutien-gorge-and-corset ensemble altogether.

Marie Tucek's Thoroughly Modern Bra

In 1893, Marie Tucek of New York City was granted a patent for a breast-supporting garment specifically designed for wear under lightweight, revealing fashions. She explained that her invention was "a breast supporter, which is simple and durable in construction, designed to take the place of the usual corset, and to be worn more principally with loose dresses." Tucek's breast-supporting garment included separate pockets for the breasts, straps over the shoulders and around the back, and strap-fastening hook-and-eye assemblies. It was, in its function, structure, materials, and overall look, the modern bra. Even now, a hundred years later, Tucek's thoroughly modern design would not look out of place on the shelves in the lingerie section of major department stores.

Beyond fashion centers such as New York City, other more utilitarian inventors were also working on breast-supporting devices of a generally similar structure. In 1898, Ebenezer Murray of Deadwood, South Dakota—one of the coldest places in the U.S.— submitted an application to the Patent Office for what he called a "breast shield." It was a two-cup-and-strap system designed to support, augment, and warm the breasts. In addition, he explained that each cup could also be made with a fabric flap opening at the nipple to facilitate the needs of nursing mothers. Murray explained that it was his intention to create a garment that "will be simple,

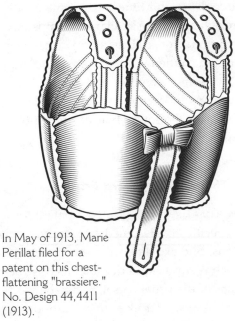

Patent Office records indicate that the term "brassiere" in the first two decades of the 1900s was used to describe a chest-compressing device which did not individually cup, separate, support, or shape each breast. Instead, it flattened both breasts tightly against the chest wall. By the late 1920s, the meaning of the word "brassiere" changed, becoming synonymous with "breast supporter," a term that previously was used to describe support garments that had the components of a modern bra.

In May of 1913, Marie Perillat filed for a patent on this chest-flattening "brassiere." No. Design 44,4411 (1913).

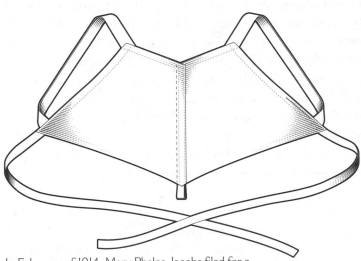

In February of 1914, Mary Phelps Jacobs filed for a patent on a lighter-weight chest-flattening "brassiere." No. 1,115,674 (1914).

economic, easily applied, and worn with comfort (and will) prevent the breasts from sagging."

The turn of the century was a watershed for women's fashions as the multi-layered, body-enveloping clothing of the Victorian era gave way to completely new kinds of attitudes and dresses which celebrated bare limbs and highlighted intimate body contours. This posed a new set of problems for large-busted women as well as the potential for new products for makers of undergarments. In May of 1913, Marie Perillat of Ye Lady's Outfitterie in New York City applied for a design patent for what she called a "brassiere." But the purpose of the device was to tightly flatten the breasts against the chest in keeping with slim-lined, minimalist fashions of the day. Perillat's bust-reducing brassiere had stiffening stays like a corset, but only wrapped around the breast area and was held in place by shoulder straps.

In November of 1913, Mary Phelps Jacobs—still listed as the "inventor of the bra" by many American reference books—became involved in the series of events that made her famous. Jacobs was the daughter of a wealthy New York family that maintained a seasonal residence in the opulent "Home Club" apartments on East Forty-Fifth Street. Part of that complex included two brownstones that had been gutted and fashioned into a ballroom and dining club, which hosted glittering social events regularly attended by Jacobs and her circle of debutantes.

Jacobs said that one day, while preparing a diaphanous gown for the evening's ball, she was so distressed by the fact that her corset showed through the top of the dress that she decided to not wear a corset. In her memoirs, she wrote that her personal maid thought this was not a good idea. The maid was a Frenchwoman and, according to Jacobs, said, "Mademoiselle cannot go without a *soutien-gorge*," under her dress. Jacobs said she and her maid then began using handkerchiefs, ribbon, and pins to construct a soutien-gorge. She described how this device was wrapped tightly around her chest to compress her breasts so that "in the glass I saw I was flat and I was proper."

A short time later, assisted by a lawyer from her social set, she filed a patent application for this device, which she called a "brassiere." She told the patent examiners that her invention was "for the purpose of covering the top of the corset and holding the wearer in proper form." On November 3, 1914, she was granted the patent she would later claim was the first bra.

Viewed in relation to the other documented developments that had preceded hers in its field, Jacobs's invention is actually remarkable for what it is not. It is not a system that cups the individual breasts, or independently supports or separates them. It is not designed to be worn in place of a corset as an independent breast garment, but rather as an accessory to a corset system. It is a breast compression wrap that seems as mechanically different from a modern bra as a boot is from a sandal. Nor is it even particularly original as a compression wrap, but rather a lighter-weight improvement on the bust-reducing chest-wrap "brassiere" patented earlier by Marie Perillat of New York.

For a short while after she received her patent, Jacobs opened a small sewing factory to manufacture her invention. She included her maid as a full partner in the venture, but sales did not go well. She ended up selling the patent rights for $1,500 to the Warner Brothers Corset Company of nearby Connecticut, which made and distributed traditional undergarments. Warner Brothers went on to become a major player in the field.

After World War I, Jacobs moved to Paris, married financier and poet Harry Crosby, changed her name to Caresse Crosby, and started the first of two book publishing companies that would establish her social standing in the highest literary and media circles of the time. Mrs. Crosby, whose publishing enterprises brought out the early works of such luminaries as Ernest Hemingway and William Faulkner, was also famous for her tales of hobnobbing about the continent with artists such as Max Ernst and Salvador Dali. A gifted promoter, Crosby made much of the fact that she was a descendant of a passenger of the Mayflower and, in her 1953 autobiography, wrote: "I am also descended from Robert Fulton, inventor of the steamboat. I believe that my ardor for invention springs from his loins—I can't say that the brassiere will ever take as great a place in history as the steamboat, but I did invent it."

In her decades of intimate association with key members of the New York publishing and media industry, she repeated her story in such an effective manner that it became perceived as historical fact.

A Backless Bra?

Some recent authors, like Anne L. Macdonald in her 1992 book, *Feminine Ingenuity: Women and Invention in America,* have begun to shift Jacobs's role in history from inventor of the bra to inventor of the "backless bra." But even this distinction seems questionable. For one thing, the device depicted in the patent that is the basis of Jacobs's claim is not, in its structural form or essential compression function, recognizable as a "modern bra" to most Americans. For another, a backless strap system was included on a bra-like device shown in a patent issued to Dora Harrison of Lansing, Michigan, in 1907, seven years before Jacobs's patent.

Nor was Jacobs the last to make such broad claims about inventing the bra. Ida Rosenthal, founder of the Maidenform Company of New York in the 1920s, claimed *she* was the first to use individual cups to independently support each breast in a brassiere-like structure. In fact, Marie Tucek's 1893 patent shows the same level of cup structure, as does a patent issued in 1919 to Edith Hillman Lowman of Los Angeles, California, years before Rosenthal's claim.

Both Ms. Jacobs and Ms. Rosenthal *were* pioneers—in the modern mass marketing and public relations business. But it does seem more accurate to say that Jacobs was the first to widely promote, rather

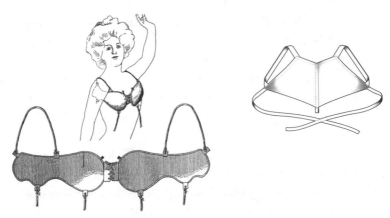

Some writers have recently begun calling Mary Phelps Jacobs the inventor of the "backless bra" (above, right), but even this claim seems questionable. The patent issued to Dora Harrison (above, left) shows a similar backless strap arrangement seven years prior to Jacobs's patent. No. 861,115 (1907)

than invent, the concept of a backless corset-replacing device that restrained only the breasts, and that Rosenthal was the first to widely promote and popularize, rather than invent, a bra that featured independent support cups.

The files of the U.S. Patent Office clearly show that the first American device that was unmistakably recognizable as the "modern bra" was registered by Marie Tucek in 1893, several years before Jacobs was born. Other devices, documented in Patent Office files as early as 1859, can also make strong arguments to the claim of being the prototype of the modern bra. And still others, documented in period fashion illustrations, show that modern bra-like constructions were incorporated as separate upper sections of corsets as early as 1844 and also qualify as a bra "prototypes."

A Bra by Any Other Name

Much of the early mechanical history of the bra has also been obscured by the confusing array of terms used at the Patent Office and elsewhere to describe and classify bra-like structures before the word itself was coined in the 1930s. These older terms included "breast pads," "bosom pads," "chest protectors," "breast forms," "bust supporters," and "breast supporters."

By the latter 1800s, numerous inventors were making padding or breast prosthetic devices whose structures were virtually identical to modern bras. Like the previously mentioned Charles L. Morehouse of Brooklyn, inventors took individual breast cups made of flexible material, hooked them together with a link in the middle, and suspended them on shoulder straps so they fit around the upper torso as a single, secure unit. George M. McCleary's patented breast forms of 1897 are another good example of this. They were rubber cup devices designed to be worn over the breasts to augment their size or take the place of amputated breasts. An inflatable cup fit over each breast and had a oval valve resembling a nipple in front. The cups were joined in the middle by a small fabric bridge and held about the body by elastic rubber straps that went around the back and over each shoulder. Clearly, the structure of this form is the same as the bra and would have provided inspiration for anyone thinking about creating new garments to support the individual breasts.

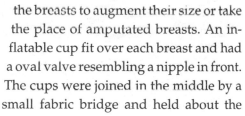

George M.
McCleary's
Breast Forms
No. 577,311 (1897)

The word "brassiere" as used by Jacobs and other inventors at the turn of the century was an ambiguous one because its meaning had changed over time. "Brassiere" is a French term used since the 1600s to mean the same as the English word "bodice." It originally described a garment, or a part of a garment, that wrapped around the trunk above the waist. In turn-of-the-century America, patent office records indicate that the term"brassiere" was used to describe a trunk-encircling compression device—an abbreviated or lightweight corset—that specifically flattened the body above the waist. In that same era, other American inventors, such as Tucek, used the term "bust supporter" to describe what they perceived as a completely different device from a brassiere. Their "bust supporter" was a garment that primarily covered, supported, and shaped only the breasts. The rest of this double-cupped structure consisted of the minimal number of straps required to hold it securely on the body.

In her 1919 patent for such a garment, Lowman called her device a "brassiere" that was "adapted especially for use as a bust supporter." She was one of the first to merge the meanings of the previously separate terms "brassiere" and "bust supporter." By the 1920s, the term "brassiere" was being popularly used to describe the new kinds of independently cupped breast-support garments that were being widely promoted by Maidenform and the Warner Brothers Corset Company. Both firms no doubt found it useful to their marketing campaigns to claim responsibility for the invention of what was becoming a wildly popular garment in an increasingly competitive market.

The growing sales, popularity, and commercial profits of the brassiere quickly drew the attention of other manufacturers, distributors, and inventors. During the 1920s and early 1930s, the new inventors were women who ran or worked in dress shops. Their patent applications—which now used the terms "bust supporter" and "brassiere" interchangeably—were for designs that made the device more comfortable or practical. These utilitarian improvements can be seen in patents issued to Katherine E. Cunningham of Chicago in 1929 for a bandeau bust supporter, or to Blanche Denise Ferrero in 1931 for a breast-separating brassiere, or to Helene Pons of New York City in 1931 for an elastic fabric-cup bust supporter

Cup bra by Helene
Pons No. 1,798,274
(1931).

"suitable for wear upon different types of figures so that a merchant need only carry in stock a limited number of sizes and yet be able to provide a brassiere suitable for the use of any customer."

But by the mid-1930s dramatic changes were occurring throughout American industry, including the businesses that supplied clothes to the nation's women. By 1935, the brassiere had become known by the new slang term "bra," and a new wave of male inventors and corporate marketing departments took control of the garment's evolving design features. Ultimately, they would seek to not only re-engineer the nature of what the bra was, but the nature of how American women perceived themselves as well.

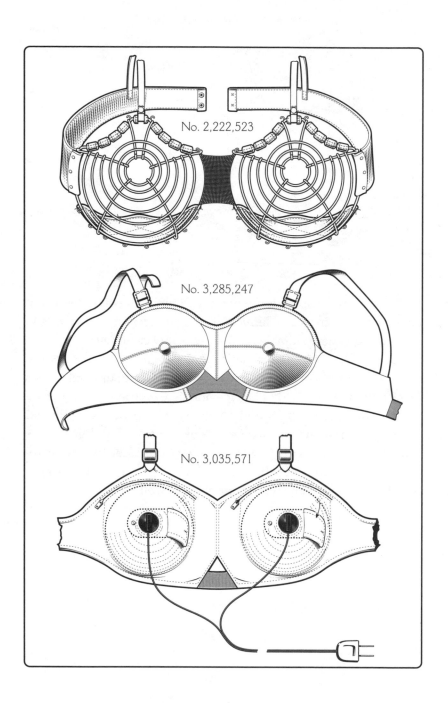

11

The Industrialization of the Breast

The shift from corsets to brassieres was just one small event in a panorama of change that swept society in the wake of World War I. The process of wide-scale industrialization that began during the Civil War had, by the 1920s, physically overwhelmed the landscape. America was fast evolving as a 3000-mile wide, self-contained, perpetual-motion machine for the financing, manufacturing, selling, purchasing, and discarding of machine-made goods. In fact, it was the first nation in history to reorganize its culture as a direct extension of mass-production business enterprise. Even the nature of government changed to accommodate this new reality of daily life; if tens of millions of Americans did not buy increasing amounts of factory-produced items every day, the economy—and the country—would collapse.

The New Sales Communications Business

It was thus inevitable that new sciences aimed at measuring, understanding, and directly influencing the population's purchasing impulses would emerge. Although advertising, market research, graphic design, photography, and public relations enterprises had been growing in sophistication since before the turn of the century, it was not until the 1920s that they began to coalesce into a single continent-straddling entity—later loosely referred to as the "media"—able to project a coordinated stream of images and messages at specific segments of the population. Crafted in accordance with the emerging principles of psychology, these messages were designed to alter the target audience's sense of personal security, daily reality, and need.

When a convention of department-store executives gathered in Philadelphia in 1923 to learn more about these new selling techniques, they were told: "Sell them their dreams. Sell them what they longed for and hoped for and almost despaired of having. Sell them hats by splashing sunlight across them. Sell them dreams of country clubs and proms and visions of what might happen if only. People don't buy things to have things. They buy hope—hope of what your merchandise will do for them. Sell them this hope and you won't have to worry about selling them goods."

By the 1930s the business of creating and projecting such illusions became one of the nation's largest industries. The first "modeling" agencies came into existence to provide the required idealized female shapes. Fashion photography emerged as a distinct genre, providing a flood of exotic photos of feminine forms that became the visual staple of almost all retail publications.

And the central feature of this carefully crafted national dreamscape was the breast, the body part about which women universally felt least secure; the body part that was used as visual code for the sexual innuendo that had come to underlie almost all sales campaigns. Thus, America's magazine pages and billboards suddenly burst out with sumptuous images of melon-breasted women hawking everything from baking flour to Oldsmobiles.

The New Bra

At the same time, the "brassiere," which had become known as the "bra," underwent a number of structural changes fostered by the latest fashions. Styles emphasized bare expanses of the shoulders, upper chest, and back and obviously required new forms of strapless, backless breast support devices. Initially, standard brassiere shapes with low back bands and a tighter cinch were used to anchor strapless cups reinforced with wire. But this approach was found inadequate by the new wave of male designers who dominated the field of bra invention.

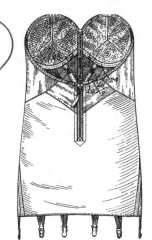

Otto Mowry
No. 2,045,401

For instance, in his 1935 patent, Jacob L. Alberts of Yonkers, New York, told the Patent Office that strapless designs that only gripped a narrow band around the breast level of the trunk were "unsightly" because they frequently created a sudden and sharp indentation in the profile of a woman's trunk. Instead, Alberts proposed a garment that combined the body-encasing structure of the traditional corset with the breast-hefting features of a bra top. Spring steel wire was sewn into the seams of the garment. Anchored firmly to the lower portions of the body, this superstructure of spring wire and elastic cloth reached up to hold the breasts in place without straps at the shoulders or back. It was, in its application of lift and stress conduction principles, not altogether unlike the structure of a cantilever bridge. In addition, it was an item of substantial size and complexity that would command a far higher price and profit margin than a mere fold-up fabric bra.

The following year, Otto D. Mowry received a patent for a similar device that incorporated a metal rod that ran down the center of the corset structure to more securely support the double arches of steel wire that branched out to encircle each breast cup from above. Henry

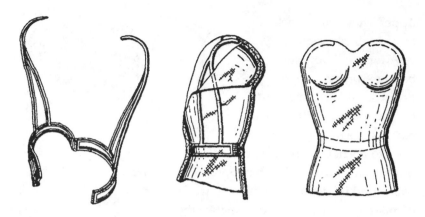

Henry Folb, No. 2,414,590

Folb of Brooklyn, New York, later boiled this concept down to its essentials, eliminated the actual cloth garment, applying for a patent on a stiff plastic "skeletal structure" that was installed around the waist to support ribs that curved upward and around the breasts. Various items of shoulderless, backless clothing could then be attached to the skeleton to drape over the breasts.

Industrialized Breast Forms

The corporations that designed, manufactured, and marketed women's foundation garments increasingly approached bra structure as a matter of industrial engineering, often selecting shapes that best fit available production machinery. This also helped establish the external shape of the female bust line as an item of fashion that could be changed as easily as the color and cut of the clothing itself. Many breast shape fashions were dictated by nothing more than the sudden availability of new materials—such as a certain plastic—or new factory production processes that could be geared up to stamp out breast-covering formats. In his design for a bra produced with injection-molded cups, Joseph Conde of New York City explained,

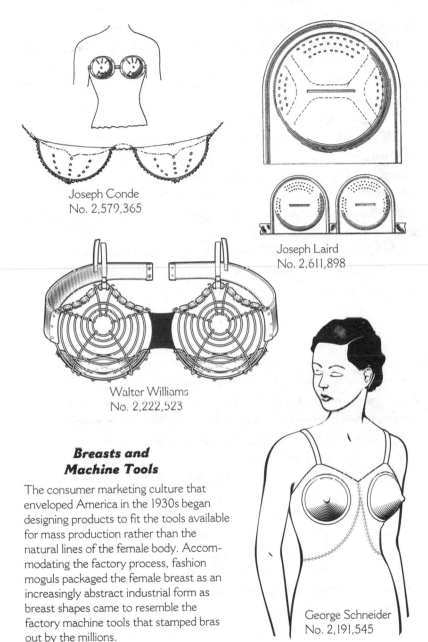

Joseph Conde
No. 2,579,365

Joseph Laird
No. 2,611,898

Walter Williams
No. 2,222,523

George Schneider
No. 2,191,545

Breasts and Machine Tools

The consumer marketing culture that enveloped America in the 1930s began designing products to fit the tools available for mass production rather than the natural lines of the female body. Accommodating the factory process, fashion moguls packaged the female breast as an increasingly abstract industrial form as breast shapes came to resemble the factory machine tools that stamped bras out by the millions.

"The desired illusion of an attractive breast line can be produced by using a conventional form such as a substantially true hemisphere (because) the manufacture of molds for making the form is thereby simplified, as they may be turned out more easily than molds of complicated and irregular shape." Conde's bra featured plastic cups, each shaped like one-half of a large rubber ball.

Another engineering effort by Joseph Paul Laird of Philadelphia, Pennsylvania, determined that the patented factory process used for manufacturing polyethylene toilet tank balls made shapes that were potentially useful for bra manufacture. His own patent shows breast forms that look like two halves of a toilet tank ball attached to a chest strap.

In 1937, George Schneider of Montclair, New Jersey, wrote that the method then being used to create breast-shaping cups on standard fabric bras was complicated and costly because it involved the joining of "a relatively large number of small pieces" of fabric sewn together in such a way they created a soft shape. Schneider was an employee of the Celanese Corporation as well as a pioneer in the evolving science of hard-substance breast forms. His invention used a "thermoplastic derivative of cellulose . . . to produce a brassiere . . . which is reinforced to give an 'uplift' effect." His bra—a landmark of artificial breast architecture—featured plastic cones that climbed in concentric rings to sharp points. Like inverted funnels, they presented the breast in the abstract shape of an industrial tool.

Later that same year, Walter Emmett Williams received a patent for a wire-frame bra that included rows of glass beads intended to create a constant "mild massage." Each wire-frame breast cup contained a chemical pad on its underside "to nullify perspiration in the angles caused by the tendency of breasts to sag." With its rows of massage beads, Williams's creation appears to be the first to define the concept of the bra as a mechanical device for delivering sensual stimulation to the breast.

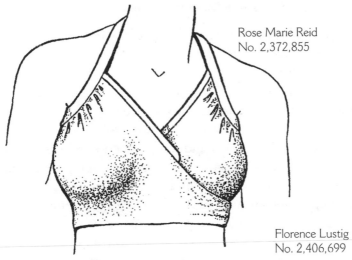

Rose Marie Reid
No. 2,372,855

Florence Lustig
No. 2,406,699

A Boom of Female Inventors

There was a boom of female invention during the World War II era as women worked in industry in record numbers. They filed a flurry of bra patent applications which, unlike those filed by the male designers of the previous decade, emphasized comfort and the practical aspects of wearing a breast support garment.

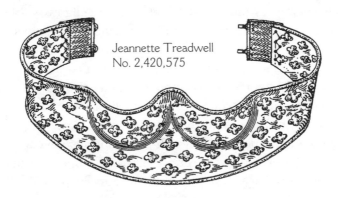

Jeannette Treadwell
No. 2,420,575

Bras from Rosie the Riveter

World War II abruptly changed life for American women as they were hired en masse in the offices, factories, and laboratories vacated by men gone to war. Widely promoted as Rosie-the-Riveter heroines of the war effort, these women were, for the first time, not only encouraged to be technologically creative, but financially rewarded for it as well. Their work as crucial members of the industrial teams designing and manufacturing everything from B-17s and jeeps to periscope lenses and howitzer barrels also resulted in a burst of patent applications from women across all fields of commercial enterprise.

For instance, women were suddenly filing bra improvement patents again, and they were quite different from those of the male designers of the 1930s. As with the previous wave of bra patents granted to women in the 1920s, the new designs of the 1940s were concerned with the utilitarian issues raised by the actual daily wearing of bras.

In 1944, Rose Marie Reid of Idaho filed for a patent for a completely soft wraparound brassiere that contoured the natural shape of the breasts and was designed to accommodate a wide range of breast shapes and sizes. Her criss-cross wrap bra was as comfortable to wear as it was practical to work in. Iva L. Blalock and Leila E. Ewing of Portland, Oregon, received a patent for a "saddle for brassiere straps," a wider, cushioned pad for the narrow bra straps that routinely cut into a woman's shoulders. Utilizing lightweight body strap designs similar to those used by parachute riggers, Florence Lustig of New York patented an elegantly simple bust separator harness that large-breasted women could wear beneath their bras. And, addressing another frustration, Jeannette E. Treadwell used new rubber production concepts for non-slip rubber bath mats to create a strapless bra design that resisted downward slippage by holding itself to the body with hundreds of tiny suction cups.

Gladys M. Hart utilized the bra structure as a support system for the first low-priced hearing aid systems introduced by Zenith Radio

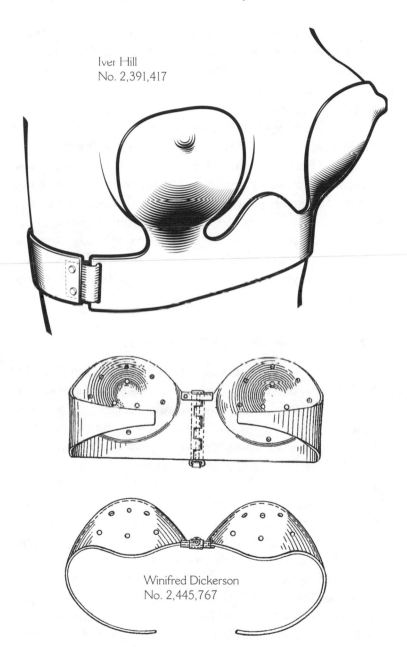

Iver Hill
No. 2,391,417

Winifred Dickerson
No. 2,445,767

Company in 1943. In 1945, Hart applied for a patent for a brassiere that included a sewn-in compartment for batteries and an amplifier. Her invention would, she wrote, "not only serve as an uplift brassiere but, also, as a comfortable and convenient support for the parts of hearing aid equipment, other than the ear piece, so that the wearing of such equipment by women afflicted with impaired hearing is rendered inconspicuous, without in any way diminishing the operating efficiency of the equipment." Etta E. Harvey of Pennsylvania also recognized the potential for building useful fabric compartments into bras. In her 1947 patent application for a bra with a zippered pocket, she explained, "in current styles, the outer feminine garments are usually devoid of pockets in which valuables could be stored, so that ladies, particularly when traveling, are inclined to 'hide' such valuables in the upper end portion of their stockings, inside their brassieres, or in other poorly accessible locations."

Post-World War II Patents

However, this period of utilitarian bra patents was a brief one that ended shortly after the war as women were encouraged once again to recognize housewifery as their most meaningful career. Males, who once again came to dominate the field of bra invention, appeared to have been particularly keen to apply a range of new wartime technological developments to the task of creating mechanically ideal breasts.

Influenced by the loosening bounds on public sexual expression as well as by the major advances in acetate plastics fabrication made during the war, Iver F. Hill of Stratford, Connecticut, applied for a patent on a new sort of strapless bra. Made from a single piece of molded plastic rigidly shaped with the curves of symmetrically perfect breasts, it was strapped on to provide a cantilever support system that eliminated the need for shoulder or back straps. It also included a set of machine-perfect nipples, which protruded distinctly

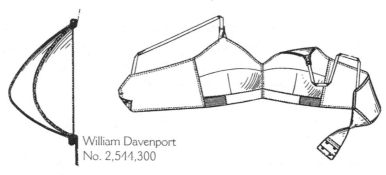

William Davenport
No. 2,544,300

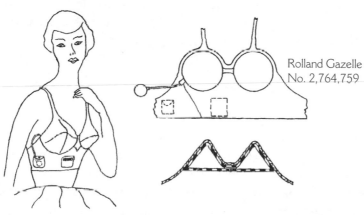

Rolland Gazelle
No. 2,764,759

Blowup Bras

During the 1950s, air inflation bladders of new plastics were used to make breast-augmenting bras. Gazelle patented a hand bulb version that allowed the wearer to pump more air into the unit whenever necessary, thus allowing her to make her bust contour larger, even while attending social functions. Buckley patented multi-compartmental bladders to eliminate the problem of exploding bra bladders experienced while flying on the era's poorly pressurized airliners.

William Buckley
No. 2,864,372

through the outer layers of the wearer's dress. Winifred S. Dickerson of Atlanta, Georgia, applied for a patent on similar bra-manufacturing technique evolved from production methods for plastic aircraft parts. His strapless, backless bra was a rigid, hinged device that was clamped and locked around the wearer. The hinge, resembling that used on door frames, was attached with bolts or rivets. Each breast was contained in rounded pyramid forms punctured with holes to facilitate ventilation. The inventor explained that although the preferred configuration was made with molded plastic, the patent claims also sought to protect the rights to similar hinged bras made from "thin stainless steel" as well.

Postwar Breast Mania

American society emerged from the war with a fixation—like none before it—on breast size as the ultimate statement of a woman's worth. The postwar advertising and sales colossus continued to promote breast imagery as one of the consumer culture's most potent totems. The fashion industry designed and churned out an endless stream of breast improvement products aimed at a population of women whose sense of breast insecurity was now so acute and widespread it almost qualified as a kind of mass psychosis.

Products for "Defective" Women

In his patent application for foam rubber breast pads for women whose "natural form is defective," Lewis Wilkenfeld of New York City explained to the patent examiners: "It is well known that some women have naturally small and meager breasts; this causes them to endure embarrassment due to their appearance." Among the many others who sought to capitalize on this same marketing concept, William F. Davenport and Howard A. Smith of Connecticut filed a patent application in 1950 for a bra with a new kind of pneumatic enlargement bladder in each cup made from high-tech plastics. They explained that their invention "relates to an improved brassiere, particularly intended for women having a bust which is underdeveloped, flat, unsymmetrical or otherwise lacking in normal or natural configuration, and has for its object to provide a brassiere having a predetermined external shape designed to give an accepted ideal contour." The enlargement bladders were inflated with tubes that could be attached to a small hand pump or blown up by mouth.

Such pneumatic breast augmentation devices became their own specialty field. In 1954, Rolland J. Gazelle of New York City applied for a patent on a pneumatic bra that allowed for resizing while it was being worn. The bra had a special rubber hand bulb and valve for pumping in more air, which fit into a special pocket built into the side of the bra. Thus a woman who arrived at a social function could, in those instances when deemed necessary or appropriate, excuse herself to the ladies' room to pump in a few more pounds of pressure to further increase her apparent breast size.

However, pneumatic bras had their own peculiar disadvantages at times, such as when flying in airplanes. In his 1958 patent application, William J. Buckley of Connecticut indicated that the standard types of pneumatic bras frequently burst when exposed to the lower air pressures experienced at high altitudes in that era's poorly pressurized aircraft. Buckley's invention was designed to avoid this embarrassing situation by constructing breast-enlarging air bladders honeycombed with individually sealed air cells. He explained that because each cell had a relatively small amount of air and stronger plastic walls, the overall breast pads were far less likely to experience structural failure at high altitudes. It was one of at least two products he devised for female customers who felt they had "a bust which is underdeveloped, flat, unsymmetrical or otherwise lacking in normal or natural configuration."

The Emergent Nipple

Other inventors were focusing on bras as items of erotic equipment emphasizing or revealing the formerly taboo nipple—a trend that first appeared in the previously mentioned plastic-nippled breast forms of Iver Hill in 1945, and quickly became the subject of heated competition among inventors. That same year, Robert O. Ferguson of Bristol, Tennessee, received a patent for a bra with unusually low-slung cup tops and cut-outs that bared the nipples. In 1948, Ceyl Anselmo of Atlantic City, New Jersey, patented a standard bra with special holes so that "the nipples may protrude" and "be more noticeable under a dress or sweater." Henry M. Herbener of Georgia in 1951 invented a bra with foam rubber cups molded to enhance the size of the breasts as well as the apparent size and protuberance of the nipples to "create the appearance of a full, youthful bust." Henry Morin of Eau Gallie, Florida, followed with a patent for a bra with foam-rubber pads that more than doubled the apparent size of the breast and included plastic simulated nipples to poke through outer garments.

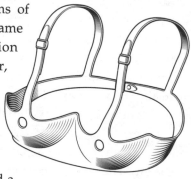

Robert Ferguson
No. 141,777 (Design)

Henry Herbener
No. 2,563,241

Perhaps the most technologically ambitious nipple-related bra innovation was that of William R. Jones who, in 1959, applied for a patent on a bra with electrically powered nipple stimulators. It even plugged into

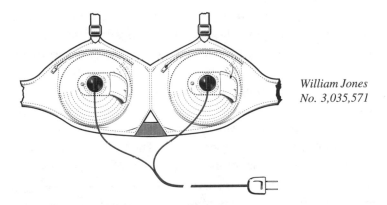

William Jones
No. 3,035,571

the wall. He explained to the Patent Office examiners: "It is well known that the bust appearance of a woman may be enhanced by increasing the circulation of blood in the breast areas, said increase in circulation promoting enlargement or dilation and firmness of the breast. Due to the massaging effect the device is also a muscle-stimulating corrective for sagging of breasts, a condition encountered often during and after middle age. I obtain these results by providing pouches in conventional brassiere pockets within which are inserted thin metal or composition cups to which are in turn connected electrical vibrator devices." After a thirty-seven-month review of his application, the patent examiners granted Jones's patent in 1962.

Bras for Children

By the 1960s, the bra manufacturers' national marketing programs were extending their sales activities from mature women with breasts to prepubescent girls without them. From a sales point of view, these female children represented an enormous potential consumer base. It seemed inevitable that inventors would create bra products which sought to directly address the special insecurities of young females.

In his 1964 patent application for a bra for immature teen-age and pre-pubescent girls, Morton Sloate of Cedarhurst, Long Island, explained to the patent examiners: "Such foundation garments as are presently available fail to consider the psychologically advantageous aspect of being so constructed and arranged that they at least present the appearance of a bust of some proportion, rather than the minimal proportions actually existing."

Such efforts to convince mothers that their pre-pubescent daughters should be strapped into chest-enhancing products was the subject of Betty Friedan's early 1960s observation, "The tragedy of children acting out the sexual fantasies of their housewife-mothers is only one sign of the progressive dehumanization that is taking place."

Friedan's book, *The Feminine Mystique,* provided the first comprehensive picture of how the sciences of psychology, marketing, and communications had been brought together to systematically manipulate the daily behavior and attitudes of women in America. *The Feminine Mystique* also provided the prism through which large numbers of women were able to focus their amorphous sense of discontent into a sharp-edged rage against the status quo. That anger exploded into public view in 1968 on the boardwalk in Atlantic City, New Jersey, the site of the High Mass of breast worship—the Miss America Pageant.

On the afternoon of the final day of the pageant, a small group of women dragged a large trash can and armloads of bras into the center of the crowds of spectators and reporters milling around the front of Atlantic City's convention hall. As a few TV cameramen set up their tripods and newspaper photographers gathered around, the women ceremoniously threw their bras into the trash can.

The event was rowdy but small; hardly one hundred women joined in. It received only a smattering of press coverage, most of it dismissive or derogatory. But, as it turned out, it was from that spot on the boardwalk that the public persona of a new feminist movement rose up as a visible political force.

The nation's bra business was never quite the same after Atlantic City. A large portion of a whole generation of women soon ceased or severely curtailed the buying and wearing of bras as a personal political statement. Increasing numbers of women who *did* wear bras demanded more simple styles emphasizing natural shape and comfort. Patent applications for improvements in traditional bra-related items dropped off precipitously by the end of the 1960s. But the commercial battle for profitable breast-enhancement products wasn't over. A new school of invention was rising in place of the old, and its mechanical vision was like something from a science fiction movie. The women of America would soon see how inventors could build the perfect breast from the inside out.

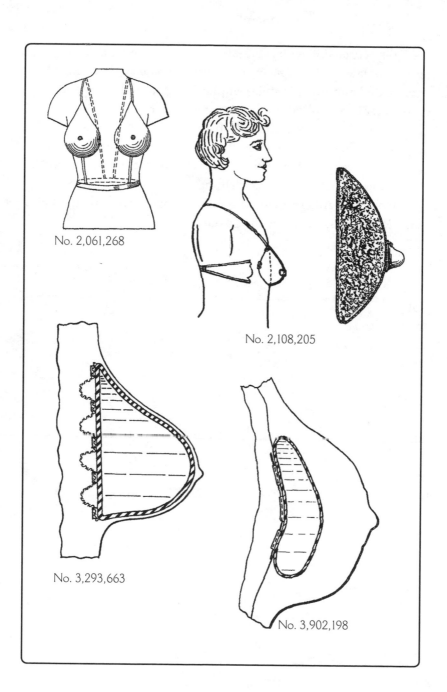

No. 2,061,268

No. 2,108,205

No. 3,293,663

No. 3,902,198

12

Artificial Breasts and the Silicone Nightmare

The quest to replicate the shape and feel of real breasts with artificial materials is as old as the anguish caused by missing or misshapen breasts themselves. The harsh realities of farm life, disease, and the dangerous nature of early factory machinery frequently resulted in breast injuries and amputations. Thus, artificial breasts were often needed. The earliest homemade versions consisted of little more than a tight wad of rags placed beneath the clothing. Even then, it was obvious that whatever material made a good replacement for a missing breast could also be used to augment the size of smaller ones.

In the second half of the nineteenth century, inventors began registering designs for improved artificial breasts made possible by new industrial materials and processes. For instance, advances in rubber fabrication techniques resulted in inflatable rubber pad systems such as that patented by Frederick Cox in 1874.

Stuffed fabric pads were the era's most popular form of artificial breast. In his 1878 patent application, Michael A. Bryson of St. Louis noted that the pads then available were stuffed with "curled hair of horses, goose feathers, cotton, granulated cork and wool (or had) springs with a suitable covering." For his own invention, he treated various sorts of animal hair with caustic chemicals to enhance their spring and "elasticity." He reported that the processed hair of deer,

Utilizing the latest advances in rubber fabrication, Frederick Cox invented inflatable breast augmentation pads. (Left) No. 146,805 (1874)

Ribbon was attached to the sides of Henry Hayward's horsehair felt "Chest Protector" to hold it in place on the breasts. (Above) No. 181,261 (1876)

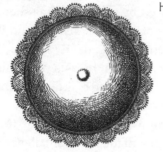

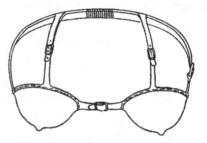

Michael Bryson's pads were stuffed with the treated hair of deer, mountain sheep, elk, or antelope. (Above) No. 212,184 (1879)

Mabel Heuchan's bust forms were made of sponge rubber. (Above) No. 1,250,875 (1917)

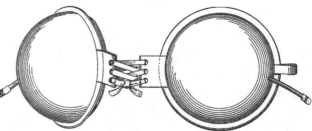

Dora Harrison's rubber breast augmentation device (Right) No. 599,180 (1898)

mountain sheep, elk, and antelope made a more life-like breast stuffing than any other known materials.

By the 1880s, breast pad harness systems had become increasingly sophisticated and continued to be improved during the next fifty years. Precursors of modern bra structure, they featured individual breast forms connected to elastic shoulder and back straps. Designs such as the bosom pads of Dora Harrison or bust forms of Mabel Heuchan had cups molded of soft rubber and could be used for either augmentation or breast replacement purposes.

Artificial Breasts for the Consumer Age

In the 1930s, the changing nature of American society created a market for new kinds of exterior prostheses: devices more suitable for the lightweight, breast-focused fashions that had come to dominate the culture. In the late 1930s, designers like Elsie L. Martin explained that the single largest drawback of all the available artificial breast systems was their lack of "the plasticity of a normal human breast." Ms. Martin received a patent for a new kind of breast form made of a fabric bag filled with shredded foam rubber.

Others were experimenting with new kinds of bra-mounted plastic pouch systems filled with water, liquid soap, or oils they hoped would mimic the plasticity of flesh. The real breakthrough in the field came immediately after World War II, when Ella H. Burnhardt of New York City informed the Patent Office she had created a revolutionary prosthesis that reproduced the weight, shape, movement, and tactile feel of a real breast. Her invention was a vinyl plastic bag filled with "conformable gel." She said she had found the proper viscosity for simulating the feel of living tissue with "Dow Corning DC 200 silicone fluid."

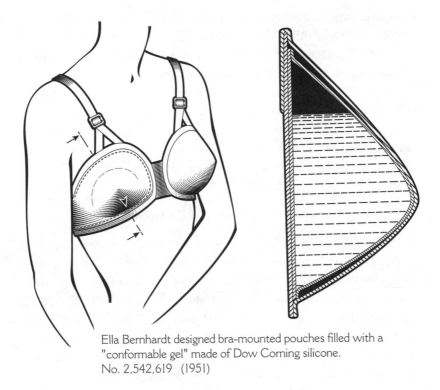

Ella Bernhardt designed bra-mounted pouches filled with a "conformable gel" made of Dow Corning silicone. No. 2,542,619 (1951)

Silicone: The Lifelike Liquid

Silicone was an odd, rubber-like compound created by chemists in the early 1900s from silicon, oxygen, and hydrogen. Silicon is a common mineral substance found in sand and clay deposits and the basic material for manufacturing the synthetic, silicone. By making slight alterations in its chemical structure, silicone could be made in a range of consistencies from runny liquids to solid blocks. In the 1930s, the Corning Glass Company experimented with a gummy form as a caulking material for clear glass construction bricks. During World War II, Dow Chemical and Corning Glass formed a new joint venture called Dow Corning Corporation to manufacture silicone products such as the seals required for the instrument panels of high-altitude aircraft. Because it was a highly efficient insulator, liquid silicone came to be widely used in the military's electrical transformers.

Immediately after the war ended in Japan, this last item became a highly valued black-market commodity among the prostitutes who clustered around the ports and airfields taken over by American occupational forces. The women had been seeking ways to make their breasts larger because they believed American GIs preferred melon-breasted females. The prostitutes' doctors first tried injections of goat's milk. Then they switched to paraffin wax. Both methods resulted in serious medical problems including uncontrollable absorption, migration, and massive infections. Then, they tried silicone.

Silicone liquid was silky and smooth like goat's milk. It also had a rubbery "body," not unlike soft paraffin wax. And better yet, silicone was believed to be inert: a substance that was not supposed to interact with human tissue, decompose, or be affected by water or heat. When injected directly into the core of a living breast, the silicone fluid initially formed a pool that increased the size of the breast, and at the same time retaining a remarkable life-like resiliency. Suddenly, containers of silicone transformer fluid began disappearing from U.S. supply depots.

By the late 1940s, it had become known in the United States that industrial-grade silicone was being used as an injectable cosmetic in Japan. Some American surgeons also began offering silicone injections to movie stars and affluent socialites.

It seems likely that this information was known to inventors such as Ella Burnhardt. At the same time she was testing Dow Corning silicone, two other inventors—Walter O. Kausch of Detroit and Ruth Freeman of New York—were working on similar plasticized-fluid-in-a-bag designs. These inventions of the early 1950s served as the inspiration for two plastic surgeons who pioneered a new era of breast augmentation technology in the 1960s. In essence, these two surgeon-inventors—William Pangman and Thomas Cronin—moved

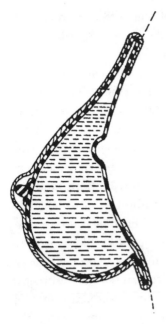

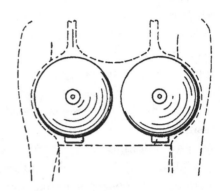

Walter Kausch was one of several inventors
who sought to create life-like external breast
prostheses from pouches filled with various kinds
of thick fluids.
No. 2,543,499 (1951)

the gel-filled bags from the outside to the inside of the human body.
For this they received patents that spawned competing product lines,
which would ultimately change the profession of plastic surgery into
a multi-billion dollar mass-production industry and alter the aspirations, bodies, and sense of well-being of millions of women.

Toward Bionic Breasts

In 1950s Beverly Hills the latest developments in plastic surgery were
of keen interest to movie moguls, starlets, and assorted hangers-on in
a business culture fueled by sex, money and the illusion of youth.
Beverly Hills surgeon Dr. Pangman was one of a growing number of
American surgeons experimenting with ways to surgically augment
the living breast. One method involved grafting flaps of fat or muscle

from other body sites. Another involved the use of what were known as "body cavity fillers." These were chunks of raw, sponge-like materials cut to a rough shape and implanted to create a permanent bulge. In a patent application for a new polyethylene mesh implant material in 1950, Jens Herman Bing noted that the raw sponge materials caused chronic tissue inflammation.

In 1951, Dr. Pangman invented an implant sponge made of a polyvinyl alcohol and formaldehyde polymer he believed to be inert and unlikely to cause such unwanted body reactions. He was wrong. It *did* cause the same problems, and was subsequently abandoned.

In February of 1954, Dr. Pangman filed a patent application for a new invention he called a "compound prosthesis device." It was a breast-enlarging surgical implant consisting of a sponge saturated in saline solution sealed inside a polyethylene plastic bag. The bag was covered with an external layer of plastic foam. The era of the liquid-filled breast implant bag had arrived.

Dr. Pangman told patent examiners his invention solved the tissue invasion problem because such growth could not penetrate the plastic bag around the main body of the device. The tissue that *could* infiltrate the thin outer foam layer would secure the implant in place. Meanwhile, the inner sac would theoretically remain permanently soft. In addition, the salt water filler would make it more pliable and lifelike. The doctor's upbeat assessment noted he was already implanting the device in his Hollywood patients and that such surgery "has proved highly successful."

It was a short-lived euphoria. By 1962 Pangman had encountered serious medical difficulties with the device. That year, he filed a new patent application, admitting to the patent examiners that the external layer of plastic sponge used on his previous invention had proven "deficient (and) prone to infiltration by germs. Because of this, infections occurring in (patients) cannot generally be cured with antibiotics or other medical treatments."

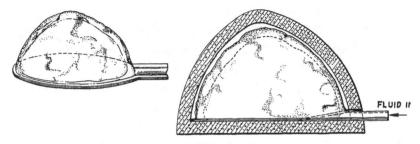

FLUID II

William Pangman, a plastic surgeon from Beverly Hills, California, was the first
to patent a liquid-filled breast implant.
No. 2,842,775 (1958)

The doctor's new, improved design retained the same general
concept of a sealed-off liquid core surrounded by a thin layer of
sponge-like foam, but the new material he employed for this outer
layer was "polyurethane foam." It would prove a fateful development that would later make Dr. Pangman's invention famous—but
for all the wrong reasons.

Dow Corning Silicone

Meanwhile, in Houston, Texas, Dr. Thomas Cronin was working on
a competing breast implant design in association with Dow Corning
Corporation. It was 1962 and although some American plastic surgeons were still using direct injections of silicone for cosmetic surgical procedures, government health authorities had recognized that
liquid silicone loosed amidst body tissues could lead to medical
complications. This would soon result in a national prohibition
against silicone injections.

Nevertheless, silicone fluid continued to hold the imagination of
plastic surgeons because of its uncanny similarity to living flesh. In
his experiments, Dr. Cronin used a mix of Dow Corning silicone
fluids to make a gel that he contained inside a flexible bag, or
"elastomer," made of another kind of rubber-like silicone. Working

with Dr. Frank Gerow, Dr. Cronin surgically inserted the first "natural feel" silicone gel bag implant in a Houston woman in 1962.

The following year, Dr. Cronin and Dow Corning filed for a patent on the device which, unlike Dr. Pangman's foam-covered implant, was completely smooth except for tufts of Dacron on its rear surface. Dr. Cronin explained to patent examiners that the walls of the silicone rubber bag were "substantially" impermeable. That is, he admitted that the rubbery silicone bag material was not a complete barrier to the fluids it contained. Thus, some level of fluid migration could be expected between the interior of the bag and the exterior living tissue spaces of the recipient's body.

Marketed under the Dow Corning "Silastic" trade name, the device was perceived as a landmark new product. After performing seventy-six breast implant operations, Dr. Hugh A. Johnson of Rockford, Illinois, wrote in a journal article: "Nothing says it quite so well, 'I am feminine,' as a nicely formed breast. The flat chested girl is painfully aware of this; with padded brassieres, she is ridiculed by her more generously endowed sisters. The Cronin Silastic breast prosthesis has, however, done much to solve this psychological problem."

Thomas Cronin, a surgeon in Houston, Texas, patented the silicone gel breat implant that started a national craze. No. 3,293,663 (1966)

The 1970s: A Bull Market in Breasts

Between 1962, when the silicone gel bag prosthesis was invented, and 1973, at least 50,000 sets of gel bags were implanted in women. At as much as $4,000 per procedure, this represented roughly $200 million in gross sales for the surgeons and prosthesis manufacturers. And this was widely perceived as just the beginning of a boom market.

Plastic surgeons' publications of the time indicated that the women who were receiving silicone implants were ecstatic with them. The 1979 edition of *Plastic Surgery* said a poll of a group of implant patients found that "93 percent reported increased self-confidence, 84 percent reported increased feelings of elation and joy, and 80 percent had increased feelings of equality and self-worth."

However, there was another side of the picture that was not receiving quite the same kind of high-profile promotion. By 1979, twenty-one additional breast implant patent applications had been filed that addressed the serious problems encountered during the widespread use of the devices.

The Scar Capsule Effect

The most serious problem facing plastic surgeons was the scar capsule effect. Months after their breast-enlarging operations were over, women began to notice that their implants were changing in texture.

Despite the frequent characterization of silicone rubber as an "inert" material that would not trigger tissue response, the actual response was dramatic. Shortly after the bags were inserted, the body marshaled a constant attack on all portions of the implants with a process that created thick, fibrous layers of scar tissue. Over time, this scar tissue completely enveloped the bags in a ball, or capsule, whose thick walls eventually contracted and hardened. Instead of hanging with the gentle curve of natural tissue, the breasts now protruded stiffly outward, round and firm, as if filled with baseballs.

Because "capsular contracture" so displeased patients, intensive inventive efforts were made to minimize or "neutralize" the phenomenon. And this is where Dr. Pangman's languishing implant patents finally came to life as money makers. While many aspects of the

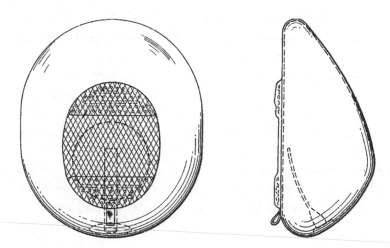

After a brief period of manufacturing Dr. Pangman's polyurethane implants, Heyer-Schulte ceased production and obtained a patent for an implant that contained no polyurethane. The firm indicated to the patent office that it questioned if polyurethane "in any form" was suitable for use in the body. No. 3,852,832 (1974)

Pangman designs were not of practical use, two of his earliest patents gave him a proprietary hammerlock on the concept of coating a breast implant bag with an outer layer of foam. Many surgeons believed that the scar capsule effect would not be nearly as hard or as spherical if there were a soft, cushioning layer of foam between the surface of the scar tissue and the surface of the silicone bag. By the early 1980s, implants utilizing Pangman's polyurethane coating had become one of the best-selling implant products in an increasingly competitive market.

Biological Implications of Implants

At the same time, increasing amounts of data had been emerging throughout the 1970s about the potential health effects of the silicone fluids that were seeping through the osmotic bag material or leaking from bag tears, cuts, or burst seams. One internal memo written by a

Dow Corning marketing executive in 1977 detailed how the company's silicone implant bags were so permeable, they developed "appreciable oiling" on their exterior surface even as they sat on tables at medical trade shows. Dow Corning salesmen were advised to conceal this problem by frequently wiping off the samples they put on display.

A year later, in 1978, Dow filed for a patent on new kind of breast implant gel—a "water swellable" gel made from non-silicone chemicals. According to the patent, these new "hydrophilic," or water-soluble, materials were designed as "non-toxic gels for medical use ... as a mammary prosthesis filler." Dow explained to patent examiners that the silicone gels then being used in implants "are not readily dispersed by the body if they should move across the prosthesis walls ... some seepage is not surprising."

Despite its development of non-silicone implant materials in 1978, Dow, like other manufacturers, continued to sell silicone gel bags in a market that, by the 1980s, had superheated into a national craze. More than two thousand American women each week were paying thousands of dollars each to have bags of silicone put in their breasts. National sales for the implant industry rose to more than half a billion dollars a year, with implant procedures accounting for half or more of the gross annual billings of many of America's five thousand plastic surgeons.

In Washington, scientists at the U.S. Food and Drug Administration appeared to be getting increasingly uncomfortable with the widespread use of an invention they had never actually reviewed or approved as safe. By the late 1980s, FDA staff had gathered enough data about silicone implant hazards to write internal memos indicating their findings were "alarming." They recommended that the agency immediately issue public warnings about the potential dangers of implant surgery.

In 1988, after FDA scientists obtained an internal Dow Corning study that showed injected silicone gel caused high levels of cancer in rats, they leaked copies of the confidential document to the consumer advocacy group Public Citizen, which released the findings to the press. The resulting explosion of publicity made breast implants an issue of national controversy.

1991: The Year the Implant Business Collapsed

1991 was the year the market for silicone breast implants began to fizzle. The Pangman polyurethane side of the business went first. FDA scientists documented that polyurethane foam coverings began reacting with human body fluids immediately after implant, breaking down into a substance called 2-toluene diamine, or TDA. Classified by the federal government as a "hazardous waste," TDA is a carcinogenic chemical previously found to cause liver and renal cancers in rats and other research animals.

The FDA began by prohibiting the sale of polyurethane-coated implants. Reports at the time indicated that at least 200,000 American women had already been implanted with Pangman's polyurethane-covered breast bags. A year later, in January of 1992, after tumultuous national public hearings featuring horrific details about the biological effects of loose silicone fluids in the body, the FDA formally prohibited the selling or surgical use of most silicone gel bag breast implants.

On March 19, 1992, twenty-three years after it was granted the patent that launched a mega-billion dollar silicone breast implant industry, Dow Corning announced it was abandoning that business and would no longer make or sell implants.

New Trends

Despite a marketplace switch by plastic surgeons to salt-water-filled bags—which remain legal—the breast implant business has dramatically declined in America.

The American fashion industry, meanwhile, adjusted rapidly to these changed market conditions. Now leery of surgical solutions to their breast insecurity problems, large numbers of American women were once again potential customers for alternative breast-enhancing products. By 1994, fashion-show runways and women's magazines heralded the arrival of "new" product lines of uplift bras and even full upper-body corset devices that were, in actuality, mechanical strategies as old and enduring as our peculiar cultural quest for the perfect breast.

13

Anti-Rape Technology

In June of 1993, in an event that propelled its participants into the upper reaches of modern American folklore, Lorena Bobbitt took a kitchen knife and cut off the penis of her sleeping husband who, she said, had been raping and abusing her for years. Ultimately, Mrs. Bobbitt's slashings cut as deeply into the collective American psyche as into her spouse: her arrest and prosecution becoming the flash point for an explosion of national debate about how America deals— or fails to deal—with rape.

Since the 1970s, when rape was first acknowledged as a serious national issue, various groups have attacked the problem in different ways. Some have marched, demonstrated, lobbied, and campaigned for stricter laws, more equitable court procedures, and stiffer sentences; others have organized sex crime prosecution units, rape crisis centers, and self-defense clinics. Some, like Mrs. Bobbitt, have struck back personally. And some—the group of inventors documented in this chapter—have gone to the U.S. Patent Office to register their entrepreneurial vision: an America where legions of women routinely purchase and wear vaginal devices designed to slice, rip, or puncture penises that enter that space without authorization.

That such extraordinary engineering and product development efforts have gone unpublicized for two decades is largely a function of the traditional press taboos which made "penis" one of our

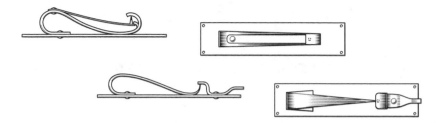

Natalie Teeple's anti-molestation device No. 1,109,264 (1914)

language's most proscribed words. Newspaper reporters were forbidden to write it; broadcasters to speak it; advertisers to even allude to it. Thus, the anti-rape patents inspired by 1970s feminists have existed in an official netherworld of the unspeakable: technology judged serious enough to be granted patent protection, but so horrific in purpose that it, like its target organ, was deemed unfit for public mention.

But the media carnival of Lorena and John Bobbitt's trials in 1993 and 1994 changed all that. Lorena Bobbitt's knife, much like this collection of anti-rape patents, was a mechanical manifestation of the extreme levels of desperation felt by women who live in daily fear of sexual violence.

While Patent Office records indicate the general idea of using weapon-like devices to even the balance of power between men and women is not new, the nature of the threats appears to have changed significantly. For instance, an application for one of the earliest female anti-molestation inventions was filed in 1913 by Natalie A. Teeple, who sought to strike back mechanically against males on Philadelphia's trolleys. She explained: "Rude and flirtatious youths and men, 'mashers,' frequently avail themselves of the crowded condition of cars and other means of transportation to annoy and insult ladies next to whom they may happen to be seated by pressing a knee or thigh against the adjacent knee or thigh of their feminine neighbor, who, as often happens, is too timid or modest to create a disturbance by calling attention to the fact. It is the object of my invention to guard against undue familiarity of the character designated by the provision of means whereby the offender is automatically warned, punished, and deterred from persistent offense." Ms. Teeple's invention was a spring-loaded spur device that could be pinned to an underskirt. When a male pressed against the woman's leg, the pressure triggered the device, which drove a sharp, pin-like point into the offending male's leg or hand.

Against Our Will

In her landmark 1975 book, *Against Our Will: Men, Women and Rape*, feminist Susan Brownmiller provided the first comprehensive history of rape in all its physical, psychological, social, cultural, and criminal aspects. Based on hard scientific data, the book painted a jarring and panoramic picture of a male-dominated society that had, for centuries, ignored the manner in which its women were routinely subjected to forced sexual encounters as a fact of daily life.

Brownmiller's book transformed the previously taboo subject of rape into a mainstream political issue and a keystone of the feminist movement. And, as always in America, the publicity alerted entrepreneurial inventors to a potentially vast and lucrative market for mechanical anti-rape products.

Anti-Rape Products

For instance, shortly after the 1969 National Commission report on the causes of violence, which described the shockingly high rate of rape in America, Charles Petrosky of Arlington, Virginia, applied for a patent for a device that looked like a wedding ring, but was actually a flesh-ripping hook. He told the patent examiners: "With the rising crime wave, it is extremely desirable that people who must be exposed to heavy crime areas have some sort of defensive weapon which is innocuous appearing, which is not extremely dangerous to either party, which cannot be used against the party carrying the weapon and which will inflict damage upon the attacker so as to ward off an attack while at the same time marking the attacker for future identification for prosecution purposes."

Charles Petrosky's finger ring blade No. 3,648,371 (1972)

In the wake of the often shrill national debate sparked by the 1975 Brownmiller book, a growing number of inventors also sought to mechanically perfect and legally protect anti-rape device designs. At the Patent Office, the applications fell into three categories: external devices for interrupting a rapist and allowing the victim to escape, barrier devices to prevent physical access to the female genitals, and intravaginal mechanisms designed to trap and mutilate unauthorized penises.

Clark Luke of Hollywood, California, filed for a patent on a device that looked like a wristwatch, but was actually a dispenser for pressurized pepper gas. A strong marketing point of Mr. Luke's "gas watch" was that it was not stored in a pocket or handbag like the pen and cigarette lighter products previously created for dispensing tear gas. Because it was worn on the wrist, it was always ready for use.

Working on the same premise of "instant availability," Dale Smith of Atlanta, Georgia, and Steven Kimmel of Granada Hills, California, applied for patents on two different kinds of chemical-dispensing anti-rape rings. One was flower-shaped with a center "stone" that was a pressurized gas-dispensing chamber. It was triggered by moving one of the petals. The second ring used a larger "stone" setting to hold an ampoule of a volatile, noxious chemical. Its

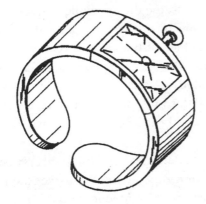

Clark Luke's pressur-
ized, irritant gas-
dispensing wristwatch
No. 4,058,237 (1977)

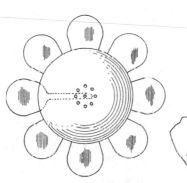

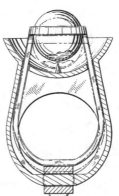

Dale Maxwell Smith's
pressurized, irritant gas-
dispensing flower ring
No. 4,061,249 (1977)

Steven Kimmell's
noxious odor-
dispensing ring
No. 4,135,645 (1979)

safety catch was flipped off with the thumb while a squeeze of the finger broke the ampoule, mechanically propelling the chemical outward, preferably into the face of the attacker. Others patented anti-rape jewelry devices such as a heart-shaped locket with a trigger on the rear that, when activated, ejected a noxious, brightly-colored chemical designed to both deter and mark the rapist. Yet another invention was an anti-rape credit card that emitted noxious chemicals when folded in half.

Edward L. Withey of Santa Barbara took a different approach by creating chemical-dispensing anti-rape devices that soaked the *wearer's* body with ammonia or concentrated synthetic skunk scent to make it repellent to a would-be rapist. Withey's device was shaped like a large brooch or belt buckle and contained a substantial quantity of noxious liquid. It could be opened by hand with a pull cord, or the woman could attach the cord to an item of clothing an attacker was likely to remove. Once triggered, the device released intensely foul chemicals that soaked the woman's clothes and body.

Another milder variation on this chemical deterrent theme was patented by Paul and Anne Martineau of Pocasset, Massachusetts. Their invention was a small wax egg filled with concentrated citric acid to be carried in the mouth. When confronted by an attacker, a woman bit into the egg, spilling the citric acid into her mouth, and then spit it into the eyes of the attacker. Theoretically, the citric acid temporarily burned the rapist's eyes, breaking the momentum of the attack and providing an opportunity for escape.

A more straightforward genital barrier approach to rape prevention borrowed heavily from the technology of medieval chastity belts. Although the concept doesn't seem all that new, chain mail anti-rape panties were granted a patent in 1986. Made of the lightweight, high-tech material used for butchers' gloves and anti-shark scuba diving suits, the mail was as soft as fabric yet could not be cut with razor sharp knives. Inventor Harry Bouwhuis included a special locking belt that he said ensured that the panties "cannot be removed

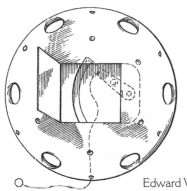

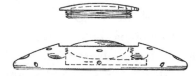

Edward Withey's anti-rape body-soaking device
No. 4,428,506 (1984)

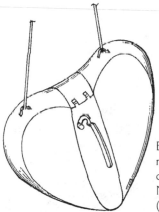

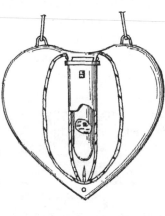

Eugene Speer's
rape deterrent
chemical locket
No. 4,241,850
(1980)

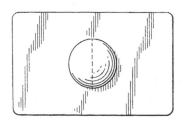

Gary Wollrich's chemical-
spraying credit card device
No. 4,816,260 (1989)

from the wearer's body in the absence of a key without the use of tools normally not carried by persons intent upon sexual attack."

Intravaginal Anti-Rape Items

The debate about rape often resonates with extreme and irrational emotions. The broad-based public sympathy—even adulation—afforded Lorena Bobbitt vividly demonstrated this. It is hardly surprising then, that the mechanical efforts of some inventors have been energized by the same sort of sentiments. This discussion of anti-rape implements is not for the squeamish. It consists of genuinely ghoulish machinery designed to halt a rape in progress by inflicting maximum mutilation and pain on the attacker's penis.

At the end of 1975, as the initial shock waves of *Against Our Will* were still reverberating, George Vogel of Buzzards Bay, Massachusetts, applied for a patent on the first such device: an anti-rape vaginal spike. "One of the important accomplishments of the women's rights movement is the increased public attention being focused on the subject of rape," he wrote. "Thousands of rape cases are reported

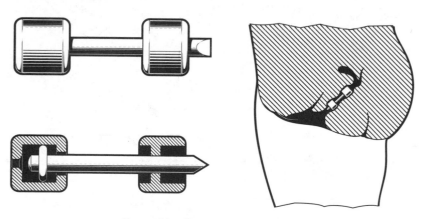

George Vogel's anti-rape vaginal spike
No. 4,030,490 (1977)

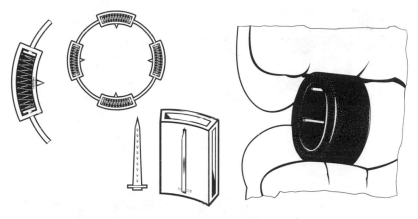

Alston Levesque's penis locking and lacerating vaginal insert
No. 4,016,875 (1977)

every year and the number is continuously rising. Perhaps even more important, however, is the recognition by the public that our system of justice and the psychological constraints imposed by our society have caused thousands more rapes per year to be unreported. While most women regard the possibility of being raped with a terror and a disgust bordering on psychosis, these feelings are almost equally strong against the possibility of being forced to publicly pursue conviction of the attacker. While the problem is by no means new, it appears that society is either unwilling or unable to cope with it. It appears, therefore, that, if rape prevention is to be accomplished, it must occur on the individual level."

He declared it was his intention to "provide a rape prevention device of the passive type, that is to say, a device that carries out its function without the necessity for violent aggressive action by the user, so that the device is effective when used by timid, frightened, or unconscious victims." Inserted in the vagina like a tampon, the device was a spike-like shaft of plastic sharpened to a cutting edge. It was held in place by two donut-like plastic padded rings.

Vogel went on to suggest that the "widespread and well-known

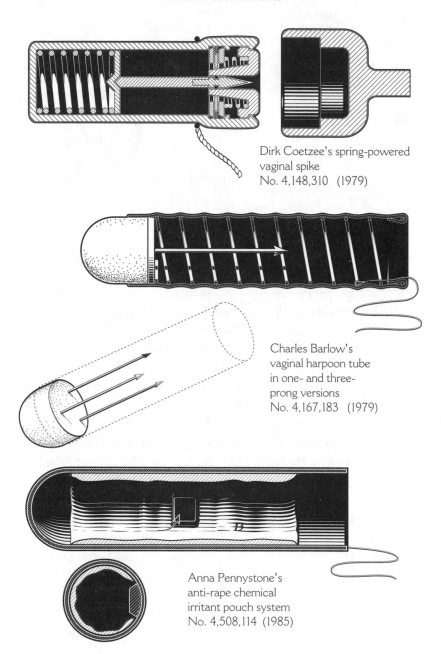

Dirk Coetzee's spring-powered
vaginal spike
No. 4,148,310 (1979)

Charles Barlow's
vaginal harpoon tube
in one- and three-
prong versions
No. 4,167,183 (1979)

Anna Pennystone's
anti-rape chemical
irritant pouch system
No. 4,508,114 (1985)

use of this device would create a deterrent effect far beyond the actual capability of the device because of the psychological factors such a pointed instrument would generate. It is also suggested that use of the present device can provide psychologically a sense of security for those women who are terrorized by the potential dangers of rape in our modern world."

Alston Levesque of Burlingame, California, followed with an invention he called a "Penis Locking and Lacerating Vaginal Insert." Shaped not unlike a circular, thin-walled cheese slicer, the mechanism of intricate springs and retracting blades fit unobtrusively inside the vagina. There, according to the inventor, "the penis may enter this device without great resistance and will activate the blades only upon the attempt of the man to withdraw the penis."

Levesque wrote: "This device may find use for those women who have enormous fears of being raped. It may also be of value for those women who have extreme discomfort in the presence of a man even on such intimate terms as dating. With this device in her possession a woman may feel secure that a male becoming intimate with her shall not receive pleasure from the experience."

A higher-powered lacerator was introduced by Dirk Coetzee, whose spring-loaded penis piercer was enclosed in a plastic, tampon-shaped container. It featured a heavy industrial spring cocked behind a nail-sized spike of surgical steel. When pressure was exerted against the front portion of the container by an unauthorized penis, the spring released, launching a two-inch spike.

The Vaginal Harpoon Tube

Charles Barlow of Tucson, Arizona, employed a similar spike idea, but a less complicated mechanical system, with his vaginal harpoon tube invention. Shaped like a vagina-lining sheath, its far end consisted of a plastic plug embedded with one to three two-inch surgical steel shafts fitted with double harpoon barbs at their points. The

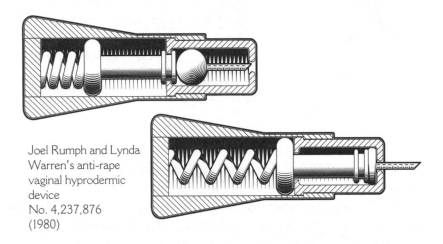

Joel Rumph and Lynda
Warren's anti-rape
vaginal hyprodermic
device
No. 4,237,876
(1980)

device had no moving parts and depended on the rapist impaling his own penis on the waiting spikes that penetrated the penis.

Turning to a form of chemical warfare, Anna Pennystone of Cincinnati, Ohio, devised a vaginal sheath device that contained an adhesive pouch of liquid irritant. The irritant was not exposed until the force of a penis entering the main sheath broke a protective covering. Thus, the rapist's first deep thrust resulted in a pouch of burning chemicals being glued around the forward surface of his penis. Pennystone explained: "The irritant contained within the pouch is a material which when it contacts the penis of a rapist will be immediately felt and the pain associated there will be such as to cause the rapist to terminate his attack and to withdraw."

Despite the fact that it was formally recognized as a new mechanical idea by the Patent Office, Pennystone's design—like the others in this category—would qualify as either a medical device or a dangerous weapon. Thus, it could only be offered for sale as a commercial product after various sorts of federal and state government approvals were granted. Given the issues of safety, product liability, and reasonableness raised by such implements, it is unlikely any of them would be approved for sale or use by any government authority.

Perhaps the most diabolically clever idea of the group was that of Joel Rumph and Lynda Warren of Elk Grove, California, who told the Patent Office: "Rape victims are frequently threatened with deadly weapons during the act of rape so that resistance is futile and sometimes fatal. It is not unknown for rapists to kill the victim to keep his identify unknown. Few rapists are ever caught at all, much less in the act, so that victims are discouraged from reporting the rape." To prevent a rape as well as ensure the easy capture of the rapist, the couple devised a vaginal, spring-loaded hypodermic needle device. Shaped somewhat like a flask to seat firmly in the vagina, it contained a spring-powered hypodermic needle loaded with a quick-acting anesthetic drug such as scopolamine to swiftly render a male unconscious.

When an unauthorized penis entered the vagina and pushed the front of the plastic device case, it triggered the spring, slamming the hypodermic needle an inch or more into the organ while injecting a knockout drug. The inventors note that not only did the victim escape as the rapist collapsed into unconsciousness, but the attacker was "left at the scene of the crime, with the evidence in hand, to be picked up by police."

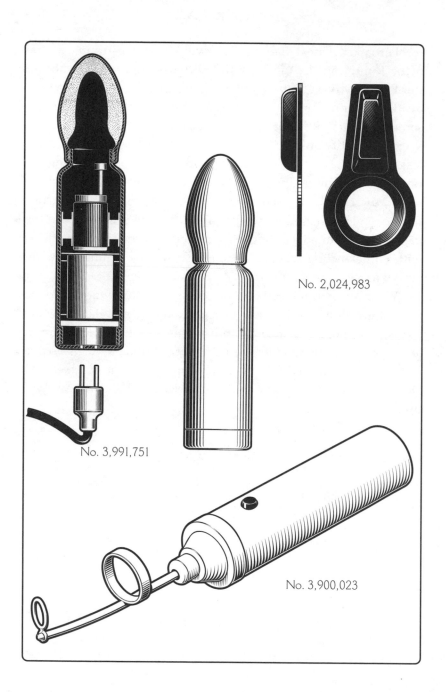

No. 2,024,983

No. 3,991,751

No. 3,900,023

14

Mechanical Stimulators

A study of American sex practices published in 1994 indicated that more than 16 percent of American women between the ages of 18 and 59 found the idea of using a dildo or vibrator at least "somewhat appealing." Four percent of those women reported actually using dildos or sex toys during the previous year. Four percent of this age group in a population of 250 million amounts to several million women.

Although the study was the first scientific one to gather credible data about the use of mechanical sexual stimulators, the findings seem to be in concert with a long record of invention as documented in the trading records, art, and literature of older civilizations.

For instance, during the time of the Greek city-states around 500 B.C., the demand for such implements made of wood and leather had become so great that at least one city in what is now Turkey set up phallus factories whose products were exported throughout the Mediterranean world. In China, one tubular plant was so commonly boiled and hardened for this purpose it became known as "Cantonese groin." Myths from Polynesia include stories of goddesses impregnated by the bananas they fondled beneath their flowing garments. The *Arabian Nights* included the ode: "O bananas, of soft and smooth skins, which dilate the eyes of young girls . . . you alone among fruits are endowed with a pitying heart, O consolers of widows and divorced women."

Hand-crafted phalluses were marketed throughout Europe in the Middle Ages. Clerics sternly denounced them as tools of the devil. Italy was the major manufacturing center for what was called a *passatempo*, or *diletto*. The same product was exported and sold in France as a *godemiche*, and in Germany as a *samthanse*. In England the item was known by several forms of the bastardized Italian word *diletto*, including *dildol*, *dil-do*, and *dildoe*.

By the eighteenth century, dildos were all the rage for hedonistic, socialite women of Europe's upper classes. Often complicated devices, they were hand-crafted of silver and ivory with internal chambers for warm water and other mechanical features that made their function more life-like. Sexual aids were popular outside of Europe as well. In his 1899 report on sexual habits in other cultures, Havelock Ellis indicated that affluent women in Japan, China, and India had long used motion-activated stimulators—hollow brass balls with central pendulum weights that were inserted in the vagina and vibrated in response to body movement.

Although it is now a mundane thing that goes without notice, the ability to mechanically produce controlled vibrations was one of the truly wondrous developments of the early industrial age. Initially, vibration was one of the great problems plaguing engineers who struggled to understand and eliminate the destructive movements caused by off-center drive shafts, unexpected vacuum actions in water lines, and improperly balanced wheels and gears. The same data provided the understanding later used to create controlled vibration mechanisms.

Vibrators: A New Technology

By the end of the 1800s, this knowledge had opened new frontiers of treatment and marketing for traveling healers and formal physicians alike. Massage, one of the oldest forms of physical therapy, had long used crude mechanical devices such as wooden rollers or spring-loaded pummeling boards to better knead a client's flesh.

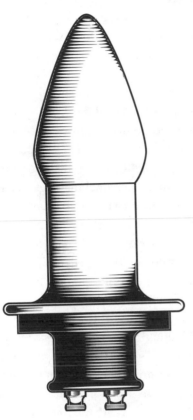

John Keough of Los Angeles applied for the first patent on an electric vaginal vibrator in 1911. It was granted in 1912.
No. 1,032,840 (1912)

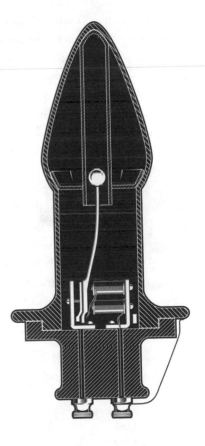

In turn-of-the-century America, hand-held vibrator units driven by hose-supplied water pressure were used by physicians, mystic healers, and barbers. In some cases, water power was used to turn internal mechanisms that created an air vacuum along with vibrations. Healers applied this seemingly magical vibrating suction as an enhanced therapy. Barbers used it to massage scalps as well as vacuum their clients' heads of dirt, dandruff, and insects.

The advent of indoor plumbing in the homes of the wealthy also created a new consumer market for hand-held vibrator devices that could be attached to the faucet of a bathtub or shower. In his 1907 patent application for a "Liquid-Actuated Vibrator," Clarence Richwood of Boston wrote that his invention would make personal massage available in a bathroom or sleeping room. It featured a rounded blunt head as well as a nubbed pad for vibrating various parts of the body as desired. Paul Hoffmann of New York was one of several inventors who improved the faucet-powered home vibrator; his unit was small enough to fit in the palm of the hand, had a variable-speed vibration control, and was, he said, designed to be "practically indestructible."

Meanwhile, others were exploring the idea of the electric-powered vibrator. For example, John T. Keough of Los Angeles tried to improve an existing medical implement—the dilator, which was used to gently expand or exercise the anal sphincter or vaginal muscles. In a 1911 patent application, Mr. Keough combined the concept of a dilator with that of a vibrator to create the first electric-powered vibrating vaginal insert. Shaped like the blunt tip of a large asparagus, his "vibratory dilator" had a metal and hard rubber body that contained an electrical apparatus that vibrated an armature against the outer casing. Aside from being a vibrating vaginal probe, the unit was designed as a tool for the then-popular practice of "electric medicine," and could be wired to send a mild electrical current into the walls of the vagina as well.

Into the Age of Aquarius

In the decade prior to World War II, the new field of "sexology" emerged as the broad body of the medical profession readjusted its thinking about sexuality and human health. For the first time, respected professionals began offering therapy sessions and workshops for sexually troubled married couples, who were encouraged to frankly discuss their sexual practices and frustrations. This revolutionary new approach not only acknowledged the desirability and positive effects of the female orgasm, but counseled that masturbation and mechanical sexual aids were a legitimate means for women to understand and better manage their own sexual functions as well as their marital relationships. The importance of clitoral stimulation was stressed to males and, almost immediately, gave rise to the invention of new passive clitoral stimulators such as that patented as the "Device for Promoting Marital Accord" or the "Helper Device."

In the 1960s this trend toward increasingly open discussion of sexual function rapidly combined with space-age technology—ranging from the processes needed to synthesize LSD to the miniaturization of the electronic components that made electric guitars possible—to create revolutionary changes in sexual technique.

New plastics, tiny motors, and more efficient battery systems had a significant impact on inventors working on fully automated sexual aids. In 1966, in a patent application for a product that could well stand as *the* symbol of the Age of Aquarius, Jon H. Tavel of Encino, California, presented the Patent Office with drawings for a cordless, one-piece, moisture-proof, battery-powered, variable-speed, torpedo-shaped, vibrating plastic dildo. The culmination of ages of artificial phallus design, the Tavel concept became one of the best-selling and most popular sexual stimulators of all time.

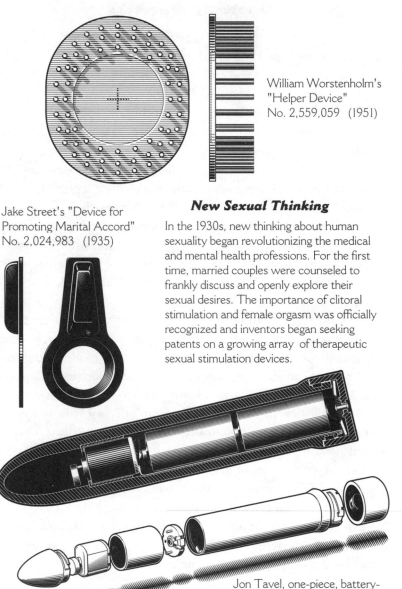

William Worstenholm's
"Helper Device"
No. 2,559,059 (1951)

Jake Street's "Device for
Promoting Marital Accord"
No. 2,024,983 (1935)

New Sexual Thinking

In the 1930s, new thinking about human sexuality began revolutionizing the medical and mental health professions. For the first time, married couples were counseled to frankly discuss and openly explore their sexual desires. The importance of clitoral stimulation and female orgasm was officially recognized and inventors began seeking patents on a growing array of therapeutic sexual stimulation devices.

Jon Tavel, one-piece, battery-
powered vaginal vibrator
No. 3,549,920 (1968)

With a battery pack that straps on the belly, and various attachments, the "Medical Gynecologic Oscillator" provides continuous stimulation to both the clitoral and vaginal regions.
No. 3,504,665 (1970)

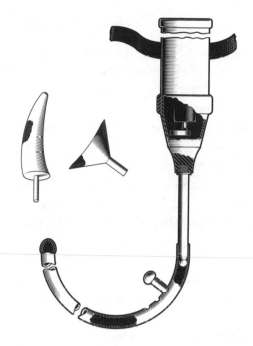

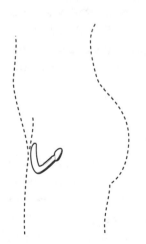

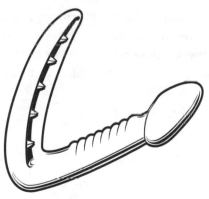

Mark Sekulich's "Self-Contained Gynecologic Stimulator" is inserted and worn beneath the clothes.
No. 3,996,930 (1976)

Gynecological Oscillators

Using the same sort of battery-powered and miniature-motor technology, but a uniquely different structural design, Maurice Bakunin, Leonard Napoli, and Raphael Costanzo of Connecticut patented what they called a "Medical Gynecologic Oscillator." The battery pack was held in place on the belly by a waist strap. A long, vibrating stem stretched from there to engage the clitoral area with a special protrusion, then continued to curve under for insertion into the vagina. When switched on, the unit delivered variable-speed vibrations to the clitoris as well as the forward wall of the vagina. A series of differently shaped attachments were also included for use at either the clitoral or vaginal position.

In a separate communication to the Patent Office, Mark Sekulich of Long Beach, California, criticized such belly-mounted, battery-powered gynecological units because they were "cumbersome to carry about and inconvenient to use, as well as having an initial negative psychological effect on the female partner." Sekulich sought a patent for his own unusual stimulator design, which was simple yet sophisticated in its use of unique materials and shapes to create a non-powered but automated mechanical clitoral stimulator. A V-shaped inverted trough device of soft plastic, one of its legs fit within the labia to cover the clitoris while the other leg was inserted into the vagina, where it pressed against the forward wall in the vicinity of the reputed "G" spot.

Male Stimulators

The 1960s also saw the invention of automated male stimulation devices that fell into two categories: those that were attached to the penis to turn it into a living vibrator for exciting female partners and those designed as imitation vaginas for male masturbation. In 1964, Meyer Katz of Melrose Park, Pennsylvania, submitted a design for an electric-powered vibrating collar that fit around the base of the penis. The rubber collar was attached to a thin solid rod that was, in turn, attached to an electrical vibration generator powered by standard 110-volt wall current. During intercourse, the rod fit between the male and female partners, delivering vibration to the penile collar. This caused that male organ to vibrate vigorously, stimulating the female organ it was penetrating. This idea was refined further in 1974 by Ralph McBride of Houston who made the entire affair much smaller and powered it with a D-cell battery pack shaped like the handle of a flashlight. It could be held in one hand to vibrate the penis at the push of a button. A third version by Bireswar Bysakh extended the collar into a cone shape that partially penetrated the vagina along with the penis. It was designed as both a mechanical clitoral stimulator and a penile vibrator.

Automated imitation vaginas were initially suggested by large-scale mechanized massage machines built earlier this century for hospital use, particularly with paraplegic patients. These instruments featured pneumatic rubber "cuffs" that fit around an arm or leg or even an entire torso and pneumatically undulated to create pressure waves. In 1966, Cesareo Barrio filed a patent application for a small version of such a machine with a plastic donut-like sleeve to receive the penis. A few years later, P. Brav Sobel of Miami Beach, Florida, patented a sophisticated penis-rotating/swinging stroking device that included a variety of attachments such as a padded tube into which a penis could be inserted to be "massaged by gentle movement" of the battery-powered system.

A tabletop-sized hydraulic orgasm machine was patented in 1975 featuring a vagina-like rubber massage sleeve. Among other things, the inventor envisioned such equipment being sold to sperm banks to automate collection procedures—a suggestion that conjures up the image of groups of males hooked to such devices in a commercial establishment much like herds of dairy cows attached to automatic milkers in high-tech barns.

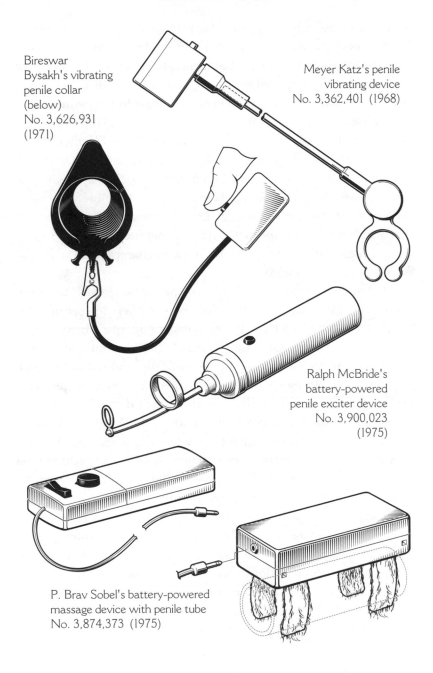

Bireswar
Bysakh's vibrating
penile collar
(below)
No. 3,626,931
(1971)

Meyer Katz's penile
vibrating device
No. 3,362,401 (1968)

Ralph McBride's
battery-powered
penile exciter device
No. 3,900,023
(1975)

P. Brav Sobel's battery-powered
massage device with penile tube
No. 3,874,373 (1975)

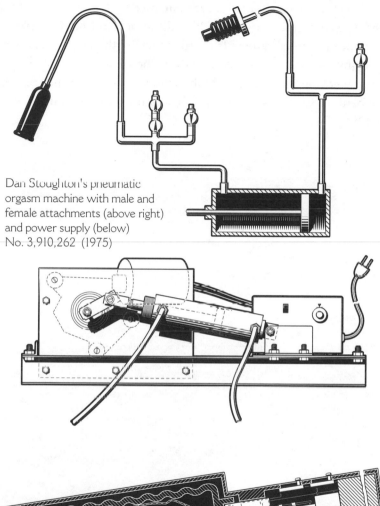

Dan Stoughton's pneumatic orgasm machine with male and female attachments (above right) and power supply (below) No. 3,910,262 (1975)

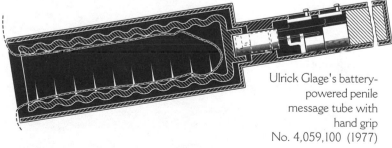

Ulrick Glage's battery-powered penile message tube with hand grip No. 4,059,100 (1977)

The final male stimulator was patented by Ulrick Glage in 1976 and was the exact inverse of the dildo: a hand-held, one-piece, moisture-proof, vibrating plastic tube lined with flesh-like rubber to fit firmly around the whole length of the penis. Holding it by its convenient handle, one can slip the vibrating device to and fro along the penis or simply leave it in place, vibrating quietly until its work is done.

15

Coital Harnesses and Sex Furniture

One of the most cherished notions enshrined in our patent system is that just about anything can be improved if sufficient amounts of Yankee ingenuity are applied to the task. This enduring belief—as well the possibility that a good buck might be scored in the process— has made America a land of indefatigable amateur inventors forever in search of some new device that answers a previously unarticulated public concern—say, the routine hazards and discomforts inherent to lovemaking. We're talking about *real* lovemaking here, not the kind you see in movies or read about in novels, about what *really* happens across America each day as millions of human couples of wildly varying shapes, weights, and dexterity come together as single, thrashing units of intertwined limbs and precariously shifting centers of gravity.

Major height or weight differences between a male and female can be a critical factor in their level of mutual enjoyment during sex, particularly when they assume a traditional position with a female beneath a male. It was this very of situation that Bernie Gallant of San Diego was addressing when submitting a patent application for his "Dual Occupancy Cradle." He explained, "In the past there have apparently been numerous devices developed very privately by some wealthy persons to minister to their needs and whims in the matter of the most private facet of family life, but there is no known

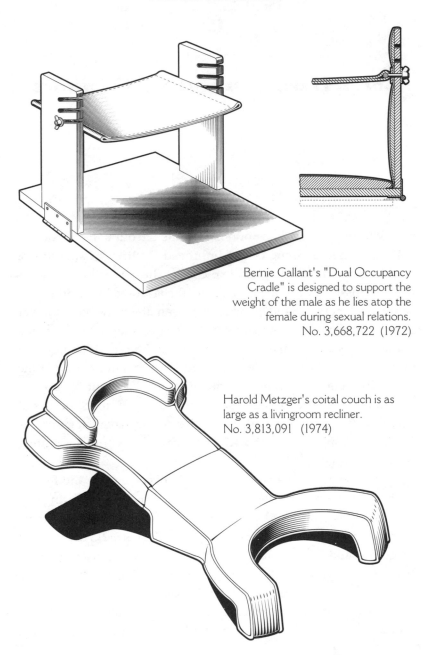

Bernie Gallant's "Dual Occupancy
Cradle" is designed to support the
weight of the male as he lies atop the
female during sexual relations.
No. 3,668,722 (1972)

Harold Metzger's coital couch is as
large as a livingroom recliner.
No. 3,813,091 (1974)

large production of any equipment for the specific purpose of supporting the weight of the superimposed love partner."

Gallant's invention was actually more of a sling than a cradle—a double-decker piece of padded furniture that could be placed on top of a bed. The female partner lay on the bottom, while the male lay his body in a small hammock-like sling that supported his weight yet allowed freedom of movement.

The Coital Couch

Along similar lines, Harold Metzger of Alabama created what might be thought of as a "Coital Couch"—a piece of furniture as large as a living room recliner for what he termed "recumbent copulative purposes." The Metzger coital couch was designed to cradle the body of a female in a partially reclined position with her legs spread. Leg rests extended outward from the low end of the couch like the prongs of a "Y" executed in upholstery. A male, resting on his knees, was able to comfortably penetrate the woman in this position. Although the idea of such a piece of furniture seems amusing to many, it had a serious purpose. Along with simply enhancing the sexual relations of a normal, healthy couple, it also allowed a female disabled by disease or age to continue to have sexual relations with her husband in a manner that was reasonably enjoyable for both.

Sex Harnesses

In 1952 the Patent Office granted the first patent for a sex harness to Lewis Twyman of Miami, Florida. A construction of canvas straps, quick-release mechanisms, and fasteners that seems to owe much to advances made in the field of parachute rigging during the war, Twyman's invention was a girdle-like device that fit around the waist of the female and trailed a large single stirrup at ankle level. In operation, this allowed a male to climb between a female's legs and

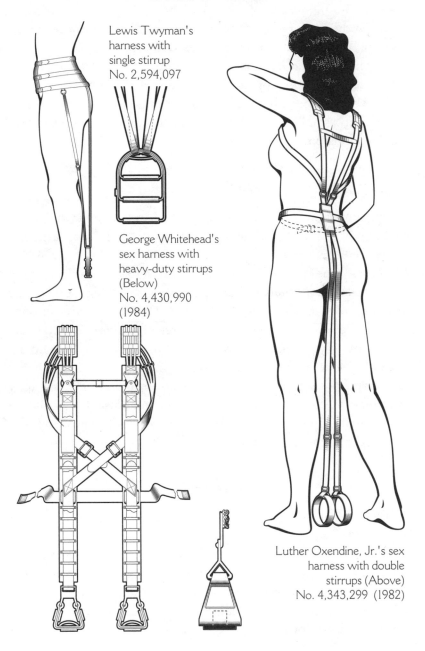

Lewis Twyman's
harness with
single stirrup
No. 2,594,097

George Whitehead's
sex harness with
heavy-duty stirrups
(Below)
No. 4,430,990
(1984)

Luther Oxendine, Jr.'s sex
harness with double
stirrups (Above)
No. 4,343,299 (1982)

anchor one or both of his feet in the stirrup. Thus, the two partners were effectively held in a position that eliminated slippage across the bed surface as they performed the sex act.

Other inventors who followed with improved sex harnesses indicated that the major market for such devices was among older persons suffering from heart and other diseases that limited their ability to engage in physically strenuous activities. Ronald Withers of Virginia introduced a sex harness system that was a solid piece of furniture that fit against the headboard of a bed and had adjustable shoulder pads as well as a set of double stirrups. He explained, "Because of this apparatus, the use of the back, chest, shoulder and arm muscles, normally associated with sexual activity and which could be injurious to the overall health of a cardiac patient, is substantially reduced by transferring at least about 50 percent or more of the physical exertion associated with the use of these muscles to the legs of the individual." Two similar therapeutic stirruped sex harnesses have also been patented in recent years.

Ronald Withers' headboard sex harness with double stirrups
No. 3,896,787 (1975)

Sex Handles

In a somewhat lighter vein, Elaine Lerner of Stoughton, Massachusetts, in 1985 received a patent for a unique harness-like device that could be called "sex handles." The invention had a waistband and

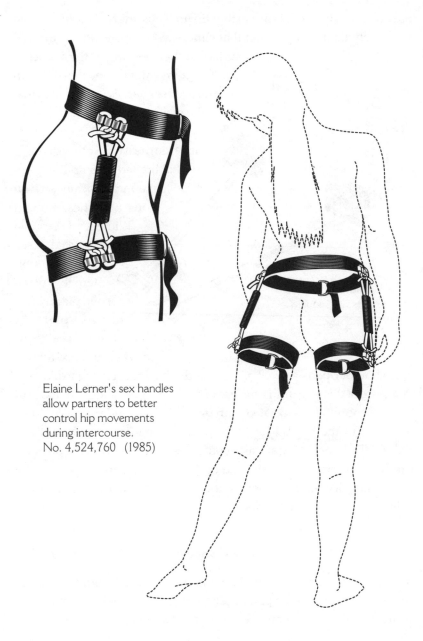

Elaine Lerner's sex handles
allow partners to better
control hip movements
during intercourse.
No. 4,524,760 (1985)

thigh bands connected on the outside of each hip by the same kind of padded handles found on suitcases. While engaged in the sexual act, the device allowed the male to take a firm hold of the female's lower body and precisely move it around in ways that enhanced the pleasure of both partners. Lerner told the patent examiners, "None of the various sexual aids heretofore known, as far as I am aware, provide a means whereby one sexual partner can actually control the hip movement of the other during intercourse."

Although such inventions as these may initially seem goofy and make us smile, they are also among the best examples of how American ingenuity *has* crossed with real sexual need to create solutions to widespread problems that have otherwise gone unacknowledged by society. In their intention to create original new mechanical concepts with the potential to improve the lives of large numbers of ordinary people, these harness and furniture inventors are perfect examples of the kind of practical innovation the U.S. patent system was originally established to encourage.

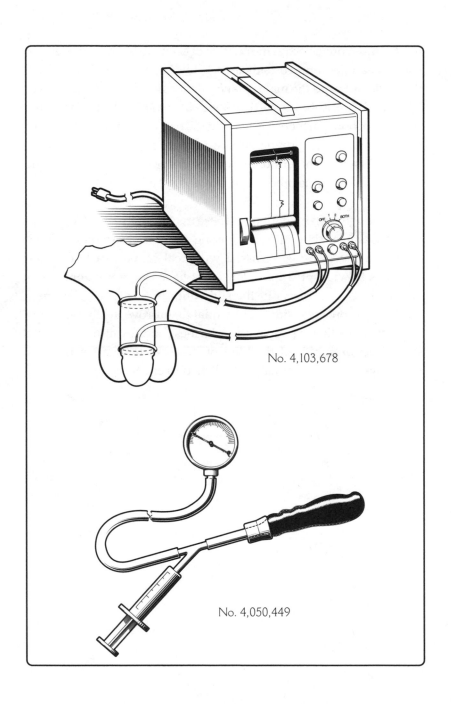

No. 4,103,678

No. 4,050,449

16

Exercisers and Monitors

A woman's sexual response is, to a large degree, a mechanical matter of muscle tone. The basket of bones framing the female pelvis is criss-crossed with slings of muscles that are themselves penetrated by three additional muscle systems: the vagina, urethra, and rectum. These interconnected hammocks and tubes of muscles, in unison with their complex nerve systems, physically support the functions of urination, defecation, sexual excitement, and orgasm. Throughout most of our history, the critical importance of such muscles was often not obvious to women who never saw, felt, or consciously used them. It was known that prolapse of the uterus was caused by muscle failure. And earlier in this century, it was recognized that weak or damaged muscles in this area could dramatically affect a woman's health in other ways as well. For instance, pregnancy results in urinary incontinence as muscles that close the urethra are weakened.

By the 1920s it became a standard practice among some physicians to include vaginal muscle-strengthening exercises in the overall treatment for various gynecological problems. Initially, female patients were simply told to squeeze their vaginal muscles repeatedly each day, but for many women who had never visualized or tried to access these invisible muscles, such exercises proved difficult. Thus, it was inevitable that creative doctors would begin to think about mechanical exercisers that provided a more positive sense of muscle engagement.

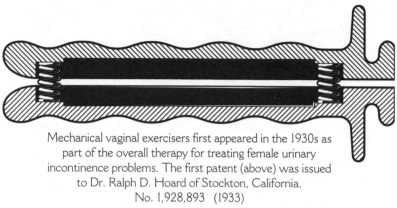

Mechanical vaginal exercisers first appeared in the 1930s as part of the overall therapy for treating female urinary incontinence problems. The first patent (above) was issued to Dr. Ralph D. Hoard of Stockton, California. No. 1,928,893 (1933)

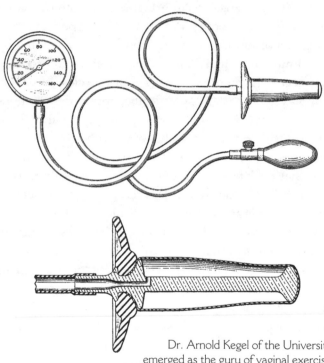

Dr. Arnold Kegel of the University of California emerged as the guru of vaginal exercise in the 1950s. He invented air-pressure devices that exercised and measured the strength of vaginal muscle systems. No. 2,541,520 (1951)

The first patent for a vaginal exercising machine was issued to a California physician in 1931. He told the Patent Office: "I have practiced obstetrics for some years and have recognized the value of exercising the vaginal muscles. Heretofore, however, such exercising has been performed by the patient by a squeezing action of the part affected and without the aid of any mechanical appliance. This has proved of great benefit but as far as the possible effectiveness of an exercising treatment is concerned, it may be compared to performing dumbbell exercises without using the dumbbells themselves." His vaginal exercising insert was a simple two-sided tubular affair held slightly apart by springs. The sides could be squeezed shut against spring pressure, forcing the muscles to work against an actively resisting force.

Therapy for Female Sex Muscles

In the 1950s, gynecologist Arnold H. Kegel of the University of California began developing a comprehensive vaginal muscle exercise program that became so widely used it is still known as "Kegel's" today. Initially, the doctor was seeking a means to assist women in overcoming urinary incontinence. However, the same women reported that the rigorous exercises had also increased their sexual response, intensifying orgasms in some and making orgasms possible for the first time in others. Thus was discovered the true importance of the previously ignored female sex muscles. In fact, later studies would find that large numbers of the women who sought treatment for frigidity—the lack of sexual response—had functional use of as little as 10 percent of their vaginal muscles. It was the lack of tone and strength throughout these invisible muscle systems that had diminished or eliminated the mechanical ability of the patient's body to respond in a sexual manner.

Dr. Kegel's exercises were soon being widely used for treating female sexual dysfunction. And in order to monitor the progress of

Howard Sasse's personal vaginal exerciser was shaped much like a fluid-filled dildo with a pressure gauge on its end.
No. 4,048,985 (1977)

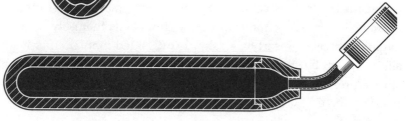

Philip De Langis's vaginal exerciser delivered two kinds of electrical pulses that contracted the vaginal muscles, automatically performing exercises for the user.
No. 3,640,284 (1972)

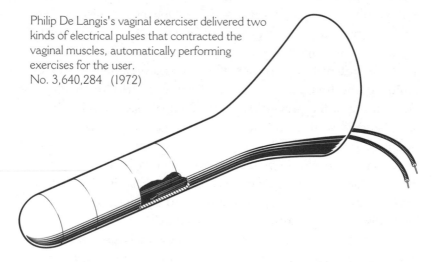

patients, he invented and patented an air-pressure instrument which measured the strength of the "grip" of flexed vaginal muscles. A hollow rubber probe inserted into the vagina was connected to an air-pressure gauge that provided direct feedback that helped women initially find and control the correct muscles. Then, as their exercise programs continued, it also provided a measure of their progress in strengthening those muscles.

Over the years, a number of gynecologists and medical equipment specialists patented variations on the same idea of an instrument that exercised and/or measured the gripping function of female sexual muscles. Some later inventors faulted Dr. Kegel's system because, they said, "clinical interviews have uncovered patient complaints about the large size of the sensing member of Kegel's apparatus. This is a factor that contributes both to a patient's physical and psychological discomfort. As with any device designed to be inserted vaginally, two patient psychologic objections must be overcome, phallic fear and masturbatory guilt. Ordinarily physician reassurance helps to allay these objections, but flesh color and the penis-like stem of the Kegel apparatus aggravate these objections."

Other inventors went the other way and *sought* to make vaginal exercise devices that were more penis-like. For instance, Howard Sasse of Buffalo, New York, created a small, economical exerciser that amounted to a fluid-filled dildo with a pressure gauge on its end. He told the patent examiners, "The device may be utilized to develop pressure skills in complete privacy. Such practice on a periodic routine basis with the device can give the user knowledge and skill in applying such pressures so as to give maximum enjoyment to both sexual partners when such skills are used in actual sexual encounters."

Space-Age Vaginal Electronics

A new, high-tech approach to such therapy was unveiled in Dr. Philip A. De Langis's 1972 patent for a vaginal electrode device that

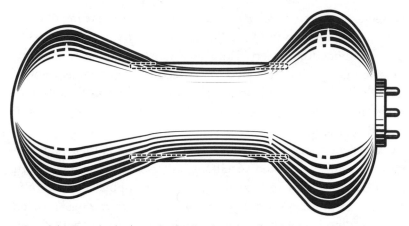

John Perry's electronic biofeedback system "reads" the electronic
activity of the vaginal muscles, providing real-time audio or visual
signals that allow a woman to more efficiently train her sex muscles.
No. 4,396,019 (1983)

automatically administered low-level electrical pulses caused the
vaginal muscle systems to automatically contract. It was a machine
that, in effect, performed the exercises for the woman. As sleekly
shaped as a space-age implement, the De Langis device was pro-
grammed to use two kinds of electrical impulses to exercise both
smooth and striated muscles and, according to the inventor, its use
resulted in "significant reduction in female frigidity, relief from
urinary incontinence difficulties, and improvement of other urogeni-
tal anomalies."

However, some gynecological authorities objected to the concept
of electric shock and automated vaginal exercises. John Perry, Jr., told
the Patent Office that such electrical devices "require the application
of an electrical shock to the human body which, however mild in
intent, necessitates close supervision of the manufacture, design and
application of the devices. In addition, such electrical shocks are
strongly feared and objected to by many patients."

Dr. Perry patented an electronic vaginal "myograph" that detected the changing electrical impulses naturally generated by muscles as they contract and relax. It was designed as the central piece in a biofeedback system that provided women with real-time audio or visual feedback on exactly what their vaginal muscles were doing.

Male Sexual Muscle Measuring Systems

Meanwhile, similarly sophisticated sex muscle measuring devices were also being created for males. Their focus was documentation of the frequency and length of nocturnal erections.

Erections that occur during sleep are now recognized by the medical profession as a barometer of many aspects of a male's sexual health. For instance, there are two kinds of impotence—one caused by psychological problems and the other caused by malfunctions of the actual biological plumbing and muscular systems that create an erection. It is often difficult for physicians to identify the root cause of a man's impotence as organic or psychological because psychological dysfunction can so completely block the operation of the muscular machinery that the two are indistinguishable. However, it was discovered that males who are psychologically prevented from having erections during their waking hours still have several involuntary erections at night—like all other physically healthy males. At the same time, males suffering some form of organic malfunction cannot support erections at any time. Thus, as a matter of diagnosis in impotence cases, it has become important to quickly ascertain whether the patient has erections as he sleeps.

The Postage Stamp Penile Test

Initially, several low-tech systems were used to monitor a given male patient's nocturnal penile behavior. Some clinics maintained sleeping rooms where nurses watched throughout the night, monitoring

Electronics came to play an
important role in monitoring the noctural penile
activity of impotent men.
Here, a strip chart records
the collected data.
No. 4,103,678 (1978)

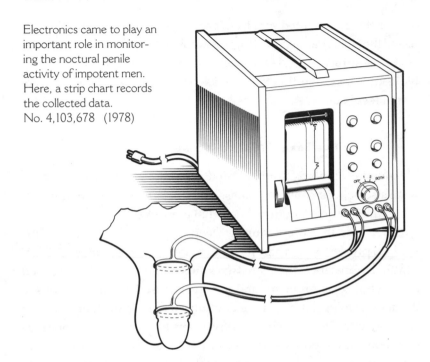

and recording visible penile activity. However, authorities report
that this method proved "both expensive and embarrassing to the
patient." Other physicians began using the "postage stamp tumescence test." This method is as simple as it sounds. A patient was
advised to wrap a row of postage stamps around his penis before
going to bed. The leading edge of the last stamp was wetted so that
it adhered to form a closed paper ring. During the night, if the penis
become erect, it would break the perforated stamp ring. Patients were
usually told to conduct the test three nights in a row. However, this
procedure was subject to a number of variables, some stamp types
were strong enough to resist breaking, while others broke from the
simple movements of sleep without an erection.

In 1977 a team of medical instrument designers applied for a
patent on a bedside strip chart recorder that was attached to the

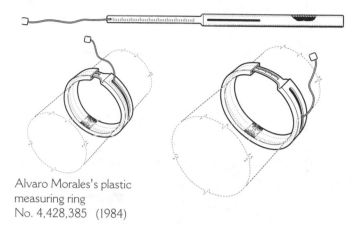

Alvaro Morales's plastic
measuring ring
No. 4,428,385 (1984)

Erection Measuring Technology:
From Very Simple to Very Complicated

In the 1980s, the long-ignored national problem of male impotence came out of the closet to be addressed by a growing number of physicians and clinics. Because of the importance of nocturnal erection data to the diagnosis of the cause of impotence, a number of tumescence measuring inventions appeared in the 1980s, ranging from the very simple plastic items on this page to the involved desktop computer system shown on the facing page.

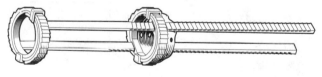

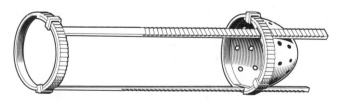

Abraham Goldstein's erection girth and length measuring device
No. 4,469,108 (1984)

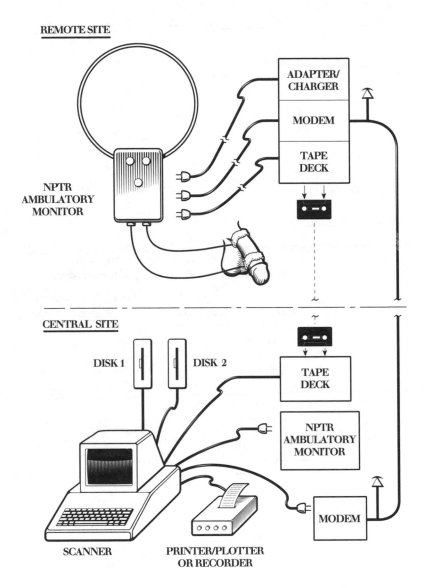

REMOTE SITE

ADAPTER/ CHARGER

MODEM

TAPE DECK

NPTR AMBULATORY MONITOR

CENTRAL SITE

DISK 1   DISK 2

TAPE DECK

NPTR AMBULATORY MONITOR

MODEM

SCANNER   PRINTER/PLOTTER OR RECORDER

Gerald Timm designed this desktop system for monitoring nocturnal penile tumescence for the Dacomed Corporation, a medical instrumentation company. No. 4,515,166 (1985)

patient's penis with electronic "strain gauges." These encircled the penis in two places and produced different electrical signals as they were expanded or contracted. A long set of wires connected the gauges to the bedside recorder. The machine then documented all changes that occurred in the circumference of the penis throughout the night.

Another inventor patented a simple penis-encircling plastic device that functioned much the same as postage stamps, but with more accurate results. Put on the penis in a manner not unlike the way a watch is put on a wrist, the inexpensive, lightweight plastic band moved to accommodate penile expansion. Ruler-like measuring marks allowed the patient to note the exact extent of the widest penile expansion documented during the night. Inventors of other, similar plastic band devices added improvements like extensions to indicate the length of a night's longest erection.

In the mid-1980s, as the desktop computer revolution took firm hold across the country, Dacomed Corporation of Minneapolis received a patent for a complicated system that allowed a computer to be connected to a penis via electronic monitoring collars with snap couplings. The constant stream of output was then sent to the desktop computer that collected and collated it in a database program.

Electronic Sex Sheath

The use of such electronic sensing systems to study and record the operations of human sexual organs is a field that has become ever more sophisticated since the 1960s, when Doctors William Masters and Virginia Johnson began comprehensive studies of human sexual response. They used all manner of electronic, photographic, and thermal devices to record the biological functions occurring in, on, and around human sexual organs during all stages of sexual excitation and orgasm. When Masters and Johnson began publishing their findings—the first in-depth mechanical documentation of what actually happens during sexual arousal and intercourse—they created a publishing sensation that helped popularize the idea that sexual "efficiency" was something to be achieved through better mechanical controls. Clinics offering sex therapy became a growing market for instruments that could provide diagnostically useful sexual data.

One of the inventors who addressed this new market was Rafael Carrera of Bethesda, Maryland, who, in 1968, received a patent for an electronic sex sheath that monitored and recorded activity along the surfaces of the penis and vagina during intercourse. Worn by the male like a condom, the sheath had miniature pressure-monitoring sensors embedded along its surface, each outputting a signal to a central data collection instrument. The Carrera electronic sex sheath gathered data about the friction pressure generated along the sex organs by each penile stroke. For instance, a strip chart recorder could capture and show the exact patterns and intensity of pressure experienced in the clitoral area. This, Carrera indicated, allowed clinicians to assist male patients in adjusting their body positions or strokes to better stimulate their female partners. The device also tracked and recorded the waves of muscle spasms that occurred in both male and female during orgasm. Carrera told the patent examiners that his product was designed for "training married couples to achieve maximum efficiency in sexual relations."

The Future

The inventors of these various systems of sex muscle exercising and monitoring equipment have almost all been directly involved in the professional treatment of sexual dysfunction. Therefore, they generally have a better grasp of the scope of this problem than most laymen.

In fact, although American movies, television, novels, and music bombard us with images of sexually insatiable and fulfilled women, scientific surveys indicate that the majority of females are neither.

The normal reality appears to be that American women enjoy a relatively low level of sexual gratification. The latest 1994 study of sexual behavior documented that one out of every five women felt that sex was not pleasurable at all and only 29 percent of the nation's females experience orgasm every time they have sexual relations.

In many instances, the simple lack of adequate sex muscle conditioning and control may play a significant role. This seems particularly likely in a general population renowned for its increas-

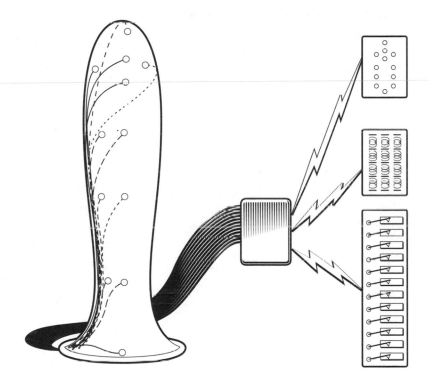

Rafael Carrera's electronic sex monitoring sheath
No. 3,417,743 (1968)

ingly sedentary habits and overall lack of exercise. Thus, it's not difficult to see the large potential national market that has already lured so many inventors into the Patent Office with sex muscle devices. Given the extensive interest already shown in the field as well as the latest breakthroughs occurring in the electronic and biological sciences, one can only wonder how long it will be before patents are issued for anabolic steroids engineered to target *only* the sexual muscles or laser-guided performance management systems that will turn the treatment rooms of sexual clinics into something resembling virtual-reality arcade games.

17

Safe Sex Inventions for the Age of AIDS

In the 1980s, a bill of sorts came due for the behavior hailed during the previous two decades as America's sexual revolution. As it turned out, one of the aspects of society most revolutionized by slackening sexual bounds was the rate of sexually transmitted disease. It sky-rocketed. First an epidemic of herpes broke out, infecting tens of millions with an incurable ailment that caused sexual organs to bloom with oozing sores. And then came AIDS.

In the fall of 1986, then-U.S. Surgeon General C. Everett Koop stunned the nation with the announcement that AIDS had not only become an epidemic, but required drastic changes in the nation's sexual behavior and attitudes if it was to *ever* be brought under control. He unequivocally urged the widespread use of condoms and the initiation of new types of open national discussions about sexual facts and practices.

As with any national catastrophe, the AIDS crisis has created winners and losers—people who lost all, including their lives, to a ruthless virus, and people who prospered by chasing the government and media-driven market for AIDS-related merchandise. For instance, in the immediate wake of Dr. Koop's public endorsement of condoms as the most effective protection against AIDS, the value of stock in condom companies increased by as much as 170 percent. It was just the sort of news that sets entrepreneurs vibrating.

Across America, the rush was suddenly on to perfect and patent the ultimate safe sex device—an idea that turned out to be easier to envision as a possibility than to execute as a profitable product. The basic problem was as maddening and curious a puzzle as any that ever confronted an inventor: how best to allow human beings to engage in sex without any actual skin contact with each other? Some of the proposed mechanical strategies were, to say the least, strange. They ranged from wet suit-like rubber body sheaths to gawky, strap-on genital barrier contraptions to fully automated sex robots. This last idea of safe sex androids was patented by two different inventors and designed to completely eliminate the need for potentially hazardous couplings with a living partner.

Some inventors have scored commercial successes of a sort. For instance, one version of the six different kinds of female condoms patented to date has been approved by the U.S. Food and Drug Administration. The subject of much national press coverage, it is being distributed by a Wisconsin pharmaceutical firm.

But other inventors have racked up large losses chasing the same elusive market. Dr. A. V. K. Reddy of Hanna, Wyoming, told reporters he spent $12 million in a comprehensive program to launch his patented female condom bikini product line. Unable to obtain the required approval of the FDA, the physician-inventor was left with a colorful collection of prototype products, slick packaging, display racks, promotional materials, advertisements, and debts.

Despite such risk, competition among inventors remains fierce. For instance, at least three different individuals have obtained patents for slightly different versions of the same essential concept of attaching a pocket to underwear shorts to hold a condom.

Pioneering New Forms of the Male Condom

The condom itself still continues as something of a touchstone of this inventive field—if for no other reason than that it is still officially

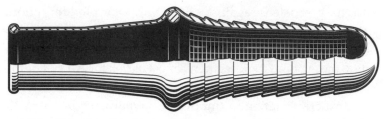

Michael Meadows' double-layered condom used lubricants and internal texturing to enhance the stimulating effect for males.
No. 4,798,600 (1989)

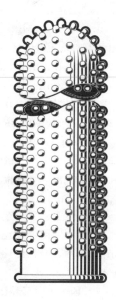

Bernard Haines' "sensory transmitting membrane" used special soft nubs to directly transfer motion across a latex barrier from the surface of one sexual organ to another.
No. 4,852,586 (1989)

Michael Stang's flavor-dispensing condom
No. 4,919,149 (1990)

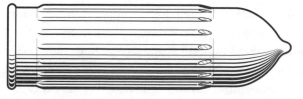

hailed as the best defense against AIDS. Despite the plodding efforts of health authorities to achieve wider acceptance of condoms, the majority of sexually active people in the country still don't use them, including those population segments most at risk for AIDS. For this reason, local and national government agencies have actively encouraged experimentation and innovation in *any* direction that might result in discoveries that make condoms more tolerable or desirable.

In his 1987 patent application, Michael Meadows of Hatboro, Pennsylvania, explained that the primary reason males still don't use condoms is because doing so lessens the sensations of intercourse. His new design was a double-layered condom that used lubricants and special texturing to internally simulate the feel of the female vagina—a condom that was also a sex toy. In use, the main sheath remained anchored in place in the partner's vagina while the second sheath on the male's organ moved in and out with a soft, fluid friction.

Seeking to achieve a similar stimulating effect with electronic action, Gary Johnson of New York patented an "electrically conductive" condom. Its rubber membrane was embedded with electrically conductive carbon particles which, Johnson said, would transmit the minute electrical impulses given off by the living membranes of the sexual organs. Johnson told the Patent Office that he had determined that the reason natural lambskin condoms were more stimulating than latex condoms was because they transmitted the natural electrical currents in a manner that latex could not.

Taking a completely different approach, Bernard Haines of Colorado devised a revolutionary "sensation transmission membrane" for condoms. The simple look of the material belied its interesting mechanical properties. Resembling "textured" or ribbed condoms previously patented for female stimulation, his condom had short, soft rubber nubs all over it. But each of the nubs extended completely through the condom membrane so that both the surface of the penis and the surface of the vagina were in contact with opposite ends of the same nubs during intercourse. The tiny rod-like

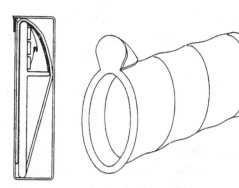

Paul Lyons' musical condom employs a sound-producing computer chip activated by pressure. No. 5,163,447 (1992)

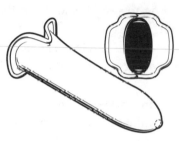

Max Freimark
No. 4,004,591 (1977)

Female Condoms

The Patent Office has issued patents to six inventors for female condoms, including the three shown here.

Roberto Quiroz
No. 4,875,490
(1989)

David Robichaud
No. 4,794,920
(1989)

nubs used their point of passage through the membrane as individual fulcrums. Slight movement against one end of a nub was directly duplicated in the reverse at its other end. Because they operated as individual units, the nubs were able to "communicate" or transmit even delicate motion directly to the surface of the organs, enhancing and even amplifying the sensations for both male and female partners.

Michael Stang of Maryland in 1988 submitted an application for a condom with a "flavor delivery system." He explained to the patent examiners that the purpose of his invention was enhancing the desirability of condoms and "adding to sexual enjoyment through the release of a pleasantly flavored composition." The sides of the Stang condom were girded with rows of flavor-dispensing tubes loaded with semi-solid ingestible compositions that became liquid when subjected to body heat.

Pursuing another novelty condom marketing idea, Paul Lyons of Massachusetts patented a condom embedded with a computer chip capable of recording and playing music. Mounted at the open lip of the condom, the musical computer chip was activated by pressure. Lyons told the Patent Office: "It is the object of this invention to provide a condom which users will like to use." He noted that the condom's miniature playback device could "incorporate musical compositions of the user's choice according to the occasion," and that "the music or voice message may be played once, or it may be repeated continuously for several minutes to coincide with the duration of coitus."

Female Condoms

As previously mentioned, the best-known alternative condom structure to emerge in the AIDS era has been the female condom—a concept initially patented in 1977 as a device to give women better control of their sexual relations. Since 1986, five more inventors have

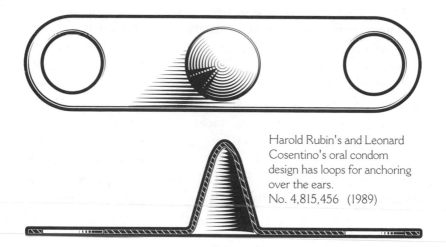

Harold Rubin's and Leonard Cosentino's oral condom design has loops for anchoring over the ears.
No. 4,815,456 (1989)

Oral Condoms

As national health authorities identified oral sex as a common route for the spread of the AIDS virus, two patents were issued for mouth condoms to be used during oral sex.

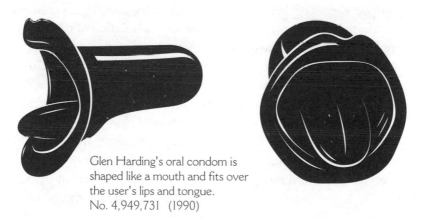

Glen Harding's oral condom is shaped like a mouth and fits over the user's lips and tongue.
No. 4,949,731 (1990)

patented improved versions of female condoms. All are similar in that they fit into the vagina like a sheath or pouch and have a plastic ring, a flange, flaps, or small leg straps that hang outside the vagina to hold them in place. The first of these was approved for sale in 1993, but despite widespread publicity, it has not been a runaway success. Women have been critical of its feel and sound (it is reported to squeak slightly when in use) and have also been somewhat put off by its reportedly low effectiveness as a contraceptive. Initial studies found that as many as 26 percent of those who used it regularly became pregnant. However, health authorities strongly recommend its regular use as a preventive device against AIDS.

Oral Condoms

Within weeks of each other in 1987, three inventors submitted applications for patents on two versions of an "oral prophylactic"— a condom designed for wearing in the mouth during oral sex. The first version of this unusual concept was designed by two Ohio men and resembled a dental dam membrane—a one-piece latex band-like device that had a condom in its middle and two loops that anchored over the ears. The inventors said they were seeking to create a product that could "provide some margin of isolation of the human mouth from various practices as may be engaged in sexually."

The second kind or oral prophylactic was actually shaped like a rubber mouth and resembled nothing so much as the wax lips sold in candy stores at Halloween. The entire soft rubber device was inserted in the mouth, fitting over the lips as well as the tongue. One version was held in place by head straps. Another had four corner tabs with low-tack flesh glue that were pressed on the cheeks to hold it firm. Inventor Glen Harding told patent examiners: "In view of the fact that fluids are passed via oral intercourse it should therefore be evident that a new device that provides prophylaxis for oral intercourse would constitute a significant improvement over the state of the art. (Mine is) shaped for the lips, tongue, and mouth and is comfortable to wear; allows for a maximum of tactile sensation; may incorporate colors, textures and flavors; and allows the comfortable swallowing and maintenance of the user's own saliva."

Condom Carriers

In order for condoms to be used, they must be close at hand in the heat of the sexual moment—a fact addressed by a number of inventors who have patented various sorts of condom-holding key chains and jewel-like pocket boxes. Perhaps the most unusual patent so far has been that of Tony Parrone of Wisconsin, whose ring-shaped condom holder was suspended at penis-level on a lightweight waist band worn under the male's pants. The holder is also an unroller ring so "that the condom may be reached and applied to the male organ with one hand without substantial interruption of activity."

Condom Pocket Underwear

Between 1989 and 1991, three different inventors filed for patents on "condom pocket underwear." All three designs were functionally very similar and included small pockets on the upper part of a set of female panties or male under shorts. Michael Katchka of Pontiac, Michigan, who was the first to receive a patent, told the patent examiners his underwear idea resulted from the fact that "as people are becoming increasingly concerned about the spread of AIDS and their use of condoms is increasing, there is currently no convenient way for a person to carry a condom."

Condom Garments

A peculiar hybrid that has also seized the imaginations of multiple inventors has been the "condom garment"—which incorporates a

Tony Parrone's condom holder
allowed the user to hang a
condom in a strap device worn
under the pants. Thus, the
prophylactic could be donned
with one hand when needed.
No. 4,875,491 (1977)

Benjamin Denno
No. D. 288,485
(1987)

Anton Davis, Kevin Simmons
and Richard Blair
No. 4,942,885 (1990)

Condom Garments

A dozen inventors have sought to
incorporate condoms into garment
structures to create more
comprehensive barriers against
skin and fluid contact.

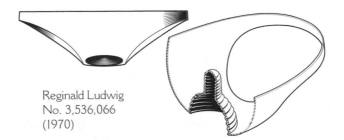

Reginald Ludwig
No. 3,536,066
(1970)

condom into a larger pubic shield or rubber body sheath-like form. The idea of a condom garment structure is not really new and was first described in a patent application submitted by Douglas Craddock of North Carolina in 1951. By the mid-1980s, three other inventors had patented safe sex structures shaped like panties with a condom built into their crotch. These systems were designed as a more effective safe sex barrier for people worried about herpes. While they might form a physically effective barrier, they also seem an awkward solution, as they would be hot and uncomfortable during the strenuous exertions of sexual activity.

Nevertheless, after 1986, this general concept of an impermeable barrier across the entire genital area took on new importance for inventors who saw it as potentially *the* new proprietary anti-AIDS product. In his 1987 application for a patent on a sex apron and face mask system, Mark Grubman of Rego Park, New York, explained: "The use of condoms, while better than nothing, leaves open considerable and major risk of infection by AIDS as a result of sloppy, careless, and/or accidental smearing and/or spilling of copulation fluids from one or more of the sex partners . . . The great publicity has made even the high-risk groups aware of the need for exercising greater care to prevent contraction of AIDS if they do not already have it."

Grubman's incredible invention was a plastic apron that tied around the waist and stretched down to the thighs. At penis level, it had a condom contiguously attached. The trailing lower edge of the apron included a special open cuff to catch fluids that ran down the front of the garment. The product also included a plastic face shield that was tied around the head and "worn in position during sex and/ or copulation, in order to avoid the touching of lips and/or saliva of the opposite mouths of the copulating partners."

Kenneth Johnson of Stamford, Connecticut, successfully filed a patent application for condom briefs—a skin-tight pants garment that covered the body from waist to mid-thigh and included special built-in expandable condom panels located at the front and rear of the crotch. The front panel could expand outward to fit a wearer's erect penis or inward to fit a wearer's vagina. The rear panel provided penetration access to the anus. Mr. Johnson wrote, "It is the object of the invention to provide a prophylactic device capable of being used by either males or females to accomplish intravaginal, orogenital, oroanal or anogenital intercourse."

In what appears to be the longest sex device patent application ever filed—thirteen of its twenty-two pages are crammed with drawings—the unsuccessful bikini condom marketer, Dr. Reddy of Wyoming, described a system that included an array of genital barrier shield variations for heterosexual and homosexual acts. Its core idea is a panty-like structure that has a condom built into its crotch and can be augmented in various versions with straps, solid shield devices, and internal pouch unrollers for vaginal and anal sex. A slightly different version of a bikini panty condom was invented by Ivan Green of New York. His device featured an accordion-pleated condom built into the panty as a flat part of the crotch. During sex, the male organ pressed inward on this panel, expanding it into the vagina. Mr. Green noted that the benefits of such a "wearing apparel" condom was that when worn it was "not subject to the possibility of being lost or forgotten," and "is employable without interruption of sexual activities such as foreplay." Other inventors have continued to try to improve upon this concept but have yet to come up with a product that can both win the approval of the U.S. Food and Drug Administration and the acceptance of the sexually active public.

Sex Robots

Without question, the most bizarre new idea patented in this field has been sex robots. Within one month of each other, inventors in Arizona and California filed patent applications for reciprocating orgasm machines that function as mechanical sex partners.

Mark Grubman's condom apron invention tied around the user's waist and extended to mid-thigh. No. 4,781,709 (1988)

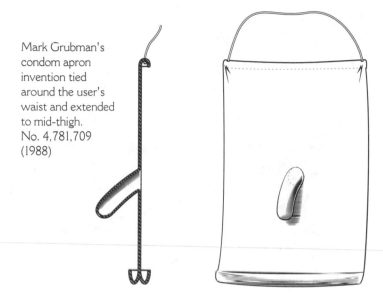

Kenneth Johnson's condom briefs with latex crotch panels that expand inward or outward at front and rear No. 4,807,611 (1989)

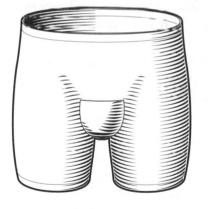
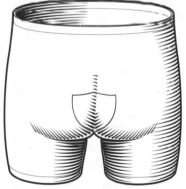

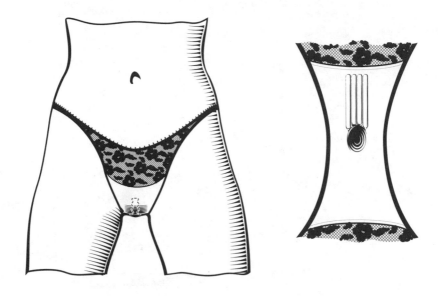

Ivan Green's bikini condom No. 4,862,901 (1989)

In his 1987 application, Daniel Segal of Malibu, California, told the patent examiners, "With the recent development and discovery of the AIDS virus, many formerly sexually active people are attempting to abstain from sexual activity. The human sexual drive, however, is such that is cannot be ignored. The fear of contracting the AIDS virus, coupled with the inhibiting and perhaps demeaning prospect of asking prospective sex partners about his or her latest sexual contacts, is changing the way many people view their own human sexuality and their relationships with others. Accordingly, there is a need for a sexual stimulation apparatus capable of providing a safe and hygienic sexual release, which also eliminates the fear of contracting communicable diseases such as AIDS. Such an apparatus should enable the user to achieve an orgasm without exchanging body fluids with a partner, and require minimum manipulation after being set up and adjusted to one's specific needs. Further, a sexual stimulation apparatus is needed

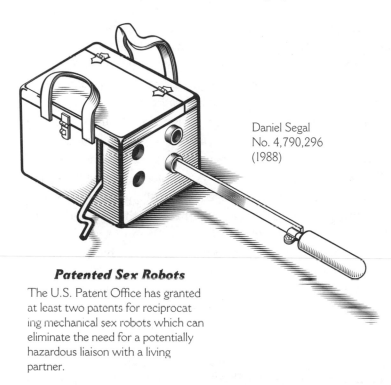

Daniel Segal
No. 4,790,296
(1988)

Patented Sex Robots

The U.S. Patent Office has granted
at least two patents for reciprocat
ing mechanical sex robots which can
eliminate the need for a potentially
hazardous liaison with a living
partner.

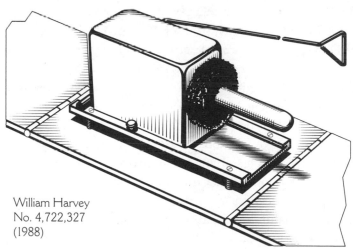

William Harvey
No. 4,722,327
(1988)

which can be powered by ordinary household electrical current, is self-contained and lightweight, is easy to clean and store, and which can be used by males or females." The patent examiners granted him a patent on a motorized box that drove either a reciprocating simulated penis or a soft rubber, vagina-like receptive sheath.

A similar motorized sex partner designed by William Harvey of Mesa, Arizona, featured a track-mounted box with a reciprocating penile shaft that included a pad of simulated pubic hair at its base. He explained to Patent Office officials: "A long-felt but unfilled need has existed and continues to exist for a therapeutic apparatus for more closely simulating sexual intercourse, which has the look and feel of a real male penis, and which can be used at any tempo, manner, or degree of gentleness or roughness, as desired by the user.... The invention may be used anally on both men and women, as well as vaginally on a female user (and) any number of positions can be enjoyed by using a little imagination and practice." His patent application was also granted.

• • •

For most people, the act of having sexual relations with a piston-driven machine or suiting up in a prophylactic body sheath is not only distasteful but, somehow, profoundly sad. Yet these patented mechanical concepts now stand as permanent markers of our technological history. As such, they seem to say as much about the individual quirkiness of American inventors as they do about the searing sexual anguish of our age. More than just machine designs, they are poignant symbols of the desperation felt by a people grappling with unprecedented levels of fear about sexually transmitted diseases.

Imagine how future historians will pore over them as they try to understand the emotions of that time in the late twentieth century when much of American society was denied the unfettered spontaneity and animal naturalness that makes sexual coupling—and expectations of the same—such a fulfilling, life-affirming event.

Afterword

The personal drive to profit from mechanical innovation is one of the most powerful and celebrated of American compulsions. For the past two hundred years it has been an unstoppable national force, overwhelming and changing all before it; so broad it could not be escaped, so relentless it could not be resisted; so important we chart much of the story of our history in terms of our famous inventors.

Propelled by greed and the rapture of their own sense of creative genius, inventors tend to be narrowly focused and disciplined by their desire to make money. They are good observers of society because they have to be. The fact that they leave behind historically significant records is an unintended side effect of their quest to document some new social need and develop a product that meets it.

We know that inventors and their work tell us something important about ourselves. But, in the case of our sexuality, what is it?

Sexually, inventors are no different from the rest of us. They live in the same society, respond to the same stimuli, experience the same fantasies, suffer the same frustrations, and enjoy the same pleasures we all do. The only thing that sets them apart is their motivation to execute their daydreams in mechanical form. What they leave us in their collective drawings and engineering narratives are not the oddball views of outsiders, but mirror reflections of the society they live in.

And the picture they capture is often not a pretty one. If, as archeologists hold, civilizations can largely be defined by the things they invent, then sexually, America seems a troubled and traumatized land. Whole schools of inventors have graphically demonstrated how our national sexual reality has been warped by religious zealotry feeding on fear and by unbridled greed feeding on ignorance.

Flogged forward by sanctimonious clerics, we are a nation that has waged the most ferocious and debilitating sort of war against a primal animal instinct. It's a battle whose logic could not have been more skewed if had it been used in similar attempts to convince a population that the passage of food into the mouth is such an inherently ugly process that eating itself should be avoided, or that the act of sleeping is such obvious evidence of sloth that it should be vigilantly resisted by the righteous.

At the other extreme, America has mercilessly exploited its sexually confused citizens with the most tawdry kinds of sales ploys. Like the larger business community they are part of, many of our inventors have viewed sexual ignorance and emotional insecurity as nothing more than favorable market conditions. The mercantile custom of hawking all manner of ludicrous products to the sexually vulnerable dates to before the first traveling medicine shows. Nor did the tradition die when that snake-oil-peddling industry collapsed earlier this century. Instead, it merged with the evolving electronic consumer culture. Now, that same spirit of predatory hucksterism energizes the flood of sexually explicit marketing campaigns that cascade through our TVs, movie theaters, newsstands, and shopping malls each day.

The illusion fostered by these enveloping commercial messages is that Americans are a people who glory in sexual playfulness and adventure. The real truth is we remain a sexually squeamish nation that has long used a system of subtle censorship to deny citizens important information about serious aspects of their sex lives. Consider the closeted agony of male impotence. Some thirty million American males are unable to achieve or sustain an erection, an ailment recognized to be "devastating on a man's emotional and psychological health." Yet most cases of impotence reportedly go untreated for two reasons—the unwillingness of physicians and health care technicians to discuss the taboo subject with patients, and the ignorance of the patients and many of these same health care professionals about the special mechanical devices available for treating or overcoming various forms of erectile dysfunction. But such machinery is not new. In fact, the history of artificial penile erection devices as documented in patent records is one of the oldest and most active areas of sex-related invention. One can only wonder how many millions of males over the years have been denied the knowledge that there are therapies and implements for treating such a common physical affliction.

In a more troubling area of American life, patents provide vivid new insights into the level of anger we feel about the sex-related violence that plagues our contemporary society. Students seeking to understand the emotional intensity of this issue need only browse the gallery of anti-rape devices. The pure fury shining through their barbs and blades and piercing points may say more about the country's sentiments than any ten thousand pages of police statistics or feminist invective.

Despite our many problems and shortcomings, the Patent Office's sex files also show that we are a country struggling doggedly toward ever-more open attitudes about sexuality as a positive and healthy force. This can be seen in the recent loosening of media taboos against the public discussion of serious sexual issues and in many of the most recently patented inventions that harness high technology to the task of improving sexual function and increasing sexual pleasure. The devices are just one result of the emerging social view that not only tolerates sexual pleasure, but recognizes it as a necessary and even curative aspect of the overall human condition.

Finally, our sex patent recipients show us that after more than two hundred years we have lost none of our enduring enthusiasm for the process of invention itself. The possibility of receiving a patent for a clever new product is one that pulls as strongly as ever at our collective imagination; it is the same financial lure that Abraham Lincoln once said, "adds the fuel of interest to the fire of genius." Inevitably, this American mania for innovation will continue to intersect in the most unpredictable and surprising ways with our ever-colorful—and forever mechanically imperfect—sexual habits and daydreams.

Notes

Chapter 1: The Original Sex Patent

Small-town Calvinism: Dirk J. Struik, *Yankee Science in the Making: Science and Engineering in New England from Colonial Times to the Civil War*, Dover 1991 reprint of 1948 original, Brown and Company, Boston, page 30. Fines and whipping: John D'Emilio and Estelle B. Freedman, *Intimate Matters: A History of Sexuality in America*, Harper & Row, New York, 1988, pages 11-25. Search for economic opportunity: James Reed, *From Private Vice to Public Virtue: The Birth Control Movement and American Society Since 1830*, Basic Books, New York, 1978, pages 19 and 20. Portuguese female pills: Linda Grossman, *Woman's Body, Women's Right: A Social History of Birth Control in America*, Grossman Publishers, New York, 1976, page 53. The market for abortion: Ellen Chesler, *Woman of Valor: Margaret Sanger and the Birth Control Movement in America*, Simon & Schuster, New York, 1992, page 63. Statistic of one in five live births aborted: D'Emilio & Freedman, *Intimate Matters*, page 65. Gut condoms: Angus McLaren, *A History of Contraception from Antiquity to the Present Day*, Basil Blackwell Books, 1990, page 183. Erie Canal as conduit for immorality: Terry Lehr, Assistant Curator for Research, Baker-Cedersberg Museum & Archives, Rochester General Hospital, letter report, June 28, 1993. Beers's arrival in 1839: Harvey J. Burkhart, "Centennial History of Dentistry in Rochester," in *The Rochester Historical Society Publication Fund Series, Vol. XIII*, Rochester Historical Society, Rochester, 1934, page 287. How Beers's device worked: U.S. Patent Number 4,729, "Preventing Conception," J.B. Beers, Rochester, NY, granted August 28, 1846. Rochester's religious elders: Porter Farley, M.D., "Rochester in the Forties," by Porter Farley, M.D., in *The Rochester Historical Society Publication Fund Series, Vol. IV*, Rochester Historical Society, Rochester, 1925, page 265. Dental crowns and gold sluicing patents: U.S. Patent Number 144,182, "Artificial Crowns for Teeth," John B. Beers, San Francisco, CA, November 4, 1873, and U.S. Patent Number 129,644, "Apparatus for Collecting the Precious Metals in Mining Sluices," John B. Beers, San Francisco, CA, July 23, 1872.

Chapter 2: America's Assault on the Solitary Vice

Rendered feeble, crippled, blind, or deaf by masturbation: Simon-Andre Tissot, *Onanism: or, a Treatise Upon the Disorders Produced by Masturbation*, J. Pridden, London, 1766, page 72. Tissot's profound effect: E. H. Hare, "Masturbatory

Insanity: The History of an Idea," *Journal of Mental Science*, Vol. 108, No. 452, Jan. 1962, p. 2. The supposed relationship between the moon and madness: John Haslam, *Observations on Madness and Melancholy: Including Practical Remarks on Those Diseases*, J. Callow Medical Books, London, 1809, pages 210-217. Masturbation as causing madness: Benjamin Rush, *Medical Inquiries and Observations Upon the Diseases of the Mind*, Grigg & Elliot, Philadelphia, fifth edition, 1835, page 24. Masturbation gave parents something to blame: Karin Calvert, *Children in the House: The Material Culture of Early Childhood, 1600–1900*, Northeastern University Press, Boston, 1992, page 141. Threatening children with knives and scissors: Ivan Bloch, *The Sexual Life of Our Time In Its Relation to Modern Civilization*, Allied Book Company, New York, 1908, page 427. Masturbators charged and tried in court: Allen W. Hagenbach, M.D., "Masturbation as a Cause of Insanity," in *Journal of Nervous and Mental Disease*, Vol. VI, Jan.–Oct., 1879, page 603. The forced removal of testicles: J. D. Marshall, M.D., "Insanity cured by castration," in *Medical and Surgical Reporter*, Vol. XIII, 1865, p. 363. Asylum conditions in 1876: John C. Bucknill, *Notes on Asylums for the Insane in America*, J&A Churchill, London, 1876, page 74. Two hundred and fifteen women in modes of restraint: The American Psychiatric Association, *One Hundred Years of American Psychology*, Columbia University Press, New York, page 115. Bromide of potassium and silver prepuce rings: Alexander Robertson, "Notes on a Visit to American Asylums," in *Journal of Mental Science*, Vol. XV, April, 1869, p. 58. Masturbators injected with opium: H. Tristam Engelhardt, Jr., "The Disease of Masturbation," in *Sickness & Health in America: Readings in the History of Medicine and Public Health*, University of Wisconsin Press, Madison, second edition, 1985, page 17. Mutilating surgery recommended up to 1936: Vern L. Bullough and Bonnie Bullough, *Sin, Sickness, & Sanity: A History of Sexual Attitudes*, Garland Publishing, New York 1977, page 69. 1994 Sex in America survey: R. T. Michael, J. H. Gagnon, E. O. Laumann and G. Kolata, *Sex in America, a Definitive Survey*, Little, Brown and Co., New York, 1994, pages 155–168.

Chapter 3: The War on Wet Dreams

Pliny and Galen accounts of lead: Herbert L. Needleman, *Human Lead Exposure*, CRC Press, Boca Raton, 1992, page 5. Early theories on semen loss and illness: Vern L. Bullough, *Sex, Society & History*, Science History Publications, New York, 1976, page 174. Dr. Acton and the need to keep dreams pure: cited in Steven Marcus, *The Other Victorians: A Study of Sexuality and Pornography in Mid-Nineteenth-Century England*, Basic Books, New York, 1964, page 23. Procedure piercing the foreskin with silk slings: Dr. Louis Bauer, "Infibulation as a Remedy for Epilepsy and Seminal Losses," in *Saint Louis Clinical Record*, Vol. 6, Sept. 1879, page 163. First spermatorrhoea rings: Dr. J. A. Mayes,

"Spermatorrhoea Treated by the Lately Invented Rings," in *Charleston Medical Journal and Review*, Vol. 9, May 1854, page 351.

Chapter 4: The Evolution of Vaginal Machinery

Families having seven children each in 1800: James Reed, *From Private Vice to Public Virtue: The Birth Control Movement and American Society Since 1830*, Basic Books, New York, 1978, page 4. Procidentia described: Edward Shorter, *Women's Bodies: A Social History of Women's Encounter with Health, Ill-Health and Medicine*, Transaction Publications, New Brunswick, NJ, 1991, page 273. Doctors keeping eyes averted from patient's genitals: Judith Walzer Leavitt, "Science Enters the Birthing Room: Obstetrics in America since the 18th Century," in *Sickness & Health in America: Readings in the History of Medicine and Public Health*, University of Wisconsin Press, Madison, 1985, page 83. Multiple meaning of term "stem pessary": Until the mid-1800s, the term "stem pessary" was generally used to describe a "stem-and-ball" or "stem-and-cup" pessary that was inserted in the vagina. The "stem" in this case was the bar that ran the length of the vagina and pressed the ball, cup, or support platform against the exterior of the womb. In the second half of the century, "stem pessary" came to assume a new meaning as a device that had a narrow stem for insertion into the uterus. As later sections of this chapter explain, these intrauterine stem pessaries were used for purposes of contraception and abortion. Throughout this book, the term "stem pessary" is always used to refer to the vaginal "stem-and-ball" type device. The term "intrauterine stem pessary" is used to describe the pessary devices which actually enter the uterus. A number of books and articles published in the twentieth century have used the single term, "stem pessary" to describe both kinds of devices in a manner that is often confusing. Decreasing national birthrate: In 1800, American women were bearing an average of 7.04 children each. By 1860, this had declined to 5.21 children per woman. And by 1900 it was down to 3.56—half of what it had been one hundred years previous. This steady decline in births parallels an equally steady increase in the use of birth control techniques throughout the century. See: James Reed, *From Private Vice to Public Virtue: The Birth Control Movement and American Society Since 1830*, Basic Books, New York, 1978, page 4.

Chapter 5: The Victorian Era of Contraception

The vagina as a Chinese toy-shop: Dr. W. D. Buck "A Raid on the Uterus," 1866 address to the New Hampshire State Medical Society reprinted in *New York Medical Journal*, Vol. 5, August, 1867, pages 464–465. Dearth of hard information on Victorian contraception and abortion products: Linda Gordon, *Woman's Body, Women's Right: A Social History of Birth Control in America*, Grossman Publishers, New York, 1976, page 67. Widespread douching: James Reed, *From Private Vice to Public Virtue: The Birth Control Movement and American Society Since 1830*, Basic Books, New York, 1978, page 10. Seaweed vaginal plugs: Norman E. Himes, *Medical History of Contraception*, Williams & Wilkins, Baltimore, 1936, page 22. Edward Bliss Foote on the womb veil: Quoted in: James Reed, *From Private Vice to Public Virtue*, page 16.

Chapter 6: The Rubber Revolution

Rubber shoes in 1820: P. W. Parker, *Charles Goodyear: Connecticut Yankee and Rubber Pioneer*, Godfrey Cabot Publishers, Boston, 1940, page 15. "Ko-chook" is the pronunciation of the word "caoutchouc." Crude rubber syringes: P. W. Parker, *Charles Goodyear*, page 13. The French and douching in the 1700s: Angus McLaren, *A History of Contraception from Antiquity to the Present Day*, Basil Blackwell, Ltd., Cambridge, 1990, page 157. Thumb-sized gobs of rubber: Ralph Frank Wolf, *India Rubber Man: The Story of Charles Goodyear*, Caxton Printers, Ltd., Caldwell, Ohio, 1940, page 44, cites Priestly's mention in the introduction to the book, *Theory and Practice of Perspective*, 1770. Quantities and prices of rubber shoes and india rubber instruments: P.W. Parker, *Charles Goodyear*, pages 15 and 22. Rubber tubes and abortion: Edward Shorter, *Women's Bodies: A Social History of Women's Encounter with Health, Ill-Health and Medicine*, Transaction Pub., 1991, page 198. Variety of commercial terms for rubber products: Patent applications filed with the U.S. Patent Office over the years mention india rubber, caoutchouc, gutta percha and, at times, gum elastic. All of these are terms used in this era to describe rubber. Comstock's diary: Heywood Broun and Margaret Leech, *Anthony Comstock: Roundsman of the Lord*, Albert & Charles Boni Publishers, New York, 1927, page 31. "All that was vulgar . . .": Broun and Leech, *Anthony Comstock*, page 75. "Stationed in a swamp . . .": Broun and Leech, *Anthony Comstock*, page 19. Seizures of "immoral rubber articles": Broun and Leech, *Anthony Comstock*, page 153. Three factories raided and closed": Broun and Leech, *Anthony Comstock*, page 155. American condom industry: James Murphy, *The Condom Industry in the United States*, McFarland & Company, Inc., Publishers, North Carolina, 1990, page 9. Volume of 1930s condom sales: Norman E. Himes, *Medical History of Contraception*, Williams & Wilkins, Baltimore, Maryland, 1936, page 186.

Chapter 7: Erector Rings

"Be thankful your studies are not interfered with": William Acton, *The Functions and Disorders of the Reproductive Organs in Childhood, Youth, Adult Age, and Advanced Life*, P. Blakison, Son & Co., Publishers, Philadelphia, 1883, page 87. Modern day impotence rate: "NIH Consensus Development Panel on Impotence," in *Journal of the American Medical Association*, vol. 270, No. 8, July 7, 1993, page 83. "Large towns harbor crowds . . .": Victor Vecki, *The Pathology and Treatment of Sexual Impotence*, W.B. Saunders, Philadelphia, 1899, page 27. Prince Lotus Blossom: James H. Young, *The Toadstool Millionaires: A Social History of Patent Medicines in America Before Federal Regs*, Princeton University Press. 1972, page 200. "Lost manhood": Stewart H. Holbrook, *The Golden Age of Quackery*, Macmillan, New York, 1959, page 76. New York Museum of Anatomy: James H. Young, *The Toadstool Millionaires*, page 183. Dr. Gross's impotence lecture: Samuel W. Gross, "On Sexual Debility and Impotence," in *Medical & Surgical Reporter*, Philadelphia, May 5, 1877, page 391. Masturbation and internal strictures: At this time, the exact nature of gonorrhea was not well understood. It would be another two years before the gonococcus microbe was isolated and identified and still later before the full range of the disease's pathology was known. Urethral strictures are one of the major characteristics of the disease. It seems likely that the strictures to which Gross was referring were those caused by gonorrhea, later discovered to be far more prevalent throughout society than was appreciated in 1877. Tonic and malt doctor: John J. Caldwell, "Impotence and Sterility, Their Causes and Treatment by Electricity," address before the Baltimore Medical and Surgical Society, September, 1879, reprinted in *Virginia Medical Monthly*, Richmond, 1879, Vol. VI, p 436. Understanding of the bio-hydraulics of erection: James H. Dunn, M.D., "Impotence in the Male and Its Treatment," in *Northwestern Lancet*, St. Paul, November, 1885 Vol. V, No. 3, page 41. Procedure of partially tying off the dorsal vein: G. R. Phillips, M.D., "Impotence Treated by Ligation of the Dorsal Vein of the Penis," *St. Louis Medical Era*, 1895–1896, page 99. Professor Bartholomew: Stewart H. Holbrook, *The Golden Age of Quackery*, page 251. 1993 NIH report: "NIH Consensus Development Panel on Impotence," *Journal of the American Medical Association*, Vol. 270, No. 8, July 7, 1993, page 83.

Chapter 8: Penile Splints

"Patent" medicines: Generally, the term "patent" medicine, does not refer to a substance that has been registered at the U.S. Patent Office, but rather to an older custom of European monarchs who granted "patents" or exclusive rights to individuals to make and sell certain substances throughout the realm. The fact that a brew or potion had been granted the favor and protection of the King or

Head of State was perceived to imply its high quality and effectiveness. Annual sales of patent medicine industry: Steward H. Holbrook, *The Golden Age of Quackery*, Macmillan, New York, 1959, page 4. $80 million in 1900 is roughly equivalent to about $5 billion in 1994 dollars. Patent medicine exposé: Samuel Adams Hopkins, "The Great American Fraud," in *Collier's Weekly*, October 7, 1905, page 95.

Chapter 9: The Bionic Penis

Discovery of effect of vasoactive drugs on erection: R. Virag, "Intracavernous Injection of Papaverine for Erectile Failure," in *The Lancet*, Vol. II, No. 8304, October 23, 1982, page 938. AMA evaluation of vasoactive drugs for impotence therapy: "Vasoactive Intracavernous Pharmacotherapy for Impotence: Papaverine and Phentolamine," A Diagnostic and Therapeutic Technology Assessment, Office of Technology Assessment, American Medical Association, *Journal of the American Medical Association*, August 8, 1990, Vol. 264, No. 6, page 752. 1993 NIH report: "NIH Consensus Development Panel on Impotence," *Journal of the American Medical Association*, vol. 270, No. 8, July 7, 1993, page 83. Federal study of impotence: Lawrence K. Altman, "Study Suggests High Rate of Impotence," in the *New York Times*, December 22, 1993, page C13.

Chapter 10: Who Really Invented the Bra?

Contemporary reference works: James Trager, *The People's Chronology: A Year-by-Year Record of Human Events from Prehistory to the Present*, Henry Holt & Company, New York, 1992, page 710; *The New York Public Library Book of Chronologies: The Ultimate One-Volume Collection of Dates, Events, People, Places and Pastimes*, Prentice Hall Press, New York, 1990, page 431. French corset maker Herminie Cadolle: "Hurray for the Bra: It's 100 Years Old," cover story, *Life*, June, 1989, page 89. Day corsets: Willett C. Cunnington, and Phillis Cunnington, *The History of Underclothes*, Michael Joseph, Ltd., London, 1951, reprint, Dover Publications, New York, 1992, page 49. "This novel application of India-rubber . . .": Willett and Phillips Cunnington, *History of Underclothes*, page 132. *Soutien-Gorge*: "Hurray for the Bra: It's 100 Years Old," cover story, *Life*, June, 1989, page 89. Jacobs's *soutien-gorge*: Caresse Crosby, *The Passionate Years*, The Dial Press, New York, 1953, page 61. "But I did invent it": Caresse Crosby, *The Passionate Years*, page 10. Bra "prototypes" of the 1840s: Willett and Phillis Cunnington, *History of Underclothes*, page 149. Backless bra: Anne L. Macdonald, *Feminine Ingenuity: Women and Invention in America*, Ballantine Books, New York, 1992, page 273. Individual bra cups: E. Vare and G. Ptacek,

Mothers of Invention: From the Bra to the Bomb—Forgotten Women and Their Unforgettable Ideas, Morrow, New York, 1988, page 58.

Chapter 11: The Industrialization of the Breast

"Sell them their dreams . . .": William Leach, *Land of Desire: Merchants, Power, and the Rise of a New American Culture*, Pantheon Books, New York, 1993, page 298. "The tragedy of children acting out the sexual fantasies . . .": Betty Friedan, *The Feminine Mystique*, Laurel Books, Dell Publishing, New York, 1983, page 281.

Chapter 12: Artificial Breasts and the Silicone Nightmare

Silicone in World War II: Aaron J. Ihde, *The Development of Modern Chemistry*, Harper & Row, 1964, reprinted by Dover Publications, 1984, page 605. Stolen silicone transformer fluid: Philip J. Hilts, "Strange History of Silicone Held Many Warning Signs," the *New York Times*, January 18, 1992, page 1. 1949 patents of Kausch and Freeman: The later patents filed by Pangman and Cronin would specifically cite these earlier designs as direct antecedents. Failure of Pangman's 1951 concept: William C. Grabb and James W. Smith, *Plastic Surgery*, third edition, Little, Brown and Company, Boston, 1979, page 719. "I am feminine . . .": Hugh A. Johnson, M.D., "Silastic Breast Implants: Coping with Complications," Rockford, IL, *Plastic and Reconstructive Surgery*, Vol. 44, December, 1969, page 588. Fifty thousand implants in first eleven years: Boyce Rensberger, "Breast Implant Study Findings Misrepresented: 1 of 4 Beagles Died in 1973 Company Test," the *Washington Post*, January 16, 1992, page A1. 1979 implant poll: Grabb and Smith, *Plastic Surgery*, page 719. Large-celled tumor masses: Harry V. Eisenberg and Robert J. Bartells, "Rupture of a Silicone Bag-Gel Breast Implant by Closed Compression Capsulotomy," *Plastic and Reconstructive Surgery*, Vol. 59, June, 1977, page 849. Dow Corning appreciable oiling memo: Dr. Frank B. Vasey and Josh Feldstein, *The Silicone Breast Implant Controversy*, Crossing Press, Freedom, CA, 1993, page 67. Implants as a half-billion dollar annual industry: Sandy Rovner, "Implant Safety: Who's Right?," by Sandy Rovner, The *Washington Post*, November 12, 1991, page Z12; Sarah Glazer, "Women's Health Battle Over Breast Implants: Fewer Women Are Seeking Cosmetic Enlargements, Plastic Surgeons Say," the *Washington Post*, January 14, 1992, page Z7. FDA's "alarming" memos: Boyce Rensberger, "Silicone Gel Found to Cause Cancer in Laboratory Rats; Citizens' Group Calls for Ban on Breast Implants," the *Washington Post*, November 10, 1988, page A3. "Guinea pigs in a vast uncontrolled clinical trial": Philip J. Hilts, "Drug Agency Questions Companies' Safety Data on Breast Implants," the *New York Times*, September 17, 1991, page B6. TDA in polyurethane implant coatings: Philip J. Hilts, "Scientists Link Breast Implant to Cancer," the *New York Times*, April 14, 1991, page 18.

Chapter 13: Anti-Rape Technology

Number of rapes in U.S.: *Violence Against Women: A Week In The Life of America*, A Majority Staff Report, Committee on the Judiciary, U.S. Senate, Second Session, October, 1992, pages 2–3. This report indicates that about 12,000 women are subjected to forcible rape throughout America each week. This calculates out to 624,000 rapes a year, or an average of about 1.2 rapes a minute, round the clock. The Judiciary Committee also cites data from the National Victim Center and the Crime Victims Research Treatment Center indicating an average of about 605,000 women have been raped each year for the last twenty years in America, or about 12.1 million women. Brownmiller's landmark book: Susan Brownmiller, *Against Our Will: Men, Women and Rape*, Fawcett Columbine/Ballantine, New York, 1993.

Chapter 14: Mechanical Stimulators

1994 Sex study: Michael, R. T., J. H. Gagnon, E. O. Laumann and G. Kolata, *Sex in America, a Definitive Survey*, Little, Brown and Co., New York, 1994, pages 146–157. Phallus factories of 500 B.C.: Reay Tannahill, *Sex in History*, Scarborough House, London, 1992, page 98. Anthropological findings in many cultures: Havelock Ellis, *Studies in the Psychology of Sex, Volume I*, Random House, New York, 1942, page 170; Norman E. Himes, *Medical History of Contraception*, Williams & Wilkins, Baltimore, MD, 1936 (1970 reprint, Schocken Books), page 125; Ivan Bloch, *The Sexual Life of Our Time In Its Relation to Modern Civilization*, Allied Book Co., NY, 1908, page 411; Ray Tannahill, *Sex in History*, page 179. Phallus implements in European history: Havelock Ellis, *Studies in the Psychology of Sex*, pages 169–170; Ivan Bloch, *Sexual Life in England*, Corgi Books, London, 1958, page 260. Handcrafted silver dildos: Ivan Block, *Sexual Life of Our Time*, page 412. Asian hollow balls: Havelock Ellis, *Studies in the Psychology of Sex*, page 167.

Chapter 16: Exercisers and Monitors

Michael, R. T., J. H. Gagnon, E. O. Laumann and G. Kolata, *Sex in America, a Definitive Survey*, Little, Brown and Co., New York, 1994.

Chapter 17: Safe Sex in the Age of AIDS

Widely publicized female condom product: Elizabeth Kaye, "Reality Dawns: With a Squeak Instead of a Roar, the First Female Condom is About to Arrive," the *New York Times*, May 9, 1993, page 8V, col. 1; Warren E. Leary, "Female Condom Approved for Market," the *New York Times*, May 11, 1993, page C5, col. 1; Mireya Navarro, "Female Condom Is Winning Favor: Among Women First to Use It as a Shield Against H.I.V., the Device Gains Interest," the *New York Times*, December 15, 1992, page B1, col. 2.

Index